READING JUDGES

Smyth & Helwys Publishing, Inc.
6316 Peake Road
Macon, Georgia 31210-3960
1-800-747-3016
© 2012 by Smyth & Helwys Publishing
All rights reserved.
Printed in the United States of America.

The paper used in this publication meets the minimum
requirements of American National Standard for Information
Sciences—Permanence of Paper for Printed Library Materials.
ANSI Z39.48–1984    (alk. paper)

*Library of Congress Cataloging-in-Publication Data*

Biddle, Mark E.
Reading Judges : a literary and theological commentary / by Mark Biddle.
    p. cm. -- (Reading the Old Testament)
ISBN-13: 978-1-57312-631-1 (alk. paper)
1. Bible. O.T. Judges--Commentaries. I. Title.
BS1305.53.B53 2012
222'.3207--dc23
                        2012015015

---

**Disclaimer of Liability**: With respect to statements of opinion or fact available in this work of nonfiction, Smyth & Helwys Publishing Inc. nor any of its employees, makes any warranty, express or implied, or assumes any legal liability or responsibility for the accuracy or completeness of any information disclosed, or represents that its use would not infringe privately-owned rights.

# Reading Judges

## A Literary and Theological Commentary

Mark E. Biddle

# Also by Mark E. Biddle

*Missing the Mark: Sin and Its Consequences in Biblical Theology*

*Deuteronomy* (Smyth & Helwys Bible Commentary)

*Polyphony and Symphony in Prophetic Literature: A Literary Analysis of Jeremiah 7–20*

*A Redaction History of Jeremiah 2:1–4:2*

To my father, Joseph William Biddle,
with loving gratitude for the example he has set as
son, husband, and father.

למד בניו ללכת בארצות ישר

And in memory of my mother, Martha Faye Miller Biddle,
whom I sorely miss.

קמו בניה ויאשרוה בעלה ויהללה

# Contents

Editor's Foreword ..................................................................................xiii
Author's Preface .......................................................................................1

Reading Judges: Issues and Approach ....................................................3
    The Problem of Cultural Values ..........................................................4
    Judges or Anti-Heroes? ........................................................................5
    Composition and Structure .................................................................7
        Book of Saviors Core (Judg 3–16[?]) ............................................8
        Deuteronomistic Framework and the
        "Deuteronomistic Paradigm" .........................................................9
        Preface/Appendices Outer Envelope.............................................11
    Framework, Envelope, and Interpretation.........................................12
    The Transmission of the Text and Interpretation .............................15
    The Structure of Judges and of this Commentary.............................17

Preface (Judg 1:1–2:5)............................................................................19
    The Southern Campaign—Judah's Preeminence (1:1-21) ................21
    The Northern Campaign—Forces of Decay and Decline (1:22-36) ..24
        Growing Internal Disharmony......................................................25
        Caleb and Achsah—A Standard for Comparison .........................26
    Foreign Influence in the South and in the North:
    A Dynamic Perspective......................................................................28

Theological Assessment(s) of Israel's History (Judg 2:1–3:6) ...................31
    Weeping at Bochim (2:1-5) ................................................................33
    Joshua's Passing (2:6-10)...................................................................35
    The "Deuteronomistic Paradigm" (2:11-17).......................................36
    God's Pity and the People's Recalcitrance (2:18-19) .........................36

The Nations: A Test of Obedience (2:20-23; 3:4-6) ........................... 37
The Nations: A Test of Israel's Military Preparedness (3:1-3) ............ 38
The Nations: A Test of Israel's Obedience—Reprised (3:4-6) ........... 38
History and Theology—History or Theology? ................................... 39

Three Judge/Savior Vignettes (Judg 3:7-31) ............................................ 41
   Othniel (3:7-11) ......................................................................................... 42
   Ehud (3:12-30) .......................................................................................... 46
   Shamgar (3:31) .......................................................................................... 51

Deborah (Judg 4–5) ...................................................................................... 53
   A Dual Tradition ....................................................................................... 53
   Deborah: The Narrative (Judg 4) ........................................................... 56
      Dramatis Personae (4:1-11) ................................................................ 56
      Plot (4:12-24) ...................................................................................... 58
         Sisera's Defeat (4:12-16) ............................................................... 58
         Sisera's Demise (4:17-24) .............................................................. 59
      Jael among the Judges ....................................................................... 61
   Deborah: The Enigmatic Song (Judg 5) ................................................ 62
      Editorial Framework (5:1 and 31b) ................................................. 64
      Summons to Attend to the Song (5:2-9) ........................................ 64
      Summons to Bear Witness (5:10-12[13]) ....................................... 67
      The Song Proper—At Long Last (5:14-30) ................................... 69
         The Battle (5:14-23) ....................................................................... 69
         Two Women in Contrast (5:24-30) .............................................. 72
   A Theology of History—Reprise ........................................................... 73

Gideon (Judg 6–8) ........................................................................................ 75
   Structure ..................................................................................................... 76
   Introduction (6:1-6) .................................................................................. 76
   Supplement: The Prophet's Admonition (6:7-10) ............................... 78
   Block I: Gideon's Successes (6:11–7:25) ................................................ 79
      Gideon's Call/Commission: Part 1 (6:11-24) ................................ 79
      Gideon and the Altars (6:25-32) ...................................................... 83
      Gideon's Call/Commission: Part 2 (6:33-40) ................................ 83
      Preparations for Battle (7:1-8) .......................................................... 87
      A Final Sign for Gideon (7:9-14) ..................................................... 91
      Triumph for YHWH and for Gideon! (7:15-25) ........................... 91
   Block II: Tensions and Conflict (8:1-27) ............................................... 93

Contents

    Conflict with Ephraim (8:1-3) ................................................................ 94
    Conflict with Succoth and Penuel (8:4-9, 13-17) ...................... 95
    Gideon's Revenge (8:10-12, 18-21) ...................................... 96
    Gideon Refuses the Crown but Makes an Ephod (8:22-27) ........ 98
  Conclusion (8:28-35) ................................................................ 99

Abimelech (Judg 9) ................................................................................ 101
  Structure ................................................................................ 102
  Abimelech's Fratricidal Power Grab (9:1-6) ............................... 102
  Jotham's Parable (9:7-15) ........................................................ 105
  Jotham's Interpretation (9:16-21) ............................................. 106
  The Usurper Usurped (9:22-29) ............................................... 106
  Abimelech Suppresses the Rebels: Part 1 (9:30-41) ................. 108
  Abimelech Supresses the Rebels: Parts 2 and 3 (9:42-49) ........ 109
  The Outcome of Disloyalty (9:50-57) ...................................... 110

Jephthah (Judg 10–12) ........................................................................... 113
  The "Minor Judges" (10:1-5; 12:[7]8-15) ................................ 114
  The Framework Statement (10:6-16) ...................................... 116
  Gilead Seeks a Leader (10:17-18) ........................................... 118
  Jephthah Negotiates Terms with the Gileadites (11:1-11) ........ 119
  Jephthah's Failed Embassy to the Ammonites (11:12-28) ........ 123
  The Spirit, the Vow, and the Victory (11:29-33) ....................... 125
  Jephthah's Daughter (11:34-40) .............................................. 128
  Conflict: Jephthah and Ephraim (12:1-6) ................................. 133

Samson (Judg 13–16) ............................................................................ 137
  The Character of the Cycle and of Its Central Figures ............. 137
  Samson's Birth Narrative (Judg 13) ......................................... 139
    Genre as a Clue to the Focus of the Account ....................... 140
    The Focal Issue, Then: Samson, the Nazirite ........................ 143
  Samson's Adventures in Timnah (14:1–15:20) ......................... 147
    Samson in Timnah: Act I (Judg 14) ..................................... 147
      Prelude to a Wedding (14:1-9) ........................................ 148
      The Marriage Feast and the "Riddle" (14:10-14) ............ 148
      Betrayal and Mistrust (14:15-18) .................................... 150
      Samson's Revenge, Samson's Character, and
      Foreshadowing (14:19-20) ............................................. 151
      Behind the Scenes 1: Reading on Two Levels .................. 152

Samson in Timnah: Act II (Judg 15) ..............................................154
   Samson's Fiery Return to Timnah (15:1-8) .........................154
   The Philistines, the Judeans, and
   Samson at Lehi (15:9-19) ....................................................156
      Behind the Scenes 2: Reading on Two Levels....................158
      Concluding Formula (15:20)................................................159
Interlude: Samson's Adventure in Gaza (16:1-3) ...............................159
Samson's Adventures in the Valley of Sorek:
Samson and Delilah (16:4-20) ............................................................161
   Samson Marries Delilah from Sorek (16:4) ...........................162
   Seduction and Complicity (16:5-20) ....................................164
   Samson in Gaza (16:21-31) ..................................................166
   Behind the Scenes 3: Reading on Two Levels .......................167

The "Appendices"—Disarray and Disorder (Judg 17–21) .......................169
   Bi-Partite Structure of the Block..................................................170
   Micah, the Levite, the Danites, and the Sanctuaries in
   Bethel and Dan (Judg 17–18) .....................................................172
      Micah, the Levite, and the Sanctuary in Bethel (17:1-13) ........173
         Micah Founds a Sanctuary and Installs a
         Cultic Object (17:1-5)....................................................173
         Micah Installs a Priest-for-hire (17:7-13)........................174
      The Danites and their Sanctuary (18:1-31) .............................175
         The Danite Espionage Mission (Judg 18:1-10) ...................177
         The Danite Raids on Micah and Laish
         (18:11-26, 27-31) ............................................................179
   The Rape and Murder of the Levite's Concubine and
   Its Aftermath (Judg 19–21) .........................................................181
      The Levite's Concubine (Judg 19) ............................................181
         A Troubled and Troubling Marriage (19:1-11).................184
         Hospitality and the Criminally Inhospitable (19:12-21) ....186
         "Worthless Fellows," Abomination, and Ambiguity
         (19:22-30)........................................................................187
      Consequences: Civil War (20:1-48) .........................................190
         Gathering at Mizpah (20:1-10) .......................................191
         Benjamin Refuses Terms (20:11-13) ...............................194
         Three Days of Battle (20:14-48) .....................................195
            The First Two Days of Battle: Benjamin Routs the
            Israelite Army (20:14-25) ........................................196

Contents

       The Third Day of Battle: Ambush (20:26-48) ............197
       Seven Wrongs Do Not Make a Right (21:1-25) ........................199
          Once More at Bethel (21:1-14) ...........................................200
          More Wives for Benjamin (21:15-25) .................................201
          Collective Punishment Gone Wild .......................................204

Works Cited ..................................................................................207

# Editor's Foreword

The *Reading the Old Testament* series shares many of the aims and objectives of its counterpart, *Reading the New Testament*. Contributors to the current series, like those to its predecessor, write with the intention of presenting "cutting-edge research in [a form] accessible" to a wide audience ranging from specialists in the field to educated laypeople. The approach taken here, as there, focuses not on the minutiae of word-by-word, verse-by-verse exegesis but on larger literary and thought units, especially as they function in the overall conception of the book under analysis. From the standpoint of method, volumes in this series will employ an eclectic variety of reading strategies and critical approaches as contributors deem appropriate for explicating the force of the text before them. Nonetheless, as in RNT, "the focus [will be] on a close reading of the final form of the text." The overarching goal is to provide readers of the commentary series with an aid to help them become more competent, more engaged, and more enthusiastic readers of the Bible as authoritative Scripture.

The title of the series prompts several comments. For the editor, at least, the term "Old Testament" is a convenient convention, since any alternative seems either awkward or provocative. The Hebrew Bible is the shared heritage of Judaism and Christianity, the body of believers whom Paul once described as branches from a wild olive tree who have been "grafted contrary to nature into a cultivated olive tree" (Rom 11:24). Since the beginnings of Christianity, questions concerning how and in what sense the Hebrew Bible/Old Testament functions as Christian Scripture have perpetually confronted the church. Nonetheless, throughout its history, in the spirit of Paul, the church has insisted that the God of Abraham, Isaac, and Jacob is the God of the New Testament. Rather than impose a detailed doctrine of the unity of the two Testaments or specify a particular hermeneutical approach, the editor and the publisher have chosen to invite contributions to the series from scholars selected because of their learning and insight, again in the spirit of Paul, we hope, without regard to faith tradition or denominational identity.

The books of the Hebrew Bible were the fountainhead for the faith of both Paul and Aqiba. May it be that, through the scholarship presented in the pages of this series, the books of the "Old Testament" water the faith of another generation.

*—Mark E. Biddle, General Editor*
*Richmond, Virginia*

# Author's Preface

Several individuals and groups who assisted and encouraged me as I researched and wrote this commentary on Judges deserve special thanks. First, my students in the spring 2010 iteration of class B1136—"Judges: Exegesis" at the Baptist Theological Seminary in Richmond accompanied me in the initial phases of deepening my familiarity with the book. They may recognize some of the insights and observations we developed together during that semester of exploration. I am grateful for their openness and curiosity. Second, I completed the bulk of the research and writing of the commentary during a sabbatical leave from BTSR graciously afforded me by the school's faculty, administration, and trustees. The absence of even one faculty member at an institution the size of BTSR complicates the work of those continuing the endeavor, and the expense alone represents a significant contribution, all in order to give one the space to research, think, and write. I cannot express my gratitude sufficiently. Third, Andy Farmer, my current teaching assistant, carefully and efficiently read the entire manuscript, calling to my attention a number of typographical and other errors. Fourth, as always, the editorial staff at Smyth & Helwys set their diligent and professional hands to polishing and preparing the manuscript for publication. No doubt, despite the thorough attention of both Andy and the publishers, my shortcomings may have survived. They are, of course, to be charged entirely to my account. Finally, I must thank my wife for her patience with the quirks of a biblical scholar agonizing with the task who was simultaneously a father confronting the first year of an "empty nest." I hope she was able to see the commentary project as an exercise needed, in part, to fill the space.

Another gaping space opened in my life during the writing of this commentary. My paternal grandmother, Ettie Jeanette Jones Biddle, passed away at an advanced age and expectedly in November 2010 to be followed only two months later, unexpectedly, by my mother. I dedicate this commentary on Judges to my father—who modeled for my brother and me what it means to "honor father and mother" and to love one's wife "as Christ loved the church," continuing thereby to teach us, as a good father does, long after we had emptied his nest—and to the memory of my beloved mother.

*—Mark E. Biddle*
*Richmond, Virginia*

# Reading Judges

Issues and Approach

For several decades, biblical scholars have been debating the merits of two contrasting approaches to biblical interpretation. In the middle of the twentieth century, scholars began to raise objections to the historical-critical approach that had dominated the study of Scriptures in the modern era. These critics proposed that a book such as Judges should be read *synchronically*, that is, as an existing whole, rather than *diachronically* by means of analyses of its constitution and composition or by redaction history. The meaning of a text for a contemporary reader, argued the synchronists, arises in the reader's encounter with the text as it exists, not from a reconstruction of the stages of its growth and the historical contexts of those stages of growth. The proper setting for reading the text is the reader's context, not reconstructed settings in the ancient past.

This commentary will reflect the position that, while the debate calls attention to the need for clarifying the various objectives involved in interpreting Scripture, it ultimately poses a false dichotomy. For the purposes of a theological reading of Judges, for example, a diachronic analysis focused solely or chiefly on reconstructing a period in the history of ancient Israel—its tribal structure, settlement patterns, international relations, religious and legal institutions, gender relations, marriage practices, etc.—may prove somewhat sterile. On the other hand, reading a book such as Judges with no attention to historical questions risks a denial of the circumstances of distance and continuity. In other words, to read a-historically overlooks the character of Scripture as a witness to God's ongoing relationship with God's people and as rooted in tradition. Furthermore, a book such as Judges exhibits such obvious and definite signs of its compositional character that leveling them threatens to produce an equally flat reading lacking sensitivity to the dynamics of polarity, complexity, and development that diachronic analyses reveal.

An admittedly crude analogy may help to illustrate the balanced approach attempted in this commentary on Judges. Does one enjoy a bacon, lettuce, and tomato sandwich as a whole or as constituent ingredients? How palatable would one find homogenized bacon, lettuce, and tomato paste? Would it even be recognizable? Part of the enjoyment one derives from a BLT derives, in fact, from the experience of layers of distinct flavors and textures—one sandwich made of distinct components with distinct characters and origins. A dynamic reading of the one book of Judges will attend to the interplay between its various components. Each flavor must be noted in order to enjoy their interaction fully. To change metaphors, each voice must be allowed to contribute to the conversation (compare Niditch's concepts of "voices" and "registers," 2008, 8–18)—even if, or especially since, these voices stem from distinct cultural and historical settings that account for their individual characters and thus color the harmony of the whole. In other words, given the unmistakable evidence of the literary growth of Judges over time, this commentary will attempt to read it as a *complex* unit, not as a homogenous uniformity. On the other hand, it will not endeavor extensive reconstructions of Israelite cultural, political, or religious history when such reconstructions do not productively inform a theological reading of the book. The vexing question of the pattern of ancient Israel's settlement in the land constitutes but one example. Such efforts have their valid place elsewhere.

## The Problem of Cultural Values

Reading the Old Testament book of Judges, in particular, presents a number of significant challenges related to social contexts, historical settings, and literary characteristics. Acknowledging and examining these difficulties provides a point of entry into the world of Judges and promises to enrich the reading experience.

For contemporary Western readers, perhaps the first obstacle to reading Judges as authoritative Scripture involves the violence, patriarchalism, and tribalism evident in the stories of Israel's judges. The reaction against such un-enlightened behavior and attitudes has prompted one commentator to remark, "the OT, especially books such as Judges, contains material that flies in the face of everything we identify as biblical morality. We do not know what to do with the rape, murder, genocide, sexual immorality, child sacrifice, lying, idolatry, and stealing" (Brown, 123). In fact, this reaction has a long history in the interpretation of the book. Like contemporary readers, pre-modern commentators and preachers also deliberated the morality of Ehud's deception and regicide, questioned Gideon's suitability for leadership given his manifest hesitancy and need of reassurance, and puzzled over Jephthah's rash vow, his daughter's facile acquiescence, and God's (non-)role in the whole affair (Gunn, 35, 94, 134–169, respectively).

The ability to approach Judges in such a way that it can be allowed to speak on its own terms requires a measure of initial restraint with respect to the application of contemporary standards. At an appropriate point in the process of interpretation, such an assessment becomes inevitable, of course. Without excusing or apologizing for the morality displayed by characters in the book of Judges, especially with regard to violence and the treatment of women, some evidence suggests, in fact, that many of the elements that readers, pre-modern and contemporary alike, have found or find objectionable were equally problematic for the narrator(s) and editors of Judges. The narrator(s) of the account of the rape and murder of the anonymous Levite's concubine and its aftermath (Judg 19–21), for example, seem(s) to have intentionally styled it to accentuate the horror and repugnance of the actions of the Benjamites from Gibeah and, indeed, of the Levite. In fact, at points, figures within the story voice the repulsion felt, no doubt, by narrator and reader alike (19:30; 20:3, 10, 12-13).

The tendency to react against moral deficiencies on the part of biblical characters parallels or mirrors a category error commonly committed in reading Scriptures. To the extent that the Bible is narrative, one must maintain the distinction between the authoritative character of its overall message and the very human failings of characters who appear in it. Put bluntly, believers hold to various understandings of the inspiration and authority of Scripture, but they surely do not value the moral authority of David the adulterer or Cain the fratricide. In fact, the power of biblical narrative derives in large part from its unvarnished portrayals of human foibles and failures—and of God's steadfast commitment to relationship with humankind nonetheless.

## Judges or Anti-Heroes?

With regard to Judges, specifically, the violence, disarray, deception, and especially the repugnant treatment of women also constitute elements of the literary genre of the book. The key figures, the protagonists, of these narratives act with the intention of benefitting their people in the struggle for territory and survival in conditions that resemble, in many ways, the

American frontier West. One scholar (Christiansen) even compares the likes of Ehud ("Loner") to the typical anti-hero of Western fiction. Prey to marauding bands of Midianites and Amelekites (Judg 6:3-6), threatened by Moabite and Ammonite expansion (Judg 3:12-13; 11:3), and pressured on the other side by the Philistines (Judg 13–16), various Israelite groups found in these "social bandits" (Hobsbawm, see also Niditch 1990) their Robin Hood or Clint Eastwood. In addition to the common role they played, individuals in this group of "judges" shared only a degree of outsider status. Apart from Deborah, the book celebrates none of them as paragons of virtue or models of faith and piety. They were not religious heroes; instead, they were, variously, non-Israelite (Othniel), left-handed (Ehud), female (Deborah), insignificant (Gideon), "illegitimate" (Jephthah), and philandering (Samson).

In this regard, the English term "judges" conventionally employed to designate these leaders as a class, while not inaccurate, does not convey the full range of the meaning of terms derived from the Hebrew root *shft* ("to judge"), and certainly not of the root *ysh'* ("to deliver, save") that appears in comparable frequency in the book of Judges. "Judge" evokes images of the legal system, of the courtroom, and of an impartial arbiter of the law. The Hebrew concept, in contrast, involves active partisanship in the interests of reestablishing proper order in communal relationships. It extends well beyond interpreting the law, issuing legal rulings, and rendering verdicts to include direct intervention such that, "in Hebrew 'to judge' and 'to help' are parallel ideas" (Köhler, 133). Judges 3:10, for example, explicates the verb "to judge" with the statement "and he went out to war" (cf. Ps 72:4, which parallels "to judge" with "to deliver"). Although the English Bible traditionally titles the book "Judges," the noun *shofet* actually occurs only in Judges 2:16-19 and 4:4, and the verbal form of the root, which appears much more frequently, does so primarily in the lists of the so-called "minor" judges (10:2, 3; 12:7, 8, 9, 11, 13, 14). The limited information in these lists does not indicate how figures such as Tolah, Jair, Ibzan, etc. functioned, although descriptions of the duration of the careers of these "judges" give the impression that they were office-holders, not charismatic leaders. In any case, the only text in the book that seems explicitly to depict a judicial or administrative function refers to Deborah's activity "under the Palm of Deborah between Ramah and Bethel . . . where the people of Israel came up to her for judgment (*mishpat*)" (4:4). Jephthah's negotiations with the Gileadites concerning his appointment as "leader" (*qatsin*, 11:6) and "head" (*rosh*, 11:8) do not involve the language of judgeship. Samson certainly does not fulfill the role of the wise adjudicator. In his case, "judging" (15:20; 16:31) means annoying and killing Philistines, "beginning to deliver (*ysh'*) Israel" from their hand.

In fact, in contrast to the lists of "minor" judges, in particular, the narratives of the activity of the "major" judges characterize them as "deliverers/saviors" (Heb. *moshia'*, 3:9, 15; 6:36) and prefers to designate them by their actions rather than with a title (verb *ysh'*, "to deliver/save"; 3:9, 31; 6:14, 15, 37; 8:22; 10:1; 13:5). Even the programmatic introduction to the book twice describes the "judges" (noun *shofetim*) as those who "delivered" (verb *ysh'*) Israel (2:16,18).

## Composition and Structure

The distribution of these two word families (*shft* and *ysh'*) points to structural features of the book of Judges, which in turn simultaneously mirror the history of the formation of the book and outline the contours of a central issue in reading/interpreting Judges. The concentration of the terms "judge/to judge" in the two lists of "minor" judges and in the programmatic introduction (2:6–3:6) contrasts with the "deliverer" vocabulary of the individual accounts of the exploits of the "major" judges. In addition to these differing types of materials, the two blocks of narrative that conclude the book, namely the story of Micah's shrine (Judg 17–18) and the account of the rape and murder of the Levite's concubine and its sordid aftermath (Judg 19–21), do not involve judge/deliverer figures or Israel's encounters with outside oppressors at all. Instead, they relate extended episodes of domestic disharmony and disarray. Furthermore, each of these narrative blocks evidence a degree of internal structure (i.e., the refrain "In those days, when there was no king in Israel," 17:6; 18:1; 19:1; 21:25, unique to chapters 17–21) and independent narrative logic.

Similarly, in its present form, the book begins with a rather enigmatic catalog summarizing the degrees of success, or more accurately failure, experienced by the various Israelite tribal groups in their efforts to control the territories allotted to them. This material stands out in context for its redundancy. It sometimes repeats, almost verbatim, sections of its predecessor in the canon (cf. Judg 1:11-15 par. Josh 15:15-19), sometimes uses presumably older materials as a model for constructing similar statements about other Israelite groups (cf. the statements that Ephraim [Josh 16:10 par. Judg 1:28] and Manasseh [Josh 17:13 par. Judg 1:27] subjected Canaanite populations to forced labor as models for similar statements regarding Zebulon [Judg 1:29] and Naphtali [Judg 1:33]), sometimes virtually contradicts its predecessor (cf. Judg 1:21 and Josh 18:11), and sometimes appropriates materials from other contexts (cf. Judg 1:17 and Num 21:3; Judg 1:36 and Num 34:4; Judg 2:3 and Exod 23:33; 34:12; Deut 7:16; and Josh 23:13), all in order to construct an exhaustive summary of the successes and failures of nine (counting the half-tribes of Manasseh and Ephraim) of the twelve tribes of Israel (omitting Levi, Isaachar, and Gad in the standard listing).

In terms of literary character and macro-structure, then, the book of Judges unmistakably represents a composite work, produced over time in several stages of collection and editing. While any reconstruction of such a process of literary development grows increasingly speculative in proportion to its degree of detail, Judges scholarship substantially agrees that the book formed in the following major phases.

**Book of Saviors Core (Judg 3–16[?])**
Noting not only that the core material dealing with the feats of the "major" judges refers to its protagonists as "deliverers/saviors" but that, in contrast to the material that frames the individual accounts, these core accounts display little interest in explicitly religious or cultic matters and focus attention exclusively on northern (i.e., non-Judahite) circumstances, W. Richter has argued that the narratives contained in Judges 3–16 represent an older form of the book of Judges, a "Book of Saviors," of northern provenance. Subsequently, Judahite Deuteronomists edited it in service of their pan-Israelite theology of history. These deliverer/savior figures were the legendary local heroes remembered from the dawn of Israel's historical consciousness of itself as a people resident in the land. While the stories about these deliverer/saviors, which recount the ingenious, daring, and often remarkable successes of the protagonists over Israel's various local enemies, attribute these victories to divine assistance, the heroes of the stories do not appear as religious reformers (with the sole exception of Gideon's cautious, even timid, destruction of the Baal site in his village, 6:25-32). Moreover, the stories themselves do not attribute the difficulties Israel faced to its apostasy, describe any act of penitence that motivates YHWH's intervention on Israel's behalf, or detail any steps undertaken to conform to Israelite orthodoxy.

Although Richter's "Book of Saviors" hypothesis has gained a degree of scholarly acceptance (cf. Römer, 37, and Rüdiger, 233, who describes the hypothesis as "controversial" but not yet falsified; for a critique of Richter and an alternative reconstruction of the composition history of Judges, see Becker), the question of the extent of this early collection continues to be debated, especially with regard to the Samson material. The accounts of the careers of Gideon (plus Abimelech) and Jephthah already constitute cycles or blocks of material evidencing internal principles of organization and editorial interests other than those that would have presumably motivated the collectors responsible for the earliest form of the "Book of Saviors." Abimelech's illegitimate seizure of power, for example, evokes associations with a strand of materials skeptical of monarchy known elsewhere (see 1 Sam 8 and 10, for example) and suggests deuteronomistic concerns. Some scholars, perhaps most notably O. Margalith (1985, 1986a, 1986b, 1987; so also Römer, 137–38), have observed that the Samson block, however, bears the marks of Hellenistic influence, especially with regard to Samson the Danite's similarities to Hercules/Herakles the Danoi (see commentary below).

### Deuteronomistic Framework and the "Deuteronomistic Paradigm"

The framework material, on the other hand, incorporates the accounts of local victories over hostile neighbors as paradigmatic examples into an overarching theological view of Israel's history that extends, ultimately, from Israel's beginnings as a people (Deuteronomy) to the end of the independent existence of the nation-state of Judah (2 Kings). In the Hebrew canon, Judges appears along with Joshua and the books of Samuel and Kings in these "Former Prophets" (in the Hebrew canon, Ruth belongs in the "Writings"). Modern scholarship recognizes these books as a continuous work in six volumes, as it were, that offers an account of the history of Israel as a nation with a view, particularly, to explaining the fall of the northern kingdom of Israel to the Assyrians and of the southern kingdom of Judah to the Babylonians. Like Judges, these books represent sometimes independent source materials combined by editors whose language and theological view of history reflect the diction and theology of the book of Deuteronomy (the literature on deuteronomisticism is abundant; see esp. Weinfeld 1972; cf. also Noth; Friedman; Peckham; Nelson). Because of the clear influence of the book of Deuteronomy on the thought and language of the editors of the "Former Prophets," scholars often refer to the collection as the "Deuteronomistic History." Its scheme of the course of the history of Israel/Judah, which scholars term the "Deuteronomistic Paradigm," most clearly and concisely stated in Judges 2:6-11, runs throughout the editorial layer of material in the collection and finds a parallel near the end in 2 Kings 17:7-23, the editorial commentary on the collapse of the northern kingdom of Israel in 722 BCE.

> This occurred because the people of Israel had sinned against the LORD their God, who had brought them up out of the land of Egypt from under the hand of Pharaoh king of Egypt. They had worshiped other gods and

walked in the customs of the nations whom the LORD drove out before the people of Israel, and in the customs that the kings of Israel had introduced. The people of Israel secretly did things that were not right against the LORD their God. They built for themselves high places at all their towns, from watchtower to fortified city; they set up for themselves pillars and sacred poles on every high hill and under every green tree; there they made offerings on all the high places, as the nations did whom the LORD carried away before them. They did wicked things, provoking the LORD to anger; they served idols, of which the LORD had said to them, "You shall not do this." Yet the LORD warned Israel and Judah by every prophet and every seer, saying, "Turn from your evil ways and keep my commandments and my statutes, in accordance with all the law that I commanded your ancestors and that I sent to you by my servants the prophets." They would not listen but were stubborn, as their ancestors had been, who did not believe in the LORD their God. They despised his statutes, and his covenant that he made with their ancestors, and the warnings that he gave them. They went after false idols and became false; they followed the nations that were around them, concerning whom the LORD had commanded them that they should not do as they did. They rejected all the commandments of the LORD their God and made for themselves cast images of two calves; they made a sacred pole, worshiped all the host of heaven, and served Baal. They made their sons and their daughters pass through fire; they used divination and augury; and they sold themselves to do evil in the sight of the LORD, provoking him to anger. Therefore the LORD was very angry with Israel and removed them out of his sight; none was left but the tribe of Judah alone. Judah also did not keep the commandments of the LORD their God but walked in the customs that Israel had introduced. The LORD rejected all the descendants of Israel; he punished them and gave them into the hand of plunderers, until he had banished them from his presence. When he had torn Israel from the house of David, they made Jeroboam son of Nebat king. Jeroboam drove Israel from following the LORD and made them commit great sin. The people of Israel continued in all the sins that Jeroboam committed; they did not depart from them until the LORD removed Israel out of his sight, as he had foretold through all his servants the prophets. So Israel was exiled from their own land to Assyria until this day. (2 Kgs 17:7-23 NRSV)

In the Judges form, the paradigm of Israel's history involves four elements. First, Israel falls into apostasy, forsaking YHWH, the God of their fathers, worshiping the gods of the surrounding nations (2:11-12). Second,

## Issues and Approach 11

they "provoke" (*kʿs*) YHWH to anger through their apostasy (2:12; a characteristically deuteronomistic statement; cf. Deut 4:25; 9:18; 31:29; 32:16, 19, 21, 27; 1 Sam 1:6, 7, 16; 1 Kgs 14:9, 15; 15:30; 16:2; etc.) so that he "sells them" to their enemies, working against rather than for Israel (2:14-15). Third, after a period, God raises up "judges" to deliver Israel from their oppressors (2:16). Fourth, despite God's intervention, the people soon relapse into their apostasy.

The deuteronomistic editors of the book of Judges likely also incorporated and may have composed the two lists of so-called "minor" judges (10:1-5; 12:7-15). The annalistic style of these lists, evidence that they stem from a source document or documents, certainly parallels the deuteronomistic use of similar chronicles and annals as structural components in its record of the reigns of the kings of Israel and Judah (cf. 1 Kgs 14:19-21; 15:1-2; etc.). Further, the first such list in Judges accompanies the most extensive formulation of the framework scheme apart from its initial statement in the introduction to the deuteronomistic book of Judges, linking the incorporation of the lists in the book with the activity of the deuteronomistic editors. Moreover, the appearance of a "Jephthah" in the source may have facilitated the placement of these lists, which bracket the Jephthah cycle (cf. Mayes 1983, 72), and, thus, the deuteronomistic editors' identification of the ad hoc heroes of the "Book of Saviors" with the "office-holders" catalogued in the lists of "minor" judges.

### Preface/Appendices Outer Envelope

Finally, the two "appendices" in Judges 17–18 and 19–21—which focus not on external threats to Israel but on internal decay, and offer no hero figures—exhibit similarities and points of contact with the "preface" to the final form of the book of Judges (1:1–2:5). As already noted, the preface, too, disrupts its canonical context. Further, like the "appendices," it portrays Bethel as a place of mourning (2:1-5; cf. 20:26; 21:2; see Mayes 1983, 79), depicts a situation of growing internal disarray, and, specifically, offers the story of Caleb's treatment of his daughter (1:12-15) as the backdrop for the deteriorating treatment of women in the book of Judges that culminates in the marital rape of hundreds of Shilonite women (21:19-24). Perhaps the most prominent commonality between the preface and the appendices, however, is their shared focus on Judah. In contrast to the older "Book of Saviors" material, which mentions Judah only incidentally in Judges 10:9 in a comment that may be secondary and reports that the men of Judah took action to curb Samson's agitation of the Philistines (Judg 15:9-11), the preface and the appendices refer to Judah ten times each. In fact, Judah is conspicuously absent in passages such as the list of tribes that participated in the campaign led by Deborah and Barak (Judg 5). The intention of the preface and the appendices in this regard seems to be to envelope the northern material with material that highlights Judah's supremacy (cf. Judg 1:1-2 and 20:18), although the account of Micah, the Levite from Judah, which does not reflect positively on Judah either, complicates the picture.

## Framework, Envelope, and Interpretation

The results of this analysis of the structure and growth of Judges represent more than speculation concerning literary history. Instead, they establish the major outlines of the hermeneutical challenge—the interpretive task—confronting contemporary readers of the book, namely how to deal with the multiple contexts in which the book took shape and which imply the multiple audiences it addresses. Taken as a group, the various accounts collected in the hypothetical "Book of Saviors," for example, reflect the interests and concerns of a frontier people struggling for survival. They celebrate valor and daring and, above all, the ironic and the surprising. Ehud, the left-handed Benjaminite (lit., "son of the right hand"); Deborah and Jael, Israel's female saviors; and Gideon the reticent exemplify varieties of unlikely deliverers. They do not, however, stand as examples of morality or piety. Instead, their acts of deliverance illustrate the willingness of Israel's God to work through the most unlikely in rather unexpected ways: assassination, trickery, opportunism.

Contrary to the impression given by the deuteronomistic framework and, probably, to the expectations of contemporary readers, these accounts do not depict a systematic paradigm for YHWH's delivering activity. According to the Song of Deborah, YHWH intervenes on Barak's behalf, apparently, through some meteorological phenomenon that nullifies Sisera's military advantage in equipment and numbers (see commentary) and, in Gideon's case, by intensifying the terrifying effect of an ingenious ruse (see commentary). The text states that YHWH "raises up" two judges (Othniel, 3:9; Ehud, 3:15) without specifying what this entailed. In contrast, YHWH gave specific instructions to two others (Deborah, 4:6; Gideon, 6:12) and to a third before his birth through his mother (Samson, 13:3-5). Alternatively, YHWH played no obvious role in selecting Jephthah, although, as with Othniel (3:10), Gideon (6:34), and Samson (13:35; 14:6, 19), the Spirit overcame him subsequent to his selection (11:29). In every instance, this Spirit-possession has the character of empowerment for extraordinary physical feats, not inspiration with wisdom or the prophetic word. In short, these accounts evidence no interest in piety, ethics, or worship. The deliverers do not represent examples of piety, nor do they champion the cause of orthodoxy; their God calls them to fight for Israel's survival and empowers them to this task, exploiting and amplifying their own cunning and courage.

It is not difficult to imagine the delight of an ancient Israelite audience in these tales of Israelite (and non-Israelite) individuals who, sometimes chosen by YHWH for the task and sometimes divinely empowered for it, knew how and when to seize opportunity. Contemporary readers may find it difficult to establish some point of contact with these frontier champions and this God of ruses and raw power. Contemporary readers do not constitute the primary, or even secondary, audience for these stories, after all. Recognizing and acknowledging the phenomenon is only a point of departure, however. The commentary will offer readers possibilities for finding meaning in these stories of daring feats of survival.

The viewpoint of the paradigm material suits contemporary tastes and expectations more readily, in a sense. It proposes a grand theological scheme of Israelite history that understands the broad sweep of events in terms of the blessing and curse model known from the book of Deuteronomy. According to it, on the condition that Israel demonstrates fidelity to YHWH and his covenant, YHWH will bestow abundant blessing (Deut 28:1-14). Contrariwise, should Israel prove unfaithful, YHWH will discipline his people with equal vigor (Deut 28:15-68). Remarkably, the deuteronomistic framework of the book of Judges devotes little attention to the details of Israel's apostasy. Further, it seems either to assume that Israel repented and reformed its behavior under the judges or, as seems most likely, to ground YHWH's deliverance in YHWH's grace and faithfulness to his people quite apart from their repentance (see commentary). The deuteronomistic editors of Judges did not find the significance of the fact that the pattern of Israel's cycle of apostasy reached back to the earliest period in the land (indeed, according to deuteronomistic texts in the Torah, all the way back to Mt. Sinai, Exod 32:1-8) in these details, but in the long history of this pattern of behavior. It evidenced not only Israel's persistent infidelity but also YHWH's extraordinary forbearance. In the deuteronomistic scheme of Israel's history, the catastrophes of 722 and 586 BCE—the Assyrian and Babylonian conquests of the northern and southern kingdoms, respectively—did not represent sudden outbursts of divine anger. Instead, they culminated a series of manifestations of YHWH's discipline that extended back for centuries. In this sense, the deuteronomistic paradigm enunciated in Judges serves the purposes of theodicy. Looking back from the perspective of the Babylonian crisis, the Deuteronomists could comment that, for centuries, "YHWH warned Israel and Judah by every prophet and every seer, saying, 'Turn from your evil ways and observe my commandments and my statutes, according to all the law that I commanded your fathers and sent to you by my servants the prophets.' Yet they would not listen, but were stiff-necked, as their ancestors had been, who did not believe in YHWH their God" (2 Kgs 17:13-14).

While this concern for theodicy may govern the Deuteronomistic History as a whole, remarkably, the deuteronomistic appropriation of the "Book of Saviors" results in a book of Judges that focuses attention only on the final element of the "Deuteronomistic Paradigm," God's deliverance. The effect, whether intended by the deuteronomistic editors or not, is subtle but unmistakable. Scholars debate whether the abrupt ending of the larger Deuteronomistic History in the comment that the last Judean king, Jehoiachin, lived out his life in Babylonian exile under the patronage of the Babylonian king (2 Kgs 25:29-30) reflects the deuteronomistic view that the long cycle of apostasy and deliverance has come to an end (so Noth, 98, and Gray, 42), or the contrary notion that the Deuteronomists saw the king's survival as an emblem of hope for a national future (so von Rad 1947, 63–64, and 1962, 343; alternatively, Cross, 277, has argued that the Deuteronomistic History, which was originally optimistic about the future of the Davidic line, later underwent a pessimistic redaction; for a review of the debate, see Levenson). Despite the reward-and-punishment character of the Deuteronomistic Paradigm, the book of Judges, at the other end of Israel's history of apostasy, attests primarily to YHWH's willingness to deliver—again and again.

The envelope around the savior-and-judge complex represents a third context. Its refrain implying some connection between Israel's misbehavior and its "anarchistic," pre-monarchial status is difficult to interpret. Together with the preface's emphasis on the relative success and failure of the various Israelite tribes in assuming control of the territories allotted them (i.e., in displacing the Canaanite populations), this refrain raises the question of the kind of (political) leadership appropriate for Israel. The judges/deliverers do not perform such roles. Indeed, Gideon rejects the suggestion that he become Israel's king, and the actions of his son, Abimelech, only illustrate the perils associated with an illegitimate claimant to royal power. Jephthah's negotiations with the Gileadites seem to involve military leadership, not necessarily governance. Nonetheless, the "no-king" refrain casts its shadow back over the whole book and forward over the entire Deuteronomistic History in its final form. While scholarship differs regarding the date and social setting of this envelope around the judges/deliverers material (see

Rüdiger, 236), its themes—the priority of Judah, the illegitimacy of the northern sanctuary, the anarchy that results from the lack of stable leadership—suggest a context of tension between North and South. Such tensions characterized much of the history of the existence of parallel Israelite kingdoms but also resurfaced in the Persian period as jealousy between Jews and "Samaritans" (cf. Ezra 4; Neh 4). Regardless of the historical setting that produced this material and incorporated it into the final form of the book of Judges, the text represents a study in negatives. Rather than propose a positive model for leadership, it illustrates the decline that can result from the absence of legitimate leadership. In canonical context, then, an understanding of the appendices to Judges as an implication that monarchy and anarchy constitute binary options cannot be sustained (see commentary). As the Deuteronomistic History unfolds, it becomes clear that the institution of the monarchy, per se, does not guarantee good order either. Canonically speaking, legitimacy does not derive from an institution.

## The Transmission of the Text and Interpretation

The text of the book of Judges, like the wording of all other books in the canonical Hebrew Bible, comes to contemporary readers in the form of a number of ancient manuscript traditions in both the original Hebrew language and in translation. Although Hebrew manuscripts reflect the original language of Judges, they should not be confused with the original document itself. Arguably, the most important witness to the text of the Hebrew Bible, including Judges, and the point of departure for this commentary are the manuscripts in the Masoretic tradition (MT) that were produced by a group of early medieval Jewish scholars and scribes known as the Masoretes ("transmitters"). They were known for their erudition and meticulous attention to the text. In the case of Judges, however, more than 1,500 years separates the completion of the process that produced the final form of the book in Hebrew and the oldest complete Masoretic manuscript of Judges still in existence (Codex Aleppo, mid-tenth century CE). Theoretically, the process of hand-copying manuscripts (lit., "hand-written") over such a long period could have been the occasion for any number of copyist's errors, whether omissions or additions, and confusions as the language of the Bible became increasingly foreign even to speakers of late Hebrew.

For these and comparable reasons, scholars also give considerable weight to ancient translations, most notably to manuscripts in the Greek tradition known collectively as the Septuagint (LXX). The value of Greek manuscripts as evidence for the original text of the Hebrew Bible derives from their relative antiquity in comparison to the MT. The magisterial Codices Alexandrinus and Vaticanus are approximately 600 years older than the comparable Masoretic Codices Aleppo and Leningradensis. To complicate matters, however, the Greek tradition of Judges exists in two forms, designated LXX A (the form found in Codex Alexandrinus) and LXX B (Codex Vaticanus). Scholars debate whether these two forms of the text represent independent translations of the Hebrew into Greek or recensions/revisions of a common predecessor Greek translation (see Soggin 1981, 18–19; Soisalon-Soininen; Trebolle Barrera 1991). Differences between the Greek and the Hebrew traditions may be evidence that the Hebrew tradition (MT) continued to develop into late antiquity and early medieval times (that is, after the translation of an earlier form of the text into Greek), that the Greek translators did not rightly or fully comprehend the Hebrew text before them at certain points, or that the process of copying Greek manuscripts suffered from the same kinds of corruption posited for the Hebrew manuscript tradition. In the end, each instance must be evaluated individually.

The manuscripts discovered in the caves at Qumran on the shores of the Dead Sea, which yielded rich stores of information concerning the textual history of much of the Hebrew Bible, included only two fragmentary scrolls containing parts of the text of Judges (1QJudg—6:20-22; 8:1; 9:1-6, 28-31, 40-43 and 4QJudg—6:2-6, 11-13; 21:12-25). Sections of these two scrolls preserved well enough to permit assessments of the textual tradition they represent seem to conform substantially to the Masoretic tradition despite predating the extant Masoretic texts by roughly a millennium. Only one passage in 4QJudg, namely 6:2-6, 11-13—which omits vv. 7-10, the deuteronomistic speech of the prophet commenting on Israel's cyclical apostasy—raises significant questions concerning the development of the text of Judges. Scholars take contrasting positions regarding whether the omission, along with the spacing of this passage in the Masoretic manuscripts that set 6:7-10 off from its context, attests to an early form of Judges that did not yet include the deuteronomistic framework of the book, including 6:7-10 (so, for example, Rofé, Hess; contra Marcos).

The commentary on this passage will examine the details of this debate. For now, the problem can serve as an example of the fluidity of the demarcation between textual criticism and literary analysis—whether diachronic or synchronic. Does the omission of 6:7-10 represent a scribal omission, or does it attest to a stage in the formation and redaction of the book of Judges? Increasingly, scholars recognize that the study of the manuscript tradition of the Hebrew Bible, including Judges, of course, requires a much more sophisticated set of questions than those based on the assumption that an "original" form of the text can be reconstructed according to the classical canons of textual criticism. Instead, "trouble spots" in the manuscript evidence such as Judges 6:7-10 often point to redactional, literary, or theological developments or to interpretative alternatives that arose around difficult texts in the transmission process. The commentary below will treat textual-critical matters primarily from this perspective: namely, it will ask what interpretive issue the ancient manuscript traditions recognized in the text and what lines of interpretation they initiated. Remarkably, just as modern interpreters hypothesized that Judges 6:7-10 constitutes a redactional insertion in the present context well *before* the discovery of 4QJudg—that is, the manuscript evidence anticipates the modern scholarly discussion by nearly two millennia—many modern critical discussions focus on passages that textual history suggests were already the topic of "discussion" among the earliest scribes.

## The Structure of Judges and of this Commentary

The structure of Judges establishes the plan for this commentary. Nine chapters will treat the introductory framework (Judg 1:1-36), the various theological assessments of Israel's history, including the "Deuteronomistic Paradigm" (2:1–3:6), the collection of three savior/judge vignettes (Judg 3), each of the "major" judges (Deborah, Judg 4–5; Gideon, Judg 6–8; Jephthah, Judg 10–12; Samson, Judg 13–16), including a separate treatment of the Abimelech material (Judg 9), and finally, the concluding "appendix" complex (Judg 17–21). The point of departure will be the Hebrew text in the Masoretic tradition, with attention to LXX and Qumran evidence only when it promises to offer insight into the theological interpretation of the text. The interpretation offered below intends to eschew the dichotomy between diachronic and synchronic approaches and to attend, rather, to both the whole and its parts. Finally, the discussion will deal with literary units rather than offer a verse-by-verse exposition.

# Preface

Judges 1:1–2:5

The opening unit of the book of Judges presents a reader with most, if not all, of the challenges encountered in reading Judges. Its arrangement into three sections dealing with the campaigns of conquest in the South (1:1-21) and in the North (1:22-36) followed by the verdict on the results of this two-pronged effort pronounced by the messenger of YHWH (2:1-5) roughly corresponds to the general impression given by the Joshua account of the conquest, namely that it began in the South (Josh 1–10). Nevertheless, Judges 1:1–2:5 does not sit comfortably in its context. From a canonical (and a historical) perspective, it manifests a number of inconsistencies (i.e., the statements concerning the conquest of Jebusite Jerusalem in vv. 8 and 21) and stands in considerable tension both with the continuation of the book of Judges and with its broader canonical context. For one, the note in Judges 1:1 to the effect that the events about to be narrated occurred *after* Joshua's death contradicts Judges 2:6-9; according to Joshua, they occurred *during* Joshua's lifetime.

Similarly, the Judges accounts of many of these events differ significantly in the details from the parallel reports in the book of Joshua. The fact that the multiple reports of the defeat of the "offspring of Anak," for example, variously credit Caleb (Josh 15:13-14; Judg 1:20) or Joshua (Josh 11:21) with the victory indicates the complicated nature of their interrelationship (see further Judg 1:19 = Josh 17:16; Judg 1:21 = Josh 15:63; Judg 1:27-28 = Josh 17:12-13; and Judg 1:29 = 16:10). Detailed examination of these parallels reveals that the texts in Judges 1 represent adaptations of the preexistent passages from Joshua (see Auld, 268–84; Rake, 34–73; Younger 1995; and immediately below). Other "continuity" problems, such as the reference to Gilgal (Judg 2:1), which seems unaware that the tent of meeting had been moved from there (Josh 14:6) to Shechem (Josh 18:1; see Lindars, 75), confirm scholars' suspicions that a process of editing produced the preface. Further, in terms of theme, substance, and diction, the second major unit in the book, Judges 2:6–3:6, tantamount in the final form of the book to a second introduction constituting the first component of a framework that structures the collection of judges materials in chapters 3–16, provides a much more suitable introduction (see already Budde, ix; cf. Auld, 261–62).

Scholars have long noted that Judges 2:6, which speaks of Joshua's dismissal of the people gathered, presumably in Shechem, to go to their inheritances, virtually duplicates the information given in Joshua 24:28-31 (see O'Doherty, 3–4). This observation and the contradictions and duplications of content between Judges 1 and Joshua have spawned a number of competing theories concerning the history of early Israel and of the literary growth of the book of Judges. Historians focus on the relative values of Joshua and Judges 1 as source material for the reconstruction of the history of early Israel. In short, they seek to answer the question of whether the Joshua version of events or the Judges version represents the older source. Literary historians grapple with the question of literary dependence. Differences and contradictions notwithstanding, the clear similarities between Judges 1 and select texts in Joshua call for explanation in terms of the literary adaptation of Joshua by Judges or vice versa.

Although the near-consensus view regards Judges 1 secondary to its context (see Rüdiger, 236), scholars disagree as to its date and function. In one view, Judges 1 constitutes the more primitive source material and Joshua represents an idealized picture, a triumphalist theology (the prevalent view in early twentieth-century scholarship, championed especially by Alt [see 26–27], who considered Judg 1 a document demonstrating the state of affairs just prior to King Saul or c. 1000 BCE). In terms of the literary history of the books of Joshua and Judges, these same observations lead many contemporary scholars to conclude that the period of the Judges is an artificial, literary construct produced by the insertion of Judges 1:1–2:5 into an originally unified context. The insertion intentionally created the distinction between the two books (see, for example, the various analyses by Smend, 506; Auld, 264; Brettler 1989, 435; *idem* 2002, 5–8; 94–96). Some scholars even argue that the entire book of Judges was inserted between Joshua and 1 Samuel as late as the Persian period (Schmid, see esp. 235, 373–74; cf. Kratz, 195; Guillaume, 227–53). In other words and in either case, Judges 1 constitutes a corrective substitute for the account of the almost total (compare Josh 11:23 and 13:1-6) conquest of the promised land in a single, albeit extended, campaign during Joshua's lifetime. Even for those whose primary interest lies in literary and theological readings of the text, the tensions between the portrayals in the book of Joshua and in Judges 1:1–2:5 require explanation. Read in canonical sequence, the contrast between

Joshua and Judges 1 highlights the idealistic quality either of the Joshua version of events or of the behavior of the Joshua generation (see Boling 1975, 66).

Whether, from a historical perspective, it represents a tradition of the conquest meant as an alternative to Joshua's account or, from a literary perspective, it reinterprets many of these traditions in relation to a period of decline much as the account of the Fall (Gen 3) follows immediately after the idyllic account of the Garden (Gen 2), the substance and thrust of Judges' contrasting depictions emerge clearly from a close examination of the material. Indeed, three central problems exemplified in the final form of the book of Judges surface in 1:1-36, namely (1) the preeminence of the tribe of Judah, which, some scholars argue, reflects the pro-Davidic, anti-Saulide tendencies evident also in the "appendices" to Judges (chs. 17–21); (2) Israel's decline from promising beginnings, as manifest especially (a) in growing intertribal disharmony and (b) in coarsening attitudes toward and treatment of women in Israel; and (3) the ambiguous presence of foreign elements within Israel. A fourth problem concerning the qualifications, strengths, and weaknesses of charismatic leadership will surface soon enough. Furthermore, although it only broaches three of these issues and does so in a relatively concise, even allusive, manner, the narrative in Judges 1:1-36 sets the stage sufficiently for the treatment in Judges 2 of the overarching question of the theological evaluation of the circumstances recounted in the book of Judges, the question of the theology of history.

### The Southern Campaign—Judah's Preeminence (1:1-21)

The central, probably older, section of the book of Judges may represent a literary collection that originated in the North; it certainly deals exclusively with northern figures, northern tribes, and northern settings (see introduction). The preface corrects this omission with an emphasis on the preeminence of Judah among the tribes of Israel that becomes apparent from the outset (cf. Auld, 285). After Joshua's death, the people seek direction from YHWH, presumably by means of the *urim* and *thummim* (see Num 27:21; 1 Sam 14:41; 28:6; Ezra 2:63) or through a prophet (see 1 Sam 9:9; 1 Kgs 22:5-9; 2 Kgs 3:11; 8:8, etc.), the two typical techniques, as to who should lead Israel in confronting the Canaanite inhabitants of the land. YHWH's response identifies the tribe of Judah as the tribe to whom YHWH has delivered the land. The tribe of Simeon, whose patronymic ancestor was the full brother of the patronymic ancestor of the tribe of Judah (Gen

29:33-34), accompanied its brother tribe in the campaign (vv. 3, 17), virtually surrendering its distinctive identity. At some point in Israel's history, in fact, Judah apparently absorbed Simeon (cf. Josh 19:1, 8, 9), a circumstance no doubt reflected in the Judges account.

Judah's multiple successes included (1) the defeat of the Canaanites and Perizzites at Bezek (vv. 4-5); (2) the initial defeat of Jerusalem (v. 8); (3) victories over the Canaanites dwelling in Hebron—including Seshai, Ahiman, and Talmai (v. 10), the "sons of Anak," a legendary nation of giants (lit., "long-necks," Biddle 2003, 23) in Debir (v. 11)—and in Zephath, which they renamed Hormah, "devoted to destruction" (v. 17; LXX translates *anathema*); and (4) the conquest of the Philistine coastal cities of Gaza, Ashkelon, and Ekron along with their satellites (lit., "daughter" villages). Judah also "took possession of the hill country" (v. 19), failing only to displace the population resident in "the plain." Perhaps extrapolating the pro-Judah tenor of Judges 1:1-21, LXX mitigates Judah's only failure by creatively translating the difficult phrase that explains it, "because they had chariots of iron." Understood literally, "chariots of iron" presents a difficulty since the weight of a chariot made of iron would far exceed the strength of the typical steed. Thus, R. Drews maintains that it refers rather to ironclad wheels. LXX resolved both difficulties by translating "because Rahab set them aside" (reading the proper name *rhb* instead of *rkb*, "chariots," and apparently reading *brzl* "iron," as *bdl* "to separate"; see Niditch 2008, 34). LXX implies thereby that Judah did not, in fact, fail to conquer the hill country. Instead, it honored its agreement with Rahab (Josh 2:12-14) who, in turn, extended her protection to the "inhabitants of the plain." This tendency in the Greek textual tradition to enhance pro-Judah elements may also account for the substitution of "Judah" in the A family of texts for "YHWH" in the Hebrew and Greek Kaige traditions in v. 22 ("The house of Joseph also went up against Bethel; and YHWH/Judah was with them"). In cases such as these, where the traditional Hebrew text is clearly superior, the significance of the Greek tradition of the text involves less its weight as a witness to the "original" text and more its value as an example of the earliest interpretive tradition. In particular, here, the Greek tendency to enhance Judah's stature provides ancient support for the modern identification of a pro-Judah tendency in Judges 1.

Although this catalogue of Judah's victories seems straightforward at first glance, it proves to be rich in complexity and nuance upon closer examination. In comparison even to claims made in Joshua, it stands out for its exorbitance, attributing successes to Judah that it would actually achieve only many years later. Israel was not able, in fact, to conquer Jerusalem until

David's time (contrast Josh 15:63 and 2 Sam 5:6-9), and the Philistine cities on the coastal plain mentioned in Judges 1, three of the Philistine Pentapolis, would beleaguer Israel until David as well (Josh 11:22; 13:2-3; Judg 16:1, 21; 1 Sam 6:17; 2 Sam 5:17-25). Indeed, the historical and canonical problem of these Philistine coastal cities seems to have motivated the LXX to transform v. 18 into a negative statement and to add a fourth city, Ashdod, to the list. Still, in comparison to the meager accomplishments Judges attributes to the other tribes in the North, the successes of Judah (and Simeon) function to affirm YHWH's decision to choose it to lead the campaign. With the exception of "the house of Joseph" at Bethel, these other tribes "did not drive out" the inhabitants of the major population centers in the North but settled, instead, for various forms of coexistence with Canaanites and Amorites. In this regard, the account in Judges 1 moves "from greatest success to deepening degrees of failure" (Stevenson, 52).

In keeping with the thesis that, like all "history," Judges engages in a depiction of "past as prelude," this focus on Judahite success suggests that Judges intends to make the case that the seeds of the later success of the Davidic monarchy can be found in the tribal dynamics of Israel's earliest period in the land (see Weinfeld 1993, 390). Indeed, Brettler (2002, 98) goes so far as to argue that "Judges is essentially a political tract which argues for the legitimacy of Davidic kingship." The contention that at least the theme of Judah's prominence, if not the other three major themes of Judges and thus the book as a whole, can be read as commentary on the Davidic monarchy finds support in how Judges 1 treats three groups other than Judah: the tribe of Benjamin, "the house of Joseph," and the tribe of Dan.

Coupled with the comment that Benjamin failed to drive the Jebusites out of Jerusalem despite the contention that Judah had previously captured the city, the Adonibezek incident (vv. 4-8), for example, bears all the marks of a sophisticated allusion to the relative merits of David's tribe, Judah, and Saul's tribe, Benjamin. Common proposals for locating Bezek (modern Khirbet Ibzek; see Zertal) do not meet expectations that this Bezek will be located in the territory of Judah, somewhere near Jerusalem. According to the only other reference to Bezek (1 Sam 11:8), it is where Saul, the Benjamite, came from his home in Gibeah in order to muster the forces of Israel and Judah for an expedition to deliver Jabesh-Gilead from an Ammonite siege. Thus, for a reader familiar with the Saul story, the reference in Judges 1:4 establishes associations with Saul and underscores the link to Benjamin. The name "Adonibezek" itself, however, offers a clue pointing in a different direction. It cannot be understood to indicate that its bearer is the ruler of Bezek where the incident took place, since otherwise the Old

Testament never refers to rulers by similar titles and since, in any case, Hebrew and Canaanite languages employ *ba'al* instead of *'adôn* in such constructions. Nor can it be easily understood as a so-called theophoric or "god-bearing" name ("My Lord is Bezek") on the model of Adonijah ("My Lord is Yah") since no deity Bezek is known.

Given the close parallels with the account of the defeat and humiliation of a king of Jerusalem named Adonizedek ("My Lord is Zedek," cf. "Melchizedek," the king of [Jeru]Salem, Gen 14:18) recorded in Joshua 10:1-27, many commentators think that Adonibezek is a derisive name given Adonizedek in the tradition or, more likely, by the editor of Judges 1 (cf. Auld, 269). If so, several options as to its meaning seem plausible. If *bezeq* is meant as a theophoric element, it may constitute word-play on *brq* (= "thunderbolt"), a possibility that hinges on the graphic similarities in Semitic alphabets between the letters *r* and *z*. Adonibezek would then be a thinly veiled reference to the Canaanite deity Baal Hadad, the Lord of the Storm, i.e., "Thunderbolt is my Lord" (see Guillaume, 91 n. 66). Alternatively, the name may be meant as an adumbration of the king's ultimate fate. Although the root *bzq* does not occur in the Hebrew Bible, it does occur in Arabic in the noun *bizqa*, "pebble, crumb." Adonibezek, the "lord of crumbs," would ironically be a fitting name for the king who forced seventy of his equals to eat crumbs from beneath the table like dogs before finding himself reduced to the same fate (see Hamlin, 26). Alternatively, the term *bzq* may be read as a composite of the Hebrew preposition *b*, "in" and the noun *zq*, "chain" (cf. Isa 45:14; Nah 3:10; Ps 149:8), in which case it would have also been meant as an ironic adumbration of the king's fate (see Hamlin, 26). It is entirely feasible that the name was meant to evoke both of these allusions. Certainly, nothing would prevent a reader from hearing echoes of both.

Altogether, the account of the Adonibezek incident, along with the comment in v. 21 concerning the Benjamite's failure to remove the Jebusites from Jerusalem despite the fact that the tribe of Judah had already subdued both the city and its king, foreshadows both the poor behavior of Benjamin described later in the book of Judges and the failures of Benjamin's representative, Saul (see also Weinfeld 1993, 390). David of Judah, like his ancestors, will accomplish what Saul of Benjamin and his ancestors could not.

## The Northern Campaign—Forces of Decay and Decline (1:22-36)

Obviously, the preface accomplishes its positive portrayal of Judah in part by means of denigrating the other tribes that competed with Judah for prominence in the monarchial period. In this context, the Bethel/Dan frame surrounding the account of the failures of the northern tribes (1:22-26, 34-36) assumes added significance. Traditions concerning Bethel in Israel's early period are confused and confusing. Some texts indicate that Bethel was the Israelite name for a city formerly called Luz (Judg 1:23; Gen 28:19; 35:6; 48:3), although Judges 1:26 seems to contradict the statement made just a few verses earlier. Alternatively, Joshua mentions two distinct cities, Bethel and Luz, situated on the boundary between Joseph and Benjamin (Josh 16:1; 18:13). Judges 1:22-26 may reflect this boundary location when it attributes the conquest of Bethel to the "house of Joseph," although Bethel is elsewhere assigned to Benjamite territory (Josh 18:22). Similarly, Bethel's association with Jacob and the ark of the covenant located there in the judges period (Judg 20:18) runs counter to the dominant attitude in the Deuteronomistic History toward the shrine located there (1 Kgs 12:26-33; 2 Kgs 10:29; 23:15-19; cf. Amos 4:4).

**Growing Internal Disharmony**
Does the Bethel/Dan frame in Judges 1:22-36 function as a device calling to mind the heterodox sanctuaries that Jeroboam I established in these cities? Joshua 22:10-34 already adumbrates concern for the danger inherent in worship at sanctuaries other than the central sanctuary authorized in the Deuteronomic code (Deut 12:10-32). Joshua describes the Transjordanian tribes' establishment of a sanctuary in the far north, west of the Jordan, presumably near Dan if the Joshua text does not intend a veiled reference to Dan itself. The allusive function of the Bethel/Dan frame draws additional energy from the end of the book of Judges, which focuses, in fact, on the shortcomings of the Danites, who "stole" their sanctuary, and of the Benjamites, who were defeated at Gibeah, later known as the home of King Saul.

Furthermore, considerable evidence suggests that Judges 2:1-5, the bridge between the opening unit of the book and the "theological introduction" (2:6-23), is a thinly veiled allusion to Bethel's heterodoxy. First, the place name "Bochim" ("weepers"), which occurs only here in the Old Testament, has an unusual definite article (e.g., "the Paris") and does not appear to have etiological significance. Taken together, these circumstances suggest that "Bochim" may be a substitute masking the actual name of the place to which it refers. Second, geographical requirements (proximity to Gilgal) and the LXX, which can be regarded once again as an early witness to an interpretive tradition, associate Bochim directly with Bethel. Third, the Old Testament also associates Bethel elsewhere with weeping (Judg 20:26;

21:2-4; Gen 35:8), with Gilgal (Amos 4:4; 5:5; Hos 4:15), and with rebuke (Amos 7:10-17; 1 Kgs 13; 2 Kgs 23:15-20). Finally, Judges 2:1-5 portrays the continued existence of the Canaanites in the land as YHWH's punishment on the north for the failures to displace the Canaanites detailed in 1:22-36, linking Bochim and corrupting Canaanite influence just as texts critical of the Bethel cult link it with idolatrous practices. Taken together, these observations lead Amit (2000, 121–31, citation 131) to conclude that "the book of Judges thus opens and concludes with a concealed polemic whose aim is to criticize Bethel." The second element in the frame, Dan's retreat from the Amorites—who were able, therefore to "continue to dwell" in the promised land—completes the foreshadowing. Canaanite presence "from Dan to Bethel" will prove to be one source of Israel's undoing.

## Caleb and Achsah—A Standard for Comparison

Recent scholarship on the book of Judges has called attention to the sweeping arch of decay and decline evident as the book progresses in depictions of inter-tribal disharmony, intimated in Judges 1 by the contrasting depictions of Judah's successes and the other tribe's failures (cf. Rake, 96–97), and in the increasingly shocking treatment of Israelite women described in the book. In regard to the latter, the account of the episode involving Caleb's reward of land and, with it, his daughter Achsah to Othniel for conquering Debir/Kiriathsepher may function to establish something of a standard of measurement (Judg 1:11-16). Its occurrence in Judges 1 represents a puzzle since it is a virtually verbatim doublet of the account in Joshua 15:16-19. With a view to developments in Israel recounted later in Judges, a translation problem involving the sequence of speakers in the account may provide a hint to understanding the function of the Caleb/Othniel/Achsah episode in the context of the whole book of Judges. The account begins straightforwardly by describing Caleb's offer of Achsah in marriage to the victor over Debir/Kiriathsepher, the success of Othniel, and Caleb's fulfillment of his promise (vv. 12-13). The crux of the problem appears in v. 14. The conventional translation of the Hebrew text of v. 14a, "When she (Achsah) came to him (i.e., to Othiel as his wife), she urged/incited (Heb. *sut*, hiph.) him (Othniel) to ask her father for a field," seems to contradict the account of how the request was actually made to Caleb in vv. 14b-15, "and she dismounted from her ass and Caleb said to her, 'What do you want?' And she said to him (Caleb), 'Give me . . . .'" Both major branches of the Greek tradition agree against the Hebrew Masoretic text, which employs only pronouns as indicated in the preceding translation, in specifying speakers by name, making it clear in its interpretation of events that Othniel encouraged

Achsah to do the asking. Furthermore, the Greek uniformly offers an apparent midrash on Caleb's name in v. 15 in the comment that Caleb granted Achsah's wish, giving her "according to her heart" (reading *kaleb* as *ka* "according to the" + *leb* "heart"?).

In contrast, the Hebrew seems to suggest that Achsah did the actual asking. Did Achsah fail in persuading Othniel to seek a boon from Caleb, or was she impatient, usurping the role she herself had assigned her new husband? The Greek avoids the apparent contradiction between vv. 14a and 14b-15, but in so doing it depicts a conquering Othniel, later to become Israel's first judge (Judg 3:9), who (cravenly? wisely?) preferred to approach his new father-in-law through his new wife's agency. Paul Mosca has called attention to another possible resolution to the difficulty apparently raised by MT. His examination of the syntax of the Hebrew verb *sut*, "to incite," reveals that in over half of its sixteen occurrences in the Hebrew Bible, it appears, as it does in Judges 1:14, with a *lamedh* preposition and the infinitive construct functioning not to indicate purpose but as a gerund complementing the main verb (cf. Deut 13:7; 2 Sam 24:1; 2 Kgs 18:32; 2 Chr 32:11; Job 2:3). He suggests, therefore, that the difficulty can be resolved by translating, "When she arrived, she beguiled him (i.e., Caleb) by asking from her father arable land."

A consideration of the nature of the transaction between Caleb and Othniel involving Achsah and land lends support to this reading of the pericope. At issue is the respective status of the territory vis-à-vis Achsah, the intended bride. Caleb does not bestow the territory but the bride. In fact, given the proximity of Debir/Kiriathsepher to Hebron, it may have been regarded as already belonging to Caleb's allotment (Josh 14:6-14; 21:12; cf. 1 Chr 6:56), a circumstance also suggested by references to the region as "the Negev of Caleb" (1 Sam 30:14) and by the fact that, technically, Judges 1:12-16 (= Josh 15:16-19) does not record the transfer of title. The verb "to take, capture" does not necessarily imply the transfer of ownership to the "taker" (see, e.g., Num 21:32; Josh 6:20; 8:19; 10:1, 28, 32, etc.). Furthermore, as v. 16 indicates, the transaction ultimately affected the incorporation of the non-Israelite Kenites, Othniel's clan, into Judah, Caleb's tribe, suggesting that the territory remained Calebite. Finally, the territory clearly does not serve as the "bride-price" since Caleb does not receive it but grants it.

In many respects, the transaction resembles the complicated exchange involving Ruth and the estate of her father-in-law: land and wife constitute a package with the expectation that the land will support the wife and any who adhere to her (including Naomi and any future progeny). The decision made by the unnamed *goel* reflects awareness of the fact that he will not have the absolute power to dispose of the property as he will, confirming that the status of the land closely resembles the status of a dowry: it is linked to the bride (Ruth 4:5-10). Notably, throughout the Judges narrative, Achsah speaks of Caleb giving *to her*. It appears, then, at least from Achsah's perspective, that the gift of springs of water (v. 15) was something like a supplemental dowry. Although the Hebrew Bible preserves no legislation concerning Israelite dowry practices, Joseph Fleishman (355, 371) finds further support for this view in "similarities in dowry trends between ancient Near Eastern laws and early Jewish law sources." Significantly, Achsah, the object in vv. 11-13, becomes the acting subject in vv. 14-15 (cf. Bowman, 23).

In the context of the fates of daughters and wives later in the book of Judges, the account of Caleb's grant of territory and bride establishes a baseline of normalcy. It relates a father's accession to his daughter's reasonable request. It highlights Achsah's agency: she speaks for herself. Unlike Jephthah's daughter, Samson's mother and concubines (except Delilah), and the Levite's concubine, Achsah has a name.

## Foreign Influence in the South and in the North: A Dynamic Perspective

Both of the major sections of the preface deal implicitly with the question of foreign elements incorporated into Israel or coexisting with it. Through its silence regarding the relevance of the prohibition against intermarriage with non-Israelite populations, the apparent incorporation of the Kenites into Judah via marriage into the Calebite clan described in the Judah section (1:12-15) and the note concerning Moses' Kenite connections (1:16) implicitly affirm the permissibility, even desirability, of such alliances. In contrast, the repeated notes concerning the northern tribes' inability to expel Canaanite populations, whom they sometimes subjected to forced labor, casts over the account the shadows of biblical injunctions to eradicate such populations in order to protect Israel from syncretistic forces and shadows of Israel's Egyptian bondage.

Biblical traditions concerning Caleb, Moses' father-in-law, and the Kenites, although difficult to harmonize, may preserve a historical memory of the perhaps gradual incorporation of the Kenites into Judah in the earliest period of Israel's existence. One strand of tradition, found primarily in Numbers and Exodus, identifies Moses' father-in-law, known variously as

Hobab, Jethro, or Reuel, as a Midianite priest (e.g., Num 10:29), while another strand, represented in Judges 1:11-16 and 4:11, identifies him as a Kenite. Genesis 15:19 lists these Kenites as a Canaanite group, and Numbers 24:21-22 addresses them along with other non-Israelite groups. In contrast, Judges 1:16; 4:11-21; 5:24 (the Israelite heroine Jael is the wife of Heber the Kenite) and another series of texts (according to 1 Sam 15:6, Saul spared them; 1 Sam 27:10 refers to "the Negev of the Kenites"; and 1 Sam 30:26, 29 reckon them among "David's friends, the elders of Judah") treat them as a friendly group living on the fringes of Judean territory and society. First Chronicles 2:55 associates the Kenites with both Caleb and the Rechabites (cf. Jer 35). A similar situation pertains to the Kenizzite group to which Caleb (and his brother Othniel) belonged according to Joshua 14:6, 14 (for a discussion of Caleb's Kenizzite connections, see McCann, 32). Genesis 15:19 also lists the Kenizzites among the Canaanite population, Genesis 36:15, 42 identify Kenaz as the grandson of Esau, and 1 Chronicles 1:36, 53; 4:13, 15 offer the genealogy—Othniel, son of Kenaz, son of Eliphaz, son of Esau. The circumstances pertaining to Judah's cordial relations with the Kenites and Kenizzites, extending even to connubium, which Judges 1:11-16 attests resemble circumstances already encountered sporadically in the book of Joshua (cf. clemency for Rahab—2; 6:22-25; the covenant with the Gibeonites, 9:15-27; the sparing of Geshur, Absalom's maternal heritage, and Maacah, 13:13; etc.).

These incorporations of non-Israelite groups into the covenant people, although apparently successful to some degree, conflict with God's express commandment against entering into covenant relationships with non-Israelite groups (Exod 23:32; 34:11-16; Deut 7:1-3), however. Indeed, one can view such incorporations as an undercurrent running through the biblical text and undermining the programmatic call for the eradication of such outsiders. Like the Caleb/Othniel/Achsah episode, many components of this countervailing undercurrent involve the marriage of key figures to non-Israelites: Joseph's marriage to an Egyptian (Gen 41:45), Moses' to a Midianite (Exod 2:15, 21; or, controversially, to a Cushite, Num 12:1), Boaz's to Ruth the Moabite, David's grandmother (Ruth 4:10), etc. In the immediate context, the Caleb/Othniel/Achsah episode contrasts starkly with the unsuccessful handling of relations with other groups such as those detailed in Judges 1:22-36. Indeed, the presence of foreign populations in the promised land and Israel's policy toward them constitutes both a major theme of the book of Judges and a major problem for historical and theological interpretation.

In fact, one approach to the book of Judges, championed by Norman Gottwald (see esp. 586–87), sees it as the testament to a sociological struggle intimately associated with the origins of Israel. Proponents of this understanding of Israel's origins point to contrasts between Israelite subsistence on the fringes of settled territories and Canaanite urban culture, between Israelite clan and tribal structures and Canaanite city-states, and between Israelite populism and Canaanite royal ideology—in short, between Israelite practices that reflect their devotion to a deity who frees slaves and Canaanite structures of oppression. For advocates of this reading, "Canaanites" functions in Judges as a code word for "forces, structures, and individuals . . . in opposition to the good order of Yahweh" (Hamlin, 14). In this context, certain central terms in the Judges account acquire connotations of political struggle: *yshb*, "to sit, dwell" = "to rule (oppressively)," and *yrsh*, "to inherit, dispossess" = "to drive out (of power)," for example (Gottwald, 531–33). Even without delving into the historical reconstruction of the sociology of earliest Israel, one cannot overlook the fact that the account of the northern campaign recorded in Judges 1:22-36 forcefully raises the problem of cultural diversity and accommodation. Ironically, the solution adopted by the northern tribes according to Judges 1, namely, the subjection of Canaanite populations to the corvée or forced labor, compromised Israel's confidence in the God of the exodus. As is often the case, in the attempt to maintain the freedom granted them, they became what they despised: they assumed the role of master, a role Pharaoh once exercised over them. In the attempt to control Canaanite groups, Israel merely sustained the corrupting influence of Canaanite religion and of the Canaanite exercise of power and domination.

# Theological Assessment(s) of Israel's History

Judges 2:1–3:6

The semi-chaotic state of affairs depicted in Judges 1 invites clarification, and Judges 2 offers a theological explanation—or, rather, several theological explanations. Like the other so-called "historical" literature in the Bible, Judges requires that interpreters keep clearly in mind the theological and therefore quasi-historical character of this material. While Judges 1 largely settles for rather straightforward reporting of human motivations and actions with the kinds of consequences one might expect, Judges 2 introduces the motivations and actions of God as a causative factor in the course of events. By definition, then, this material is not "history," since historians consider it unfair, as it were, to introduce divine machinations into their descriptions of the course of human events. For example, a historian would analyze the Babylonian conquest of Judah and Jerusalem in the sixth century BCE as the consequence of the interplay of several strictly human factors: principally, Babylonian imperial expansionism and Judah's unwise attempts to resist incorporation into the Babylonian Empire. From the perspective of the strictly historical assessment of documentary and archaeological evidence, these factors alone explain the course of events.

Biblical authors, however, found deeper significance in the Babylonian crisis. They saw the Babylonians as the human instruments of God's displeasure with Judah's long history of idolatry and apostasy. They gave historical events a theological interpretation. Similarly, Judges 2, and by extension the entirety of the book (and further, the entirety of the so-called "historical" books of the Bible), then, intentionally asserts the claim that human motivations and actions do not constitute the sole factors that influence the course of human affairs. Modern readers must bear in mind the distinction: Judges views Israel's "history" through theological lenses; it makes faith claims.

Indeed, the unsystematic, confused, and confusing chronology of events offered in Judges 2 already makes it evident that the authors/editors of

Judges did not employ the criteria of modern historiography. As has already been noted, although, according to Judges 1:1, all the events narrated in the book of Judges occurred after Joshua's death, he resurfaces repeatedly in Judges 2 (vv. 6-9, 21, 23). Does Judges 2 mean to suggest that, because of the transgressions of the generations that *followed* Joshua's, God refused to continue expelling the nations from the land (vv. 20-22) or that anticipation of these transgressions led God not to drive them out completely *during* Joshua's lifetime (v. 23)? Obviously, the authors/editors of Judges were not particularly concerned with the hallmarks of modern historiography. Instead, paradoxically like modern history and apparently owing to their "panoramic" or "paradigmatic" purview, they were willing to accommodate multiple explanations for the course of Israel's history. Indeed, as David Jobling (115) observes,

> 2:20–3:6 . . . deals with the issue of why Canaanites were left in the land after Joshua. Given that this is not an issue that will receive particular attention in the judges-cycles, why is it included in the programmatic introduction to them? Perhaps . . . because, although it is not part of the surface agenda, it is part of the deep structure problematic of the book.

In this regard, it is important to note that the editors of Judges, like the editors of many biblical books, did not choose to harmonize, although they presumably could have done so. Readers can therefore read the complicated, sometimes convoluted, final form of the text as an acknowledgment of the complexity of Israel's history.

This circumstance also invites consideration of the canonical interrelationships between the component elements of Judges 2 and other passages in the Hebrew Bible that exhibit common language and substance. Such a consideration reveals that the multiple perspectives in Judges 2 regarding the problem of the survival of elements of a Canaanite population and, more importantly, of elements of Canaanite culture and religion participate in a discussion that extends well beyond the boundaries of the book of Judges to include much of the Pentateuch and the Former Prophets.

Judges 2:1–3:6 divides readily into seven subsections. First, 2:1-5, which manifests close verbal and thematic affinities with texts in Exodus 23 and 34 and Deuteronomy 7, reports the announcement at Bochim (Bethel?) that God will not continue to "drive out [the nations] before" Israel. Second, 2:6-10 virtually reproduces the account of the death of Joshua and the passing of the generation that knew his leadership found in Joshua 24:28-31. Third, 2:11-17 expounds the so-called "Deuteronomistic Paradigm" of Israel's history, which represents the dominant (cf. 3:7-15; 4:1-4; 6:1-10; 8:33-35; 10:6-17; 13:1) but by no means exclusive viewpoint expressed in Judges and in the continuation of the Deuteronomistic History (cf. the other parade example in 2 Kgs 17), shifting the focus to the covenant infidelity of the post-Joshua generations. For the first time in the context, this unit explicitly conceives of the persistent flaw in Israel's history as idolatry. Fourth, 2:18-23 duplicates 2:11-17 in many respects (see Moore, 63–74) but specifies the cyclical nature of the paradigm. Fifth, 2:20-23 and 3:4-6 attribute the persistence of Canaanites in the land to God's decision to permit it as a means of testing generations of Israel subsequent to Joshua's leadership to see whether they would meet the standard of obedience set by their ancestors, presumably the idealized Joshua generation. Sixth, 3:1-3 uniquely explains the survival of foreign populations in the land as YHWH's plan for maintaining Israelite military preparedness.

## Weeping at Bochim (2:1-5)

Source and redaction critics typically consider the account of the Bochim incident, already discussed briefly above in relation to the Dan/Bethel subtext of Judges 1, as its continuation. In terms of the redaction history of Judges, they have good reason since it interrupts the continuity between the book of Joshua and the resumption of Joshua's chronology in vv. 7-10. From a literary and theological perspective, however, Judges 2:1-6 transitions (cf. Lilley, 94–95) from the retrospective concern with the failures to displace the Canaanite population described in Judges 1 to a focus on theological explanation of their continued presence in Israel's subsequent history. In the context of Judges 1, the shift from a purely military assessment of the failure of even the tribe of Judah (i.e., the enemy had "chariots of iron," v. 19) to a theological explanation merits attention.

Perhaps the most outstanding feature of this unit, however, apart from the probable allusions to the Bethel sanctuary, is its similarity to other texts that offer essentially the same assessment of the survival of Canaanite populations within Israel. Judges 2:2 charges Israel with failing to obey God's prohibition against entering into covenants with the inhabitants of the land and his command, instead, to "break down (*ntts*) their altars." When did God issue these instructions? Exodus 34:11-16 commands Israel to make no covenant with the inhabitants, to tear down (*ntts*) their altars, break up (*shbr*) their masseboth, and cut down their Asherim, and to refrain from intermarriage. In return, God will "drive out (*grsh*)" the population, all so that Israel's religious purity may be preserved. LXX recognizes the affinity between Exodus 34:13 and Judges 2:2, supplementing v. 2 with phraseology that echoes Exodus 34:13 (cf. Deut 7:5, 25). Exodus 23:23-33 outlines essentially the same program, but with significant modifications. It instructs Israel to "break up (*shbr*)" the pillars/masseboth of the inhabitants of the land and prohibits covenants with them. In return for obedience to this charge, God promises to "drive out (*grsh*)" the inhabitants, but only gradually ("not in one year," a practical measure intended to protect against the proliferation of the wild animal population, v. 29), "little by little" (v. 30). The stated objective of both Israel's policy toward the Canaanites and God's intention to drive them from the land, albeit gradually, is the preservation of Israel's religious purity. Deuteronomy 7:1-5 (cf. Deut 12:1-3) calls on Israel to destroy (*khrm*) inhabitants of the land, to make no covenant with them, to eschew intermarriage with them, to tear down (*ntts*) their altars, to break up (*shbr*) their masseboth, to cut down their asherim, and to burn their images. Again, in return, God will "clear away (*nshl*)" the nations in order to protect and preserve Israel's religious purity. Like Exodus 23, however, Deuteronomy 7 (v. 22) goes on to add references to the gradual program of expulsion, even employing the "little by little" phrase found in Exodus 23:30, and to the problem of the overpopulation of wild beasts. Joshua 23:13 warns that, if Israel intermarries with the existent populations, God "will not continue" to expel them.

Clearly, these texts and the continuation of Judges 2 (cf. vv. 21-22, 23) engage in various explanatory strategies regarding the continued presence of Canaanite populations. They differ along three axes: whether the gradual expulsion of the Canaanites was a provision of God's original plan or a response to Israel's disobedience, the precise nature of Israel's disobedience, and God's intention in permitting the persistence of Canaanites. According to one of these strategies (Exod 23:29-30; Deut 7:22), for example, God intended from the outset to expel the Canaanites gradually in order to forestall the rapid growth of the wild animal population. In contrast, the dominant viewpoint of Joshua and Judges holds that God meant Israel to take total possession of the land in a single, if multi-phased action, continuous until ultimately successful. The failure of this program, not God's original purpose, resulted in the continued vexing presence of Canaanites in the land. With respect to the precise causation of this circumstance, one viewpoint suggests that the process of conquest deteriorated from the successful beginnings under Joshua because the generations after Joshua failed to fulfill YHWH's commandments concerning the destruction of the Canaanite cult and the prohibition of social interaction (covenant-making and marriage) with the Canaanites (Josh 23:12-13; Judg 2:2-3). Another accuses post-Joshua generations of even greater infidelity involving not just social interaction but the worship of "other gods" (Judg 2:11-13, 17, 19). Finally, some texts describe Canaanite survival as the troublesome source of disobedience (Judg 2:3), while others assign the Canaanite population the function of presenting Israel with an ongoing test of fidelity (Judg 2:22). A careful reader will note the admixture of historical explanations, i.e., those dealing strictly with human actions and motivations, and theological rationales.

One other matter addressed in the opening unit of Judges 2 also requires contextualization. The angel of the Lord accuses Israel of having violated the prohibition against making covenants with the inhabitants of the land. If this prohibition is to be found in Exodus 23 and 34 and Deuteronomy 7, where does one find record that Israel had violated it sometime during or shortly after Joshua? The Bible reports a number of instances when one of the patriarchs or the entire nation of Israel entered into a formal "covenant" (*berit*) with a non-Israelite individual or group: Abraham with Abimelech (Gen 21:27-32), Isaac with Abimelech (Gen 26:28-31), Jacob with Laban (Gen 31:44), Joshua's generation with the Gibeonites (Josh 9), Jabesh-Gilead with the Ammonites (1 Sam 11), Solomon (as vassal) with Hiram (1 Kgs 5:12), and Asa with Benhadad (1 Kgs 15:18; 20:32). The only recorded post-Sinai and pre-Judges covenant was the agreement that the Gibeonites negotiated fraudulently. As the prohibition against these covenants seems to envision them, they imply Israel's willingness to accommodate, if not cooperate, with foreigners among them. In this regard, it resembles the prohibition against intermarriage with non-Israelites, a prohibition explicitly violated in a number of important instances viewed positively in Scripture (Tamar, Rahab, and Ruth, for example). In context, then, both prohibitions represent absolutist viewpoints that were neither strictly practiced nor even practicable.

## Joshua's Passing (2:6-10)

In comparison to its counterpart in Joshua 24:28-32, Judges 2:6-10 adds an interesting element. Every statement in the Judges passage except for v. 10 duplicates, for the most part verbatim, statements in the Joshua passage: Judges 2:6 supplements Joshuah 2:28 with the phrases "the sons of Israel went" and "to take possession of the land." Judges 2:8-9 reproduces Joshua 24:29-30, omitting only the opening adverbial phrase, "after these things," to suit the literary context. The unique statements in Judges 2:10 contend that the post-Joshua generation had no direct experience of YHWH, i.e., of what he had done on Israel's behalf during Joshua's lifetime, apparently implying that this ignorance influenced their subsequent apostasy.

## The "Deuteronomistic Paradigm" (2:11-17)

The apex of this chain of explanatory material occurs in vv. 11-17, the first full explication of the scheme that scholars describe as the thesis of the monumental work of Israelite theological historiography represented by Joshua through 2 Kings in the Hebrew Bible (that is, omitting the book of Ruth in the English order). Several surprising features of this paradigm as stated in vv. 11-17 merit comment, particularly in the context of the book of Judges as a whole, because they suggest that the purview of the paradigm extends far beyond the events described in the body of the book of Judges (see also above). Notably, from a historical standpoint, although the discussion up to this point in Judges 2 has involved the Canaanite population dwelling alongside Israel in the land and posing a temptation to apostasy, the paradigm speaks of the "surrounding" nations, a circumstance that suits certain of the accounts of the individual judges in the body of the book but is even more appropriate to the history of Israel during the monarchy. Theologically, a careful reading of vv. 16-17 reveals that, contrary to what might be expected, the initial statement of the paradigm does not attribute God's intervention to any act of repentance or any call for assistance. Furthermore, the initial statement does not claim that the intervention of the judges resulted in any actual change in the people's behavior. Rather, "the people did not listen to their judges" (v. 17).

## God's Pity and the People's Recalcitrance (2:18-19)

The supplement in vv. 18-19 clarifies the latter two of these peculiarities, meanwhile producing a depiction with added emphasis on the downward spiral of the cycle. It specifies that God intervened through the judges because he was "moved to pity by their groaning" (RSV; cf. Exod 2:23), not because he was motivated to forgive because of their repentance! The Hebrew verb *nkhm* that the RSV translates, adequately, "moved to pity," is often translated "to repent, to relent." It involves not necessarily the moral connotations of religious repentance but, in cases such as these, the softening of resolve. God cannot sustain God's anger, although justifiable in the view of the authors of Judges, in the face of the suffering of the people of Israel. "Moved to pity," not by any merit or penitential act on Israel's part, God "relents" (cf. Gen 6–9 and Exod 32–34; see McCann, 37). So much for the caricature of the wrathful God of the Hebrew Bible! Conversely, vv. 18-19 specify the ultimately nugatory impact of the judges on Israel's religious behavior. When an individual judge died, Israel immediately reverted to the patterns of behavior practiced by ancestral generations. Indeed, they "behaved worse than their ancestors" (2:19). The overall picture contrasts a deity frustrated at every turn with a recalcitrant people: the former justifiably provoked to anger but mercifully unable to sustain wrath; the latter unable to discern the significance of events or to learn from its own history.

## The Nations: A Test of Obedience (2:20-23; 3:4-6)

At first glance, Judges 2:20-23 seems to constitute a summary of the preceding composite theological analysis of the causes and effects of the persistence of non-Israelite groups and nations as the sources of temptation and oppression in and surrounding Israel. It reiterates the themes of God's anger, Israel's transgression of the covenant, and the resultant survival on the nations in the land, but it also adds a completely new explanation for God's decision to leave the nations in the land. Moreover, it further complicates the sequence of cause and effect. Now the nations remain in the land not to be expelled gradually as a precaution against animal overpopulation, nor as adversaries and "snare" (v. 3), but as the means whereby YHWH may test Israel's obedience. This novelty adds to the repertoire of explanatory material in Judges 2, but it does not introduce a contradiction as the final comment in the chapter, v. 23, seems to do. The comment reverts back, at the conclusion, to the antecedent period, the time of Joshua. Read straightforwardly, it claims that because of the apostasy of the generations to come, God chose not to drive out the nations swiftly, submitting them to Joshua's might. In other words, it seems to claim that God did not give Joshua total success because God anticipated future Israel's apostasy, resulting in something of a temporal paradox. If God had given Joshua such success, the temptation represented by the nations would not have been present in the land to entice Israel into the apostasy that motivated God to leave some of the nations in the land.

### The Nations: A Test of Israel's Military Preparedness (3:1-3)

Judges 3:1-3 offers yet another explanation for the significance of the continued existence of the nations in the land and lists them. It differs in two respects from the explanations that precede it. First, like Judges 2:20-23, rather than understanding the persistence of the nations primarily as a consequence, i.e., the result of Israel's failures (1:21, 27, etc.) or its disobedience (2:1-3), it attributes the phenomenon to YHWH's intention. The nations survive in the land in order to fulfill a divinely intended role in the future and not as evidence of Israel's past shortcomings, whether military or religious. Second, it characterizes this divine intention not once but twice: the nations are to serve as a means ("by them," v. 1) of "testing" Israel. Apparently, an early form of this explanation understood this function as a means of testing Israel's covenant fidelity (v. 4), but a later editorial insertion, like Exodus 23:29 and Deuteronomy 7:22, sought to supply a more mundane motivation. Whereas Exodus and Deuteronomy explain the continued existence of the nations as evidence of YHWH's provision for defending against exploding populations of wild animals, however, an editor of Judges 3 (vv. 1b-2) interpreted their survival in the land as YHWH's provision for educating the sedentary generation that followed Joshua in the ways of war. The implication seems to be that YHWH did not wish to see Israel become unskilled in defending itself. The nations in the land would act as a persistent irritant to keep Israel alert and prepared.

### The Nations: A Test of Israel's Obedience—Reprised (3:4-6)

The explanation of the continued existence of non-Israelites in the land offered in vv. 1-3 seems to interrupt an original continuity between Judges 2:20-23 and 3:4-6. These sections share the view that God intended the nations as a test of Israel's obedience, not as a means to sharpen its military prowess. Further, the list of nations left in the land contained in v. 5 differs from the similar list in v. 3. While the enumeration of Philistines (specifically, the so-called "Philistine Pentapolis" of the coastal cities consisting of Gaza, Ashdod, Ashkelon, Gath, and Ekron; cf. Josh 13:3; for the phrase, "lords of the Philistines," see also Judg 16:5, 8, etc.; 1 Sam 5:8, 11, etc.), Canaanites, Sidonians, and Hivites is unique in the Hebrew Bible, the list in v. 5 represents one variant (six nations) of a well-established, apparently Deuteronomic tradition (as here with six elements—Deut 7:1; Josh 3:18; 17; 24:11; with seven—Exod 3:17; 23:23; 33:2; 34:11; Deut 20:17, etc.). In addition, the Hebrew syntax of 3:1-3, which does not employ the conjunction linking clauses in a sequence, contrasts with the syntax of the surrounding material. In any case, vv. 5-6 succinctly summarize the deuteronomistic understanding of the problem posed by non-Israelite populations in the land: intermarriage that leads to religious apostasy.

## History and Theology—History or Theology?

Of course, this concluding statement, like the whole of Judges 2, is theology, not history in the modern sense. A contemporary reader may feel constrained to unravel the logical strands woven through the discussion in Judges 2:1–3:6 in order to reconstruct a more systematic analysis of causes and effects or to privilege one or more rationale(s) over the others. While theological claims and historical analyses differ in terms of their understanding of cause and effect, both may be permitted to reflect the complexity of human affairs. Methodologically sound histories of World War II need not restrict their identifications of the root causes of that catastrophe to a single factor. The most rigorous historians concede that unemployment and inflation in Germany, the worldwide economic depression, the German sense of national humiliation after World War I, Nazi manipulation and fearmongering, Japanese imperial ideology and economic ambitions, international distraction, and ineffective foreign policy—in short, a host of factors—all contributed to the creation of the circumstances that resulted in the invasion of Poland in 1939, the bombing of Pearl Harbor, and the subsequent outbreak of fullscale war. Looking back on their own history, the theologians who contributed the constituents of Judges 2 saw a similarly complex nexus of factors. Even the final redactor of Judges 2 resisted the temptation to simplify.

The remarkable range and variety of the Bible's rationales for the coexistence of the nations along with Israel in the land represents a challenge to interpreters who approach the Bible as Holy Scripture. Did God intend from the outset that the nations would be expelled only gradually, or did they survive Joshua because of Israel's failures? If the former, did God mean to forestall the dangers of animal overpopulation or to utilize the non-Israelite populations as "sparring partners" for Israel, as it were? If the latter, were Israel's failures primarily military or religious?

The proximity of these multiple rationales suggests, of course, that the editors of the Bible did not view them as contradictory but as cumulative. Their presence in the text highlights the fact that, in this as in other instances, biblical authors attempt to analyze current situations (the presence of non-Israelites among them) as the effects of prior causes, effects that God either intended or permitted. Unfortunately, for theology as for history, it is difficult to ascertain intentions from causes and their effects in the realm of human activity. Single acts have multiple effects, some reflecting the actor's original intention, some not. Fundamentally, however, biblical authors, like modern historians, began with empirical data (the present) and attempted to reconstruct a chain of events that produced it. As will become evident subsequently in Judges, the complexity and disharmony of the rationales offered for the continued existence of non-Israelite populations in the land only reflects the complexity of the data. The messiness of human affairs resists reduction to simple explanations, whether historical or theological.

# Three Judge/Savior Vignettes

Judges 3:7-31

Accounts of the activity of the individual judges/saviors begin in Judges 3:7 and continue through the end of Judges 16, the conclusion of the Samson cycle. Apart from two lists of figures, the so-called "minor" judges (on the term, see "Judges or Anti-Heroes?" above), that bracket (10:1-5; 12:7-15) the block of Jephthah of material without providing any specific information concerning the activity of these figures, the material in the core of the book ranges from brief reports of single feats of individuals (Othniel, Ehud, and Shamgar) to more complex blocks or cycles of material resembling descriptions of the careers of their central figures (Gideon, Jephthah, and Samson). Meanwhile, the story of the defeat of Sisera through the combined efforts of Deborah, Barak, and Jael lies somewhere between these poles. In a sense, the structure of the core of the book demonstrates a movement from episodes (3:7-31) to cycles (chs. 13–16). The material in this core section of the book seems to predate both the deuteronomistic introduction and the even later preface/appendices envelope (see "Composition and Structure" above). Furthermore, its themes and concerns differ significantly from them. The pan-Israelite perspective of the introduction and envelope, especially the emphasis on Judah's preeminence manifest in the preface, does not appear in the core. Instead, the heroes are local, northern figures who deal with local threats. Although deuteronomistic editorial material interspersed throughout these accounts continues to assert the theological rationale for Israel's cycle of distress and deliverance (3:7-8, 12; 4:1-2; 6:1; 10:6-8, 10-16; 13:1), apostasy, repentance, and religious reform play no role at all in the accounts of the feats and careers of the judges/saviors. To invoke the sandwich metaphor discussed in the introduction (see "Issues and Approaches" above), readers face the challenge, or the opportunity, of "tasting" each of these accounts on its own merits before or as part of appreciating its contribution to the overall work.

## Othniel (3:7-11)

Judges 3:7-11, the account of Othniel, the first "judge" of Israel, appears as the first specific case illustrating the paradigm propounded in 2:11-17. Indeed, the fact that the Othniel account conforms so closely to this paradigm coupled with indications that it represents an editorial composition suggest that it may be viewed as a parade example of the pattern. These indications of its editorial character include not only the deuteronomistic list of nations and the repetition of language found in Judges 2:11-19 concerning exogamy (marriage to non-Israelites), infidelity to YHWH, and idolatry, but also the peculiarly prototypical nature of some of the story's details and the idealized description of Othniel's role. To begin, the name and identification of the antagonist, Cushan-Rishathaim, raise the possibility that he stands as a representative figure. His name combines two terms, the first either a reference to a Midianite clan by the same name (cf. Hab 3:7) or an allusion to Cush, the biblical term for Ethiopia (cf. Gen 10:6; Ezek 38:5), which is also sometimes linked, however, to Mesopotamia (cf. Gen 10:8). The second term, Rishathaim, a dual form of the noun "wicked," describes this figure as "doubly wicked." He is said to be king of "Aram of the Rivers," a problematic designation. Aram is the biblical term for Syria; however, references to "the rivers" in the Bible usually denote Mesopotamia (Greek for "between the rivers"). Indeed, some scholars and translations (compare RSV and NRSV) conclude that "Aram" must be a scribal error and take the phrase as a reference to some Mesopotamian kingdom.

Scholars have struggled without success to find a historical scenario in which an Ethiopian or Midianite chieftain ruled either in "Syria of the Rivers" or Mesopotamia or, for that matter, in which a hero from the far south in Judah would have campaigned in the far north. Alternatively, the peculiarity of the designations and the lack of detail in the account probably mark the report of Othniel's judgeship as an idealized prototype. Some interpreters, in fact, see in the account a reflection, if not of the actual circumstances, then of Judean attitudes in the period when deuteronomistic editors compiled the book of Judges, namely, during the exile (so Täubler who argues that Othniel's heritage recognizes the incorporation of Edomite groups into Judah in the exilic period and that "Cushan-Rishathaim" is a cipher for Babylon) or earlier in the co-regency of Hezekiah and Manasseh (so Guillaume, 91, 94).

Regardless of its value as a source for reconstructing either historical events or historical attitudes, in its literary context, this account clearly serves as the exemplar against which to evaluate all subsequent accounts. Othniel serves as the prototype of the judge/deliverer figure. The account addresses, then, perhaps the central theme of the book—leadership.

This idealized literary function itself raises interpretive questions, however. Some interpreters have pointed to distinctions between the paradigm expounded in Judges 2:11-19 and reflected in the Othniel account, on the one hand, and the perspective manifest in the so-called "framework" of the accounts of the feats of judges subsequent to Othniel, on the other. Guillaume (16–22), for example, has distinguished between what he calls the "judges schema" of Judges 2 and the "saviors framework" in terms of five criteria: First, the judges scheme describes the nature of Israel's sin as the desertion of YHWH; the framework has this only in the Jephthah account, which has all the elements of both (10:6, 10-16), and in the appearance of the anonymous prophet in the Gideon story (6:7-10). Second, the scheme omits reference to "cries" while the framework mentions them consistently (3:9, 15; 4:3; 6:7; 10:10). Third, the paradigm/scheme and related materials describe Israel's leaders as "judges" while the framework calls them "saviors." Fourth, the scheme depicts the relief from oppression brought by the judges as transient whereas the framework specifies a definite period of peace. Finally, in the scheme, God delays taking action (out of pity, not in response to cries) due to Israel's spiraling decline, but in the framework, God sends saviors immediately in response to the people's cries.

For Guillaume and others (cf. Römer and de Pury, 118–19; Knauf 2000, 396), these distinctions serve primarily as indicators of the editorial history of the book of Judges: the editors responsible for the deuteronomistic scheme, and presumably for the idealized account of Othniel's judgeship, incorporated an earlier "book of saviors" into their "book of judges" or expanded the earlier book with additional material (ultimately, these options are tantamount). Granting, for the sake of argument, that these differences in style and vocabulary may reflect editorial activity, the question remains as to whether the deuteronomistic scheme and the saviors framework materials actually offer contrasting portrayals, especially when read in their current literary context. Lindars (100) argues to the contrary that Judges 3:7-11 establishes the connection between the Deuteronomistic schema and the framework material such that the first statement is to be understood as implied in the subsequent material. He identifies nine elements in the framework to the Othniel story, all of which appear in some form in the deuteronomistic introduction to the book and all of which appear in subsequent instances of the framework material, although inconsistently and with no clear pattern.

From this perspective, the supposed distinction between the paradigm's qualification of Israel's wrongdoing as idolatry over against the simple statement found in the introductions to the Ehud, Barak, and Gideon stories that "Israel did evil in the sight of YHWH" (3:12; 4:1; and 6:1, respectively) seems overblown. The phrase "to do evil in the sight of YHWH" occurs most often in the books of 1 and 2 Kings in descriptions of the shortcomings of the kings of Judah and of Israel. These accounts accuse the former of various forms of disobedience including noncompliance to specific instructions (1 Sam 15:19), murder (2 Sam 12:9), and idolatry (1 Kgs 11:8), and characterize the latter almost universally as perpetuators of the idolatrous cult established by their predecessor, Jeroboam I (1 Kgs 22:4; 15:26, 34; 16:7, 19, 25-26, etc.). Three of four occurrences in Deuteronomy (4:25; 9:18; 17:2) refer to idolatry, and the fourth (31:29), which attributes the evil to "the work of [Israel's] hands," probably does as well. What evil other than infidelity/idolatry would motivate YHWH to abandon Israel to its enemies?

Although they probably point to distinct literary origins, the scheme and the framework do not seem, therefore, to offer significantly divergent explanations for Israel's suffering at the hands of its oppressors. Can the same be said of the rationales for divine intervention to deliver Israel from this oppression? Guillaume demarcates the "cries" of the people (Heb. *ṣ'q* or *z'q*) characteristic of the saviors framework from the "groans" (*n'qh*) mentioned in the paradigm and concludes that the two terms reflect different understandings of the motivation for God's intervention. In the saviors material, YHWH responds to the cries of the people whereas, according to the paradigm, YHWH responds "only out of pity for his suffering people" (Guillaume, 21). For comparison, Exodus 2:23-24 (cf. Exod 6:5), which reports God's decision to deliver Israel from Egyptian bondage, employs both terms along with a third *'nh* that also means "groan."

It may be important to check a common assumption at this point. Commentators frequently describe an element of the deuteronomistic paradigm as the people's cry of penitence or repentance (cf. Soggin 1981, 43) although the book of Judges never refers explicitly to Israel repenting in relation to God raising up a judge. The Hebrew terms translated "to cry (out)" here commonly denote expressions of anguish or distress, sometimes implying a call for assistance, and appear in a specifically theological use in prayers of lament/complaint (TLOT, s.v. "צעק *ṣ'q* to cry out"). Biblical laments characteristically express the speaker's sense that he or she suffers unjustly; that is, their general attitude is antithetical to repentance. Guillaume's assertion that God responds to the "groans" of the people "only out of pity" and the common assumption that the paradigm describes the (cyclical) repentance of the people seem to reflect the theological bias that God extends salvation only to those who repent properly. In contrast, both the deuteronomistic scheme and the "saviors framework" portray a God moved to pity solely by the pain of God's people. Remarkably, even the deuteronomistic material in the Hebrew Bible, which one would expect to follow a rigid theory of retribution, depicts a merciful and gracious God who continues to respond to Israel's cries and groans just as God responded to Israel in Egypt, not because these cries express the people's repentance but because God remembers the promise to Abraham, Isaac, and Jacob (Exod 2:23-24).

Similarly, while source and redaction critics justifiably regard the occurrence of distinct terms designating the heroes of the book of Judges (*shôfēt*, "judge," or *môšîaʻ*, "deliverer") as evidence of (at least) two sources, this conclusion does not yet answer the question as to whether the two terms denote different offices or functions. The leadership problem is central to the book, of course, and will receive close scrutiny in the furtherance of this commentary. At this point, however, it must suffice to observe that Judges 3:5-11 conflates the terminology, describing Othniel as a "deliverer" (v. 9) who "judged" Israel (v. 10), and that it equates Othniel's "judging" activity with military leadership. Obviously, as understood here and elsewhere in the book of Judges, "judging" is not primarily a judicial or administrative function. Rather, consistent with ancient Israelite thought generally, "judging" extends to the enforcement of justice, the execution of the just verdict. A number of psalms (see Pss 75:7; 149:9), for example, describe YHWH as the judge who punishes evildoers, especially Israel's enemies, and who thereby "delivers" Israel from oppression (Pss 72:4; 82:3, 8; 96:13). In fact, at least one psalm virtually equates "judging" (*shft*) and "delivering/saving" (*yshʻ*) as expressions of YHWH's benevolence toward Israel (Ps 72:4). Affinities with the notion of judging/delivering in the book of Judges are self-evident. Othniel, Ehud, and the others "judge" on Israel's behalf by executing divine punishment against Israel's enemies, thereby "delivering."

Finally, the editors responsible for the Othniel story have ironically given priority to a figure whose connections with the tribe of Judah further the book's pro-Judah agenda but whose connections with the Kenites/Midianites (see "Foreign Influence in the South and in the North" above) undercut its nationalist program. Either these editors failed to recognize the incongruity or they were fully aware of the many cases involving non-Israelites who assimilated into Israel and proved to be faithful Yahwists and contributing members of God's people. Regardless, the mere presence of figures such as

Othniel in the biblical account subverts the exclusivist program of strict endogamy and eradication of non-Israelites.

## Ehud (3:12-30)

The account of Othniel's judgeship lacks the detail characteristic of a real narrative and appears, rather, to replicate elements of the paradigm as a parade example of it. In contrast, the story of the judge Ehud bears the marks of folk tradition, specifically, humor, trickery, and celebration of the unlikely hero, the loner who becomes the deliverer of the community. Because Israel reverted to evil, YHWH permitted a certain Eglon, king of Moab, to occupy "the city of palms" (no doubt Jericho; cf. Deut 34:3; 2 Chr 28:15) with the help of a coalition of Ammonites and Amalekites and from there to dominate the Israelites for a period of eighteen years, extracting regular payments of tribute. Together, the Moabites, Ammonites, and Amalekites were among Israel's oldest and most persistent enemies with a history of conflict in biblical tradition reaching back before Mt. Sinai in the case of the Amalekites (Exod 17:8-16). This account relates how a certain Benjamite, Ehud, was able to end Eglon's domination by assassinating him and leading the Israelites to capture the critical fords of the Jordan, presumably near Jericho, thereby regaining control of this important trade route.

Summarized in this fashion, the report seems straightforward. The details, on the other hand, add layer upon layer of nuance. Indeed, these details create an atmosphere that virtually overwhelms the plot and demands focal attention. The narrative abounds in irony.

The most obvious of these layers of nuance involves the many comic elements (for treatments devoted to the humor of the Ehud story, see Hübner; Klein, 37–39 [irony]; Handy [ethnic humor]; Brettler 1991, 1995 [political satire]; and Jull [scatology]). Consistent with other Israelite satirical treatments of the Ammonites and Moabites, their near neighbors, and, according to tradition, relatives (cf. the account of the birth of their patronymic ancestors, the sons of Lot's daughters by their father, Gen 19:30-38), Eglon's name ("little calf") contrasts with his corpulence ("Now Eglon was a very fat man," v. 17) and hints ironically at his fate. Ostensibly, Ehud has come to "present tribute" (*qrb mnhh*), but in other contexts this expression regularly denotes offering sacrifice (Lev 2:1, 4, 8, 11, 14; 6:13; 7:9, etc.; cf. Exod 29:3, 10, 13; Lev 1:2; see Brettler 1991, 294–95). This multivalent term already introduces ironic uncertainty into the account. Has Ehud come to "present tribute" to Eglon or to "make a sacrifice" of the fat little bull?

Ehud's request for a private audience with Eglon constitutes a similar case of *double entendre*. After presenting the tribute and even departing Eglon's residence, Ehud returns with a new mission: he has a *debar seter* for the king. Again, the narrative employs a phrase with a range of possible meanings. The Hebrew word *dabar* can denote a "word," a "matter/issue," or even a "thing." Thus, Eglon surely understood Ehud to mean, as most translations render the phrase, "a secret word/message," but Ehud may well have been thinking of the "hidden thing," as the Hebrew expression can also be translated, on his right thigh (the "concealed weapon"). In fact, the *debar-'elohim*, the "word/thing of God," Ehud has for Eglon proves to be the sword (v. 20). In similar fashion, the verb (*tq'*) employed to denote the act of Ehud's sword thrust (v. 21) also describes the shophar blast with which Ehud subsequently summons the people of Israel to battle against the now-leaderless Moabites (v. 27; cf. Alter 1981, 38–41).

Ehud's tribal affiliation—he was a Benjamite, a "son of the right hand"—contrasts with, or perhaps comically highlights, the left-handedness that plays a central role in the subterfuge he perpetrates on Eglon (see Soggin 1989). The Hebrew text describes Ehud as "restricted/bound in his right hand," a phrase that has caused translators and commentators some difficulty. One branch of the Greek tradition took it to mean "ambidextrous," while other translations and commentators have understood it to suggest that Ehud was "crippled" in his right hand. Halpern (1988, 35) has suggested the possibility that the Benjamites, like the Spartans, bound the right arms of trainees so that they learned to use the left in battle, which would have given them a significant advantage against enemies accustomed to fighting only right-handedly against right-handed opponents. This suggestion may also shed light on the significance of the identical expression employed in relation to the Benjamite marksmen discussed in Judges 20:16. In any case, the point is clear: Ehud, the "son of the right hand" was facile, perhaps even specifically trained, with his left hand—but the narrative implies that Eglon did not know this, an ignorance with fatal consequences.

The description of the assassination itself involves a dense concentration of scatological humor and sexual innuendo. It is literally "bathroom" humor since it occurs in or just outside Eglon's toilet. As Jull (64) has observed, the traditional translation of the *hapax legomenon* (a word that occurs only once in the Hebrew Bible so that scholars are uncertain of its meaning) in v. 20 as "cool room" disregards the climate of the region (an upper room would have been the hottest in the household). He has argued instead, in part based on Deuteronomy 23:10-15 and its context, that the term in question refers to a toilet. Apparently, Ehud interrupted Eglon *in situ*—the Moabite king was indeed "on the throne"—with the urgent announcement that there was a "secret word/thing" for him. The narrative omits details here, but, presumably, Eglon, with expectations heightened by Ehud's return, must have stepped out of his private toilet only to be met by Ehud's dagger thrust.

The scatological humor reaches its apex at this point. Eglon was so obese and the force of Ehud's blow so fierce that the dagger disappeared, blade and handle, into Eglon's belly, apparently disemboweling him since "the dirt came out." This phrase also involves a *hapax legomenon*, *prshdn*, which seems to be related to an Akkadian quadrilateral root *prsd* that denotes "exiting." Consequently, based on usages in Akkadian that connote excreting, Barré (11) translates Judges 3:22 ". . . he did not withdraw the dagger from his belly; and (as a result) the/his excrement came out (of the wound)." The response of Eglon's attendants, waiting just outside the doors, to the delay in their readmittance to his presence heightens the likelihood that term *mqrh* refers to a toilet facility. They give the locked door and the odor resulting from Eglon's disembowelment the obvious interpretation, conveniently permitting Ehud the opportunity for escape. Elijah's taunting of the prophets of Baal at Mt. Carmel with the suggestion that their god's unresponsiveness to their prayers may be because Baal is indisposed offers a ready parallel to this humor. In fact, the Ehud story may evidence undercurrents of anti-Baal satire. Eglon's name elicits associations with the bull of the Baal cult, slaughtered/sacrificed/defeated in this case by an Israelite champion. Guillame (p. 28) has called attention to parallels between Eglon and the storm-god in Psalm 104 (vv. 3, 13) who "waters the mountains" from his "upper room (*mqrh*)" (involving the image of rain as divine urine? cf. Aristophenes, "The Clouds" l. 373).

Several scholars also see sexual innuendo as a prominent feature of the account. In the ancient Near East, victors often made a point to further underscore the inadequacies of their enemies by humiliating them sexually, by "making women" of them. In such a reading of the story, Ehud girds his phallic sword on his "thigh under his clothes"; he "enters in to" Eglon; he "thrusts" his sword into Eglon's belly; doors are "opened" and "locked" (cf. Cant 5:26); Eglon's servants assume that their master is "covering his feet," an idiom for relieving oneself that employs "feet" as a euphemism for genitals; and, finally, Ehud subdues Moab under his "hand" (*yd*, vv. 28, 30; a common Hebrew euphemism for "penis"). In short, Ehud "makes a woman" of Eglon and, by extension, of the 10,000 "strong, able-bodied" Moabite men slain at the fords of the Jordan (v. 28; cf. Brettler 1991, 294–95).

Finally, Ehud's escape also highlights the comic ineptitude of Eglon's entourage. The narrative is somewhat obscure as to the architecture of

Eglon's chambers (if Ehud locked the doors from the inside, how did he exit the room?). In fact, if the understanding of *mqrh* as "toilet" holds, Ehud may have escaped through the plumbing. In any case, Eglon's attendants wait while Ehud slips away, surprisingly and boldly toward Moabite territory, the last place he would be sought (cf. Soggin 1989, 97).

What is the point? From the standpoint of the editor or editors responsible for incorporating this account into the judges scheme, of course, the details of Ehud's act have little relevance to the overall paradigm: Israel sinned, God handed them over to Eglon, Ehud delivered, and a period of stability ensued. A focus on the account itself, apart from the framework device, reveals that the tale contains no overt clues as to how the narrator viewed events. There is no moral.

Thus, interpreters regularly read this account on any of several levels. Historians adopt a variety of stances concerning the kind of historical evidence the account yields. Many are skeptical as to whether, in the absence of other source materials and given the many literary motifs and techniques manifest in the account, it can be mined for reliable data about a Moabite King Eglon and an Israelite liberator Ehud. Knauf (1991), who sees Eglon as a place name (see Josh 10; 12:12; 15:39; cf. Isa 15:5; Jer 48:34; Ezek 47:10) and Ehud as the name of a Benjamite tribe (see 1 Chr 7:10; 8:6), for example, regards the account as the folk memory of some intergroup conflict. To be sure, animosities between the Israelites and the Moabites certainly and demonstrably had a long history, were sometimes virulent, and seem to have been reciprocal (cf. the Mesha Inscription). Brettler (1991, 1995), on the other hand, finds the account a reflection of political circumstances in the period when the book of Judges was produced and identifies it as an example of "political satire." While such readings of the Ehud story may have merit for the reconstruction of Israelite attitudes toward the Moabites, they risk overlooking Ehud and his actions as testimony to Israel's model of leadership, surely a central focus of the book.

Seen from this perspective, a number of features of the story stand out. It celebrates the bold, daring, inventive—even deceptive—initiative taking of a left-handed ("sinister") loner, Ehud (see Christianson, 62), who literally single-handedly attacked the seat of power oppressing Israel. This bold action legitimated his leadership and apparently gave his people the courage and opportunity to resist. Commentators, not wishing to endorse such violence or to suggest that Scripture depicts it as an expression of God's will, quite often remark on the marginal morality of Ehud's assassination. Not surprisingly, this aspect of the story was particularly troubling to commentators who wrote in eras and societies that emphasized the divine authorization of governmental authority (see Gunn, 38–46, 50). In contrast, some, perhaps most notably John Milton (who adduced Ehud in support of the legitimacy of the trial of Charles I), have regarded the Ehud story as a biblical sanction of rebellion against unjust or oppressive authority.

As the account of such a daring trickster, however, the Ehud story stands alongside a number of similar biblical accounts about individuals who implemented risky and sometimes shocking solutions to problems that were apparently insoluble through standard approaches: Judah's daughter-in-law Tamar (Gen 38:13-30), the Moabitess Ruth (Ruth 3), David in his relationship with the Philistine king Achish (1 Sam 27), etc. Commentators might wish that Ehud had been able to persuade Eglon to grant Israelite autonomy and forego the levy of tribute, but the story, whether the account of a historical event or the legendary reflection of the circumstances and attitudes of some political situation, operates within the context of the political verities of the ancient Near East: foreign powers subjugated and exploited weaker nations and peoples as a matter of course. The options available to these oppressed peoples were submission or (violent) resistance and rebellion. Stories such as this evidence ancient Israel's admiration for individuals in crisis situations with no easy solution who were not content to submit or to wait for "help to arise from another quarter" (Esth 4:14), but who shaped events to their benefit.

These daring loner stories also attest to the theological complexity, even sophistication, of the Hebrew Bible. Contrary to the popular expectation that the norm in the Hebrew Bible involves Israel's God intervening mightily, even miraculously, on behalf of God's people, the Ehud account and its kindred call attention to the principle of "dual agency" evident at points in the Hebrew Bible (cf. Amit 1999, 172 n. 6). Apart from the notation that God "raised up" Ehud "as a deliverer" in response to Israel's cries found in the editorial introduction to the account (v. 15), God plays no obvious role in Ehud's daring-do. Instead, Ehud "made for himself" the sword designed specifically for its purpose, just as he apparently conceived and executed the entire plan on his own, just as Tamar obtained from Judah what was due her through her own wit and courage, and just as Ruth and Naomi created the situation that resulted in the birth of Obed, "the restorer of life" (Ruth 4:15)—all, apparently, with no explicit divine direction, guidance, or assistance. Yet, either explicitly or implicitly, all of these accounts attribute the positive outcome to God's gracious provision. Throughout, the Hebrew Bible consistently portrays a God who acts mysteriously to support or hinder human agency. God's involvement may not be manifest in "supernatural" phenomena in these cases such that an observer can point to God's activity, but, in retrospect, the authors of Scripture were able to discern the mysterious influence of God on the outcome.

Judges recounts a series of these stories of daring, unlikely (left-handed, female, illegitimate, etc.) loners. Ancient Israel seems to have valued such courage and inventiveness. As the book unfolds, however, it will pose the question of whether a people can rely on a succession of such charismatic figures for stability.

## Shamgar (3:31)

A single verse (3:31; cf. 5:6) recounts the judgeship of the enigmatic Shamgar, ben-Anath. Apart from his name and the fact that, like Othniel and Ehud, he also delivered Israel from an oppressor, it records only the identity of that oppressor and a single feat of heroism, the slaughter of 600 Philistines with an oxgoad. It prominently omits the typical observations concerning Israel's apostasy and the period of tranquility following the judge's intervention. Its brevity coupled with the reference to the death of Ehud in 4:1 suggests that the editors interposed the Shamgar story (see Lindars, 156 and Brettler 2002, 24), borrowing a figure from Judges 5:6 and converting a Canaanite warlord who struggled against the Philistines, the common enemy of Israelite and Canaanite, into one of Israel's saviors. The motivation for this insertion is unclear, although Brettler (25) suggests that it supplies the only specific example of the deliverance from Philistine oppression mentioned in Judges 10:11. Soggin (1981, 59) attributes it to the redactors' interest in "[indicating] that Israel is saved by someone who will soon be their enemy *par excellence*, by the work of a person of doubtful historicity, probably not even an Israelite."

Every specific in this brief notice represents a puzzle. Shamgar's name does not appear to be Hebrew. Scholars have proposed a number of etymologies (Hurrian), including proposals that reclaim the name as a relatively rare West Semitic form (shaphel) from a root *mgr*, "to submit" (so Van Selms, 299–301 and Soggin 1981, 57–58) or postulate a compound Hebrew form *sham + ger* "sojourner there" (Danelius; see also Lindars, 157; cf. the name of Moses' son, Gershom). In any case, the epithet *ben Anat*, "son of Anath," apparently refers to the West Semitic goddess of love and war, the consort of Baal at Ugarit and elsewhere. It significantly increases the likelihood that the name and its bearer were not Israelite. Based on evidence from Ugarit and Egypt concerning the martial character of the goddess Anath and from Mari concerning a mercenary group that included Hurrian elements associated with a cult-center for Anath, Craigie concludes that "ben Anath" identifies Shamgar as a mercenary. Snyman (127–28) argues to the contrary that his use of an oxgoad marks him as farmer turned warrior. Finally, Shamgar's victory over the Philistines raises a number of difficulties in chronology (the Philistines become Israel's primary opponent only in the second half of the book) and geography (Shamgar's association with Jael/Deborah suggests a northern conflict, but the Philistines had no presence so far north; see Van Selms).

Perhaps the only firm impression to be taken from the Shamgar enigma relates to his name and association with Anath. Despite the insistence inherent in the program outlined by the book's framing paradigm that Israel's history of sin resulted largely from its failure to expel foreigners from the land and to prevent any intermixture with them, the details of events refuse to support the program. Indeed, they undercut it. Shamgar the "son of Anath" joins Othniel the Kenite/Kenazite in the company of Israel's deliverers. Others will follow. Specifics are often the bane of absolutist programs.

# Deborah

Judges 4–5

Beginning with Judges 4–5, the compositional character of the material transitions from the brief comments devoted to Othniel and Shamgar or the account of a single episode involving Ehud to the increasingly detailed and extended narratives of the activities of Deborah and her associates, of Gideon, of Jephthah, and of Samson. Two features remain constant, however. Israel's deliverance by a woman, a hesitant member of one of its least clans and tribes, an outcast son, and a rash womanizer is as unlikely as the judgeships of two non-Israelites and a lone, left-handed "son of the right hand." Similarly, the element of ironic surprise features prominently throughout. A reading of the account of the judgeship of Deborah must consider both the shift in compositional techniques and the continuation of improbability and unpredictability.

## A Dual Tradition

Any reading of the account of the judgeship of Deborah must first, however, acknowledge and account for the appearance of two versions of the story, the prose narrative (Judg 4) and the poetic "Song of Deborah" (Judg 5). Scholars debate whether one version of the Deborah tradition depends literarily on the other and make arguments for all the possible permutations of interrelationship (the song derives from the narrative; the narrative derives from the song; they represent independent realizations of a common tradition; see the convenient survey of positions in Mayfield, 308–10).

While both versions clearly deal with the same incident, Baraq's victory over and Jael's subsequent assassination of a certain Sisera, the two accounts differ on several details. First, the two versions vary as to the identity and roles of the participants. Judges 4:2 describes Sisera as a general in the service of Jabin, a Canaanite king seated in Hazor; Jabin does not appear at all in the song, which focuses on Sisera and depicts him as a royal figure (cf. 5:19), although it does not explicitly call Sisera king. A full account in Joshua 11:1-14 mentions Jabin in connection with Hazor. Since he plays no active role in Judges 4, and Judges 5 does not mention him at all, many scholars (cf. Soggin 1981, 70; following Fritz) conclude that the deuteronomistic redactors likely introduced him in order to link Judges with the Joshua account.

Similarly, Judges 5:6 dates the event to "the days of Shamgar, son of Anath," while Judges 4:1 orients the episode chronologically in relation to the death of Ehud. Judges 3:31 identifies Shamgar as a judge who delivered Israel from Philistine oppression although the reference to him in Judges 5 describes an anarchic period when commerce on the major trade routes was virtually halted, presumably because of the threat posed by unchecked robbery. In other words, Judges 5 does not celebrate Shamgar as a liberator from foreign oppression but portrays him as a Canaanite bandit preying on the Philistines. Of course, the reference to Ehud in Judges 4:1 represents the work of the deuteronomistic editor who was probably also responsible for the insertion of Judges 3:31. In other words, the song has not been fully integrated into the deuteronomistic chronological scheme nor has the scheme's appropriation of the song's Shamgar figure fully transformed the outlaw of Judges 5:6 into an Israelite hero.

Perhaps the most glaring divergence between the two versions of the story involves the identification of the Israelite tribes whom Baraq mustered for battle (Judg 4) or who responded to the summons (Judg 5). According to Judges 4:10, Baraq called only on the northernmost tribes of Zebulun and Naphtali. They responded with a muster of 10,000 men. In start contrast, the song also praises Ephraim, Benjamin, Machir, and Issachar (vv. 14-15) for joining the battle while reprimanding Reuben, Gilead, Dan, and Asher for their failure to do so (vv. 15-17). Several aspects of the list of participants and nonparticipants in the song attract the attention of historians. The list altogether omits the southern tribes of Judah and Simeon and the priestly tribe of Levi, evidence of the northern provenance of the tradition. The song treats Machir, normally identified as the son of Manasseh and the father of Gilead (Gen 50:23; Num 26:29; passim), on par with the tribal descendants of Manasseh's half-brother, Ephraim. In essence, Machir occupies Manasseh's place in the list. Intriguingly, however, the song also contrasts the participation of Machir, identified elsewhere as Gilead's father and as the recipient of the territory of Gilead (Num 32:39, passim), with the reticence of Gilead itself.

Assuming the antiquity of, at least, the core of the tradition preserved in the song (on the dating of the song, see Mayfield, 324–25), these features, including the motives attributed to the nonparticipants (Dan sticking close to his ships, for example, itself a unique characterization of Dan in the Hebrew Bible), tantalize those interested in mining the song for historical information concerning the history of Israel's tribes and their interrelationships (see Mayfield, 326). From a literary and theological perspective, however, the most significant characteristic associated with the difference between the two accounts is arguably the collocation of genres. Literary studies of all varieties operate on the fundamental assumption that different genres function according to their respective rationales and with varying objectives. Prose narrative and song will treat even a single common incident in radically distinctive ways and for equally distinctive purposes.

Story intends to relate the substance of an event with some attention to chronological sequence, details concerning the main action, dialogue, etc. Except perhaps for dialogue, the precise wording employed is secondary to the effort to convey the essence of the story. Narrative involves a storyteller and a listener or reader. Song, on the other hand, aims to evoke the emotions and attitudes associated with the subject matter. It need not and often does not concern itself with chronology, detail, or dialogue. It often deals in imagery and allusion. The words of the song themselves are its essence: a song paraphrased is no longer song but narrative or, worse, doggerel.

Song evokes the involvement of its "audience" as performers. A narrative account of the American Civil War, for example, will contrast in all these ways with "The Battle Hymn of the Republic" with its references to God "trampling out the vintage where the grapes of wrath are stored," to the "fateful lightning" of God's "terrible swift sword," and so on. An interpreter of "The Battle Hymn" would be right to note the connection between the song and its historical referent, but by virtue of its genre, should not expect it to attempt an accurate and detailed account of the campaigns of the armies of Sheridan, Lee, and Grant. Instead, it interprets the whole as God's work for justice in the world. Furthermore, it can continue to be performed and heard long beyond its original setting as an evocation and affirmation of its central challenge, "As He died to make men holy, let us die to make men free." In fact, many contemporary hymnals alter the second half of this line to read "let us live" in recognition of the fact that when sung now, the hymn is being "reused" in a new context. (For an extended discussion of the implications of the fact that biblical authors appropriated the "Song of Deborah" and other such songs and set them secondarily in narrative contexts, see Giles and Doan; see also the summary of recent discussion concerning the precise genre of the song in Mayfield, 325–26.)

As will be demonstrated more clearly below, Judges 5 bears all the marks of such a song: disregard for chronological sequence; a focus not on human but on divine agency; allusion, especially to the chaos and exodus traditions; imagery such as "quaking mountains" and combatant stars; refrains and antiphonal elements indicative that the song was originally meant to be performed not read; and a related interest in celebrating the event as an example of God's ongoing victory over God's (i.e., Israel's) enemies. In short, their respective genres and intentions may account for many of the differences between Judges 4 and Judges 5. Indeed, as Lindars (165) argues, neither account could have been created based on the other, suggesting the likelihood that they represent separate traditions (narrative and lyrical) concerning the same event. Historians will certainly be interested in assessing the value of the two traditions for historical reconstructions; a literary and theological reading will attend to the distinction in attitudes and objectives between story and song (cf. Younger 1991).

## Deborah: The Narrative (Judg 4)

First, then, the story. To aid the full appreciation of all the implications of the generic peculiarities of narrative and poetry/song, it may be helpful to analyze the narrative account in Judges 4 according to the standard criteria of characterization and plot development. The former accentuates the unlikelihood that these characters will play the roles they actually perform in the account; the latter depends entirely on the element of ironic surprise.

### Dramatis Personae (4:1-11)

Both the story and the song revolve around four main characters, two women (Deborah and Jael) and two men (Baraq and Sisera). Jabin, the Canaanite, appears only in the deuteronomistic introduction to the story. As noted above ("A Dual Tradition"), in comparison to the account of Joshua's victory over "Jabin, king of Hazor" and conquest of Hazor in Joshua 11:1-15, Jabin conspicuously plays absolutely no role in either the story or the song. In addition, Sisera, described in Judges 4:2, 7 as Jabin's general, is otherwise treated as an independent agent. Together, these observations indicate that Jabin has been imported into the context of Judges 4 from the Joshua account (see Lindars, 165–66) and can be safely dismissed from further consideration. Like Jabin, Heber (Heb. "comrade, friend, companion") the Kenite (vv. 11, 17, 21) plays no active role whatsoever in the story. He is merely Jael's husband. The intrusive comment concerning him in v. 11 serves only to explain why a band of Kenites, whose home was in the southern desert, could be found so far to the north (Lindars, 191), to set the stage for the appearance of Jael in the story, and to explain Sisera's expectation that Jael will offer refuge and succour.

At first sight, Deborah (Heb. "bee"), one of the nine women the Bible identifies as "prophetesses" or reports as prophesying (Miriam, Exod 15:20; Huldah, 2 Kgs 22:14; Noadiah, Neh 6:14; Isaiah's wife [?], Isa 8:3; Anna, Luke 2:36; and Philip's four daughters, Acts 21:9), seems to be the major character in the story, the heroine. The story further identifies her as the wife of a certain Lappidoth (Heb. "torches"). Given the Hebrew convention of identifying married women in relation to their husbands (cf. 4:17), the proposal to translate the phrase "Deborah, a fiery woman" (Fewell and Gunn, 391; Guest, 152–53; Niditch 2008, 60), while plausible, is unlikely, as is the identification of Lappidoth with Baraq (Heb. "lightning") since Deborah ("the hill country of Ephraim") and Baraq (Kedesh) did not have the same home (so also Lindars, 182)—the coincidence of *lapid* and *baraq* in Ezekiel 1:13, which attests the poetic association of "torch(-light)" and "lightning" notwithstanding. The description of Deborah's work further heightens expectations that she will dominate the story. Not just a prophetess, she actively exercised a judicial/administrative role in Israel, the only "judge" in the book of Judges attributed with such a function (see Soggin 1981, 71). As discussed above in the introduction, disregarding the enigmatic "minor" judges whom the book only lists without further characterization, all the other "judges" act as champions, warriors who "deliver" Israel by defeating its enemies. Will a woman "deliver" in this fashion?

Almost immediately, the story offers the apparent answer. Deborah summons Baraq and conveys God's instructions to him that he is to muster a force of 10,000 from the tribes of Naphtali and Zebulun. From Mt. Tabor, they will march to engage Sisera, the enemy, in battle near the river Kishon. Baraq's response, however, complicates the reader's expectation that he will be the champion. He refuses to undertake the mission unless Deborah accompanies him.

Lindars (184) calls attention to the fact that Baraq's hesitancy reflects a pattern commonly evident in commissioning accounts in the Hebrew Bible. From Moses to Jeremiah, those commissioned to special tasks stereotypically resist the commission at first, requiring the assurance of some indication of God's presence (Lindars, 184). In any case, commentators puzzle over Baraq's motivation. Does his response betray insecurity (so, e.g., Marais, 101, and Wong, 156) or the recognition that Deborah is a "woman of God" whose presence promises access to a medium of revelation and power (so

Niditch 2008, 65)? Is Baraq a coward or simply a shrewd commander who seeks every possible advantage in battle? In turn, Deborah's response, which the development of the story reveals to be ironic, effectively refocuses the reader's attention on her. She agrees to accompany Baraq to battle, but she also warns him that, as a result, the course he has chosen will not bring him fame. Instead, "YHWH will sell Sisera into the hand of a woman" (v. 9), presumably Deborah herself, since she is the only woman mentioned to this point.

Somewhat surprisingly, the story manifests little interest in describing Sisera, the enemy, or the nature of his relationship to Israel, leaving interpreters to deduce his ethnicity and the circumstances that presumably made him an enemy of Israel. As narrated in both the story and the song, the battle with Sisera "has no cause and . . . no effect. At present we know neither the conditions which led up to it, nor the conditions which resulted from it" (Mayes 1969, 355). His name, the only tangible evidence, is clearly not Semitic; that is, he was not a Canaanite as the association with Jabin might suggest. Diebner (116–20) proposes an etymology from the Greek *sisura*, "goat-hair blanket," which could be an ironic reference to the covering that Jael places over him shortly before assassinating him (4:18). Lindars (177) has called attention to the appearance of a similar name in Minoan Linear A materials from Crete and concluded, with many other scholars (e.g., Soggin 1981, 63), that Sisera is a Luvian name. In this case, Sisera would have belonged to a pocket of the so-called "Sea Peoples" who inundated the eastern Mediterranean in the late thirteenth century CE and included the people that came to be known as the Philistines.

### Plot (4:12-24)

Regardless, the story deals not with the person and status of Sisera but, in the second and briefest of the three "scenes" (introduction of major characters and establishment of the setting, vv. 1-11; Baraq and Sisera do battle, vv. 12-16; Sisera's demise, vv. 17-24) narrated in the prose account, with the bare essentials of his encounter with Baraq before relating his climactic encounter with Jael. Since the first "scene" devotes itself to the figures (except Jael!) and backgrounds essential for the course of events to unfold, analysis of the action, the plot, must focus on scenes 2 and 3—Sisera's defeat and demise, respectively.

**Sisera's Defeat (4:12-16).** Hearing that Baraq had mustered a force at Mt. Tabor, Sisera mustered his own corps of charioteers (on the significance of the phrase "chariots of iron," see "The Southern Campaign—Judah's

Preeminence" above) and probably the attached infantry ("and all the men who were with him," v. 13; "all his army," v. 15). Deborah recognized the fact that Sisera had taken the bait as the opportunity provided by YHWH and, in her role as commander-in-chief, sent Baraq into battle with the assurance that YHWH had "given Sisera into [his] hand" (v. 14). As has been the case to this point in the narrative, the account of the battle itself keeps to the basics. YHWH "confused" (Heb. *hmm*) Sisera's forces, who fled in disarray, easy prey for Baraq's army. The language and idea are associated with Israel's Holy War tradition that often depicts situations in which YHWH creates "confusion," the collapse of military discipline, in an enemy force, allowing Israel's warriors a free hand on the battlefield (Exod 14:24; 23:27; Josh 10:10; 1 Sam 7:10; etc.). The idea exemplifies a major strand of the Bible's concept of God's activity in the human realm: God creates the conditions, but human beings, often acting on God's commission, execute the deed.

**Sisera's Demise (4:17-24).** Most notably, especially in comparison with the song, the story omits any detail of the battle scene, a circumstance that contrasts significantly with the next and final scene of the episode: Sisera's disastrous encounter with Jael (Heb. "mountain goat"), the wife of Heber. Without naming her, the account has already explained her presence in the general vicinity (v. 11). When the narrative finally introduces her by name, it needs only to explain why Sisera would seek refuge with her from the pursuing Baraq: Heber, Jael's husband, participated in a treaty relationship with Jabin.

Beginning in v. 18, the narrative slows its pace, richly supplying the detail heretofore lacking in the account. Irony predominates. As if to signal that Sisera is about to enter Jael's domain—that, like Baraq, he is about to submit himself to a woman's control—the account refers to "Jael's tent" (i.e., not Heber's; see Bal, 212). Baraq has vanquished his foe, to be sure, but, because he insisted on Deborah's (protective?) presence, she has warned that the victory will not accrue to his credit but to the glory of a woman. Now Sisera seeks refuge with a woman. What will ensue?

Initially and on their face, Jael's actions seem to confirm Sisera's expectations of refuge. She greets him at her tent-door, invites him to enter, and assures him that he need not fear. In maternal fashion, she covers him, fulfills his request for water with milk (!), and covers him again (see Bal, 213). Weary, now warmed and soothed, Sisera falls into a deep sleep on Jael's tent-floor while she stands watch at the door—an idyllic picture of security from imminent danger under tender and vigilant maternal care. Jael's behavior also suggests the intimacy of a lover. Not only does she invite him into her tent, creating a potentially scandalous situation in itself, but she also "comes to [Sisera] softly" later as he sleeps and, allusively, "penetrates" (*tq'*, "thrusts," cf. 3:21 and "Ehud" above) him with the (phallic?) tent stake (cf. Alter 1985, 43–49).

Turning attention for the moment from these explicit features of the storytelling craft, the text's silence with regard to the characterization of the social and political implications of the behaviors of Sisera and Jael, especially of the motivations of Jael and generally of the interpersonal transaction that takes place between Sisera and Jael, raises a number of questions. Especially since romantic notions concerning Eastern culture, particularly Eastern "hospitality," became dominant in Western biblical scholarship (Gunn, 81–87), commentators have focused on the apparent problem of Jael's transgression against the rules governing the host. According to this interpretation, Jael not only disregarded the treaty relationship that existed between Heber and Jabin, a relationship that would have extended to Jael and Sisera, but she also murdered a guest to whom she had extended refuge and provender. For this line of inquiry, the Bible's celebration of Jael's feat represents an ethical puzzle involving behavior that both championed Israel's cause and violated a fundamental principle of the culture's morality. Recently, however, Matthews (1991, 19; cf. Matthews and Benjamin) has argued the contrary position, namely, that it was Sisera, not Jael, who violated the rules of hospitality in a series of cascading breaches. First, he should have approached his treaty-partner Heber and should not have foisted himself upon Heber's wife. His presence with Jael, alone in her tent, could have invited scandal. Second, he should not have asked for anything. It would have been her place to offer. Third, and perhaps most egregiously, Sisera should not have asked her to lie for him. Ironically, Jael takes action that converts his request that she respond to any inquiry that "no one" is in her tent into the truth (see Bal, 214). Matthews speculates that, confronted with this warrior in flight, Jael may have feared rape. In yet another irony, Sisera's mother, who raises her voice in the song, celebrates her son's military prowess with a description of his raping and pillaging among his vanquished enemies.

Granting that the circumstances of the events described in this story do not conform easily to expectations surrounding the relationship between host and guest, i.e., that Sisera's behavior may have invalidated any claim to hospitality he might have otherwise been right to assert, the text also leaves the question of Jael's motivation unanswered. Here, the nature of the relationship between the Kenites and Israel becomes a factor. Earlier in Judges 4 (v. 11), the isolated statement that sets the stage for the encounter between

Sisera and Jael specifies that Heber, the Kenite, descended from "Hobab, Moses' father-in-law," thereby accentuating the long-standing presence of the Kenites at the periphery of Israelite identity (see "Foreign Influence in the South and in the North" above and cf. 1 Sam 15:6). Soggin (1981, 77–78) and Lowery (611) speculate that Jael may have faced the dilemma of conflicting loyalties. Unwittingly, Sisera found his way to a presumed ally who, unkown to him, has other, prior loyalties.

**Jael among the Judges**
From a historical perspective, this tradition concerning the relationship between Israel and the Kenites may testify to a period when Israelite identity was extremely fluid, when loosely associated tribal groups moved in and out of the orbit of the forming core of Israel (cf. Judg 1:16). In the literary context of Judges, however, Jael, the Kenite, joins Othniel, the Kennizite/Kenite, and Shamgar, of unknown ethnicity, as yet another of Israel's non-Israelite or quasi-Israelite champions. As such, Jael's feat further relativizes the absolute particularism of the deuteronomistic scheme of Israel's history. According to its foundational theory, the presence of non-Israelite elements in Israelite society constituted the occasion for Israel's continual apostasy; contrariwise, the individual tales of Israel's champions celebrate non-Israelites, para-Israelites, women, left-handed persons, and the illegitimate as Israel's deliverers.

The story of Jael shares another commonality with the only other fully executed story encountered so far in the book, namely, the account of Ehud's act of daring. Several verbal parallels call attention to the similarities between the two characters and their actions (see Webb, 137–38, and Lindars, 174). Both Ehud and Jael dispatch their opponents with a surprise "thrust" (*tq‘*) that penetrates the victim's body; both accounts relate ironic discoveries of the dead (by Eglon's attendants and by Baraq, respectively); the two accounts describe the corpse lying dead in almost verbatim fashion (*wehinneh . . . nofel . . . met*). To be sure, the differences in the contours of the two accounts are significant: Ehud plans and prepares to assassinate Eglon whereas Jael seizes an opportunity—"going out to meet" Sisera as he approached and ingeniously exploiting the soporific effects of the milk she offers him instead of the water he requests; Ehud's act precipitates Israel's military resistance while Jael's concludes a military campaign; Ehud fulfills the combined roles of champion and general (but not, explicitly, judge), roles played in Judges 4 by distinct individuals (Deborah—judge; Baraq—general; Jael—champion).

Nonetheless, the verbal parallels between the two accounts call attention to more profound similarities. Both episodes hinge on the initiative of individuals who, regardless of whether with premeditation or opportunistically, take bold action. Neither account mentions divine direction, divine intervention, or divine empowerment. Both Ehud and Jael succeed through craftiness, deception, and bravery—the capacity to decide on a course of action, in Jael's case instantaneously, and to take it without hesitation even in the face of considerable danger.

These traits place Ehud and Jael in the company of other audacious agents in the Hebrew Bible: Lot's daughters, Tamar, Rahab (see Assis, 89, for a comparison of Rahab and Jael), and Ruth, to name only a few. Together, they testify to ancient Israel's admiration for individuals who seize initiative, who take risks in the pursuit of a desired outcome, who make opportunities or quickly recognize them when they arise, who do not hesitate to exploit whatever advantage they may enjoy. From a theological standpoint, the accounts of Ehud and Jael testify to ancient Israel's understanding of the complicated and subtle interrelationship between God's purposes in human affairs and human agency. The book of Judges incorporates these stories of bold heroes who acted alone into its broader narrative of God's deliverance of Israel from its oppressors, thereby making the explicit and implicit claim that God acted through Ehud and Jael, even when God issued no word of call or commission and God's hand was not visible in the form of signs and wonders. Fager (28), who draws comparisons with this theology of history and contemporary "chaos theory," observes, "[A]s the story of Deborah indicates, divine order may emerge from the chaos of human unpredictability."

Finally, in the context of the entire book of Judges, the story of Jael and Sisera plays an additional, allusive, role. On one hand, she prefigures the anonymous woman who killed the tyrannical Abimelech (Judg 9:53). On the other, she represents the converse of the Levite's concubine. Whereas the woman Jael extended mock hospitality to Sisera as an opportunity to assassinate him, the concubine indirectly becomes the victim of a host's faulty exercise of his duties. As Judges progresses from the stories of Achsah, Deborah, and Jael, through the account of a "certain" anonymous woman of Thebez, to the tragic tales of anonymous daughters and concubines, women become first nameless, then victims instead of agents.

## Deborah: The Enigmatic Song (Judg 5)

The Song of Deborah constitutes perhaps the most difficult and puzzling section of the book of Judges. Apart from the obvious question of its relationship to the narrative account, it confronts its modern readers with a host of mechanical puzzles involving the text and translation of key passages—

difficulties that inhibit an interpreter's ability to have confidence in a given understanding of the song—and others dealing with the precise genre and intention of the unit. What kind of song is it, and what does it hope to evoke in those who sing/hear/read it? Often cited as evidence of its antiquity, one of the most obvious issues that confronts interpreters of the Song of Deborah involves the density of textual and translational difficulties it manifests. While it is not consonant with the thrust of this commentary to devote significant attention to such critical issues, the complexity of this text, a complexity that makes it almost impossible to attain certainty as to specific references at a number of points, requires some notice if only to alert readers to the dangers of over-interpretation or over-reliance on an interpretation based on uncertain ground. The nature of these problems, however, can also suggest something of the tone and flavor of the song in the original Hebrew. A sampling of the most vexing of these textual issues in the discussion to follow will serve these purposes.

The confusing state of the text, or better the limitations of contemporary linguistic and historical knowledge, cautions against overconfidence with regard to the translation of the song at many points and, especially, with regard to any reconstruction of the historical, sociological, or religious circumstances described or reflected in it. The song is not, however, entirely incomprehensible. In fact, these difficulties, along with the synoptic problem posed by the coexistence of song and story, point to the central observation that the song seems to represent a quite ancient tradition that predated its inclusion in the book of Judges and that, therefore, must have fulfilled an independent function and purpose before the compilers of Judges appropriated it. Presumably, in fact, they will have also intended to appropriate the attitudes and sentiments associated with the song. Indeed, its structure, tone, and themes offer significant indications that the song once served a liturgical purpose and that, as a piece meant for public performance, it functioned to evoke a public response.

The structure of Judges 5 confirms its liturgical origins. It divides rather neatly into seven sections that, in some instances, also point to its literary history: an editorial framework (vv. 1 and 31b); a summons for the kings and princes of the world to attend to the song (vv. 2-9); corresponding calls for the Israelite public to bear witness, for Deborah to sing, and for Baraq to take possession of his captives (vv. 10-12[13]); the song of the battle with Sisera (vv. 14-31) that includes the curse on Meroz (v. 23), the celebration of Jael's heroism beginning with a blessing for her (vv. 24-27), and the depiction of Sisera's mother as she vainly awaits his return from battle (vv. 28-30); and, finally, the liturgy's summary petition (v. 31a).

## Editorial Framework (5:1 and 31b)

The editorial framework in vv. 1 and 31b incorporates what must have been a preexistent liturgy into the narrative of the book. Notably, it attributes the song to both Deborah and Barak (v. 1) and supplies at the end of the whole Deborah/Baraq/Jael/Sisera complex the comment concerning the period of rest that Israel enjoyed pursuant to the defeat of Sisera typical of the editorial scheme of the book. Together, then, these framework elements subsume the song, quasi-parenthetically, into its literary context.

## Summons to Attend to the Song (5:2-9)

The poem proper begins with a unit (vv. 2-9) spoken by an individual, presumably not Deborah who is addressed in v. 7, and directed primarily to kings and princes (v. 3), calling on them to attend to the subsequent celebratory song. A brief refrain ("bless YHWH") that appears in vv. 2 and 9 demarcates the unit. The temporal use of the *beth* preposition (twice each in vv. 2, 4, 6) further characterizes the summons: the song celebrates a time "*when* leaders led in Israel, *when* they offered themselves willingly for the people" (v. 2), "*when* the commanders of Israel offered themselves willingly for the people" (v. 9). Significantly, this unit indicates two rationales for the subsequent song of praise. Alongside celebration of the willingness of Israel's leaders as a reason for thankfulness to God, vv. 3-5 address YHWH directly and recall a time when YHWH appeared in typical theophanic fashion: "*when* you went forth from Seir, *when* you marched . . . ."

Translators encounter the first significant linguistic puzzle in the Song of Deborah as early as the first two words in v. 2, a phrase involving play on the consonantal root *prʿ*. Verbal forms of this root most commonly denote the act of loosening, releasing, or unbinding while the related noun refers to hair (as bound or tied up). Understood in this way, the phrase would be translated "when hair was unbound (in preparation for battle?) in Israel." Scholars have also noted a possible etymological relationship with an Arabic verbal root *frʿ* with the meaning "to be eminent, to lead" and suggested understanding the noun as a references to "leaders." They translate "when leaders led in Israel." Alternatively, Janzen (1989) rejects both translations while retaining the traditional etymology of the root. Based on the connotations of occurrences in Deuteronomy 32:42; Proverbs 1:25; 4:15; 8:33, passim; Exodus 5:4; 32:25; and 2 Chronicles 28:19, he argues that here *prʿ* "means 'let go, let alone, disregard,' but has nothing to do with hair." Instead, he suggests, "it refers to the act of throwing off the yoke of domination . . ." (403).

The various etymological arguments seem equally plausible, but the structure and theme of the song may provide a helpful clue. The second occurrence of the quasi-refrain that frames the first major section of the song (vv. 2-9) repeats the reference to those who "offered themselves willingly" and the call to "bless YHWH," suggesting that the first elements of vv. 2 and 9 should also be taken as parallels. Fortunately, v. 9 refers clearly if somewhat unusually to the "commanders/leaders (*hoqeqe*) of Israel" and supports the translation of *prʿ* as "leaders." Additional support for this translation derives from the overall theme of the song, namely, the celebration of those who came forward to lead Israel in the conflict with Sisera, including the explicit expression of disapproval for those who failed to do so. Still, no translation can yet claim assured status, and caution remains the watchword.

The song's enigmatic allusions to the circumstances surrounding Israel's conflict with Sisera do not provide evidence for confident historical conclusions. Instead of "to cease," the usual translation of the verb *hdl* (vv. 6, 7), for example, Boling (1975, 109) has argued for the alternative meaning "to grow fat/plump." The second occurrence of the verb also involves the equally unclear noun *perazon*, variously translated "leading class" (Soggin 1981, 82), "warriors" (Boling 1975, 109), or "unwalled towns" (Niditch 2008, 72). The options result essentially in two contrasting depictions of the circumstances surrounding the conflict between Sisera and Israel: either normal life, especially commerce and life in villages exposed to marauders, had come to a standstill because of the activity of Sisera and his forces, or Israel's leadership had grown complacent and unwilling to stand up to outside oppression. The former supposes a setting of lawlessness and social and economic anarchy, the second a context of political oppression. In the end, the song's paucity of clear indices as to the historical background of the conflict recommends caution.

Similar caution pertains to the religious backgrounds of the song, or at least of its earliest form. The common translation of v. 8a ("When new gods were chosen, there was war in the gates") defies ready interpretation. Who is the putative subject implied in the passive construction? Is it to be understood as a reference to Israelite apostasy? What is the supposed relationship between the apparent shift in religious loyalties and the ensuing conflict? Was this conflict internal to the community, i.e., was the warfare metaphorical? Does the phrase envision the conflict with Sisera as the end of a period of oppression that resulted, in accordance with the pattern established by the deuteronomistic paradigm of the whole book of Judges, from Israel's disloyalty?

Scholars propose a number of solutions. Hillers suspects textual corruption. Written Hebrew originally had no signs for vowels. Medieval manuscripts produced by a group of Jewish scholars known as Masoretes include a system of vowel points inserted above, below, and in the middle of the existing consonants, but they are not part of the canonical text of Scripture. By omitting so-called *matres lectionis* (consonants that functioned before the invention of the Masoretic system of vowel points, not as actual letters, but as clues as to the vowel to be read in the given syllable), substituting different vowels for those indicated in the Masoretic text, and restoring one consonant presumably omitted in the history of the transmission of the text, Hillers attains a text that can be translated, "They chose new gods; indeed, they desired demons" (cf. Deut 32:17). This proposal is congruent with the notion that the text refers to Israel's apostasy.

In contrast, Margulis disagrees with standard interpretations. His objection that standard interpretations rely on the notion that Israel repented from some sin although the poem knows of no such pertains to Hillers's proposal as well. For Margulis, the key term *hadasim*, understood in standard translations as the common Hebrew word "new," refers here instead to the "hardness, sharpness [of weapons]" (see 2 Sam 21:16; Isa 41:15; Job 29:20). He further notes (70) the near synonymity of *bhr* (translated "to choose" in the standard renderings) and *brr* in 1 Chronicles 9:22; Daniel 11:35; Isaiah 49:2; Jeremiah 51:11 in the meaning "sharp/polished." Therefore, he proposes the translation "When Elohim sharpened 'arrows' then there was war in the gates (of the enemy)," which would be consonant with the song's theme of divine intervention on the field of battle (68–71). Margulis's proposal has the advantage over Hillers's suggestion in that it involves possible alternative translations of the existing text, not emendation or reconstruction. In the end, however, the statement remains both ambiguous and uncertain.

The dual motivations for the song call attention to the question of the genre of the overall composition. Source and form critics point out that—references to theophany (vv. 4-5), the participation of the stars in the battle against Sisera (v. 20), and pronouncement of the curse on Meroz by the angel of YHWH (v. 23) notwithstanding—the apparently "older" preponderance of the liturgy commemorates the heroism of human actors (Israel's leaders in general, the tribes who participated in the conflict, Deborah, Baraq, Jael) while disparaging the failures of others (the tribes who refrained from joining the battle, Meroz). Consequently, Müller (452), for example, argues that the core of the song should be described as a war epic intent on lauding its heroes, not as a hymn of praise or thanksgiving to God. Only the psalmic inclusions in vv. 4-5 and 31a transform the whole into a Yahwistic psalm (Müller, 454). Indeed, neither the narrative account of the battle in Judges 4 nor the corresponding sections of Judges 5 report a divine intervention of theophanic proportions. Moreover, the statement in vv. 4-5 has all the marks of a fixed liturgical formula (cf. Ps 68:8-9; Deut 33:2; Hab 3:3; see Lindars, 229–30).

The first section gratefully recalls a time when Israel's leadership (and YHWH) stepped forward to lead the people in a crisis. Unfortunately, vv. 6-8, which describe this crisis, involve many of the textual and translational difficulties discussed above. Apparently, the conflict with Sisera was motivated in some way by conditions affecting travel and commerce with negative consequences either for Israel's peasantry (who "ceased," i.e., suffered diminished economic well-being) or its leadership (who "grew fat," i.e., became complacent). Somewhat surprisingly, Shamgar ben Anath, previously cited as a judge of Israel, also appears here, probably in his original context. If the two references to Shamgar are to be harmonized, the fact that the crisis described here occurred during his lifetime, and presumably after he began to act as judge, diminishes his stature. Contrariwise, if the earlier, very brief, reference to Shamgar derives from the occurrence of the name in Judges 5:6, the older tradition concerning the figure, whose name suggests non-Israelite origins (see "Shamgar" above), may depict him as a marauder who was responsible for the cessation of commerce. The question of the nature of the relationship between the commercial crisis and the choice of "new gods" apparently mentioned in v. 8 (see "Summons to Attend to the Song" above) only complicates an already obtuse situation.

**Summons to Bear Witness (5:10-12[13])**
The underlying character of the "war epic" also surfaces in the call to bear witness that constitutes the second major section (vv. 10-12[13]) of the complex. From the perspective of whether it yields any historical information concerning the central event, this section continues to raise as many questions as it answers. In particular, the translation of v. 13 proves to be a significant challenge. Translators and commentators interpret the ambiguous grammar of this verse in a number of ways, each generally as plausible as the others: "Then down marched the remnant of the noble; the people of the LORD marched down for him against the mighty" (RSV); "Then down went the remnant like the mighty, the people of Yahweh got themselves down like heroes" (Lindars, 210); "Then a survivor subdues the chieftains. The people of Israel subdue for me the mighty" (Niditch, 68); etc. As with the issues surrounding the proper translation of vv. 6-7 (see "Summons to Attend to

the Song" above), the resolution of the ambiguities here results either in a picture of the Israelite peasantry rising in opposition to the marauders who represented a threat to the security of travelers, traders, and villagers, or of Israel's leading classes awakening from their complacency.

Structurally, it consists of a summons for the travelers and traders mentioned in v. 6 to testify to events (v. 10); a report that, indeed, they recount the tale of the "triumphs of YHWH, the triumphs of his peasantry/aristocracy (see "Summons to Bear Witness" above) in Israel" to musical accompaniment in the various oases along the highways in the region (v. 11a); two parallel accounts of the beginning of the engagement (vv. 11b and 13); and a summons to Deborah and Baraq to take up song and engage in battle, respectively (v. 12). The result is a second song introduction in two roughly parallel subunits, each including a call to sing the tale (vv. 10, 12) followed by a report that some group "then marched down (*'z yrd*)" (vv. 11b, 13). Verse 11a does not fit well into this parallel structure, although the information it supplies concerning the performance setting of the song (namely, in gatherings of travelers at oases, not at cultic sites) supports the theory of its origins as a popular "war epic" transmitted in oral tradition. The second report of a group marching into battle flows smoothly into the battle account that begins in v. 14, but the first continues in the summons to Deborah and Baraq.

Alternatively, especially if one is interested in reconstructing the history of the literary growth of the complex, one could take the temporal terms "when" (vv. 2-7) and "then" (vv. 8, 11b, 13, 19, 22) as clues. In such a redactional analysis, vv. 2-7 would specify the circumstances "when" the events celebrated in the song transpired and vv. 8-23* would constitute the narration proper of what happened "then." The rough transition from vv. 11b to v. 12 would then be the result of the somewhat redundant insertion (cf. v. 3), well into the body of the song, of the calls for the travelers and Deborah to sing. The excision of vv. 10, 11a, and 12 (and perhaps v. 9) produces a seamless sequence.

Whatever the case, the complex clearly preserves evidence that it represents a traditional epic first transformed into a hymn and then appropriated by the editors of the book of Judges. The logic operative in the canonical form is poetic or perhaps, better, evocative, not narrative. To be sure, the unit juxtaposes travelers called on to tell the tale of what once happened on one hand, and Deborah and Baraq called on to initiate the events later to be narrated on the other. Distinctions between report and event collapse just as the redactional history of the text has produced a juxtaposition of contexts (campfire, cult, and canon).

### The Song Proper—At Long Last (5:14-30)
Certainly by v. 14, the song "proper" has begun. It divides thematically into two sections: the battle scene (vv. 14-23) and the contrasting depiction of two women involved in Sisera's fate (vv. 24-30).

**The Battle (5:14-23).** Notably and contrary to expectations, the treatment of the battle with Sisera devotes little attention to the description of the actual battle, focusing instead on praising the willing participants on Israel's side of the conflict (Benjamin, Machir, Zebulun, Issachar, and Naphtali) and disparaging tribal groups who abstained (Rebuen, Gilead, Dan, Asher, and the otherwise unknown Meroz). Apart from its function as admonition and encouragement, this list of participants and nonparticipants attracts scholarly attention principally because of the intriguing data it offers concerning Israelite tribal structure in an early period of Israel's history. No southern group appears, confirming the view that the division between north and south that surfaced after the death of Solomon had cultural and historical roots stretching back to the earliest period in Israelite history. The catalogue primarily mentions groups recognized elsewhere as members of the tribal system, a phenomenon that raises the question of whether Machir, Gilead, and the mysterious Meroz once had tribal status in a hypothetical northern tribal confederation.

A series of text/translation issues involves options that influence the characterization of the social and political situation reflected in the poem. The most intractable of these problems involves the identification of Meroz, the subject of the angel's curse for its failure to join the tribes who participated in the battle against Sisera (v. 23). Presumably a reference to the inhabitants of a place by that name or to the members of a tribe or clan by that name, it does not appear elsewhere in the Bible or in extra-biblical sources. Scholarly speculation has produced no convincing solution. Ultimately, the name functions only as evidence of the limits of knowledge concerning Israel's earliest history.

Perhaps the most puzzling feature of this catalogue involves the brief and enigmatic charge leveled against Dan that it chose to "remain with the ships." The Bible preserves traditions concerning the migration of Dan as it sought suitable territory (see Josh 19:40, 47; Judg 1:34; 18:1-29), but there is no evidence that the Danites ever lived near the sea or engaged in maritime activities. According to biblical tradition, Dan eventually settled in the extreme northeast of Israelite territory, well inland and a considerable distance north of the Sea of Galilee.

Another series of problems represents primarily questions of translation and, collectively, may be evidence of the antiquity of the poem. For example, the last phrase of v. 14 employs the root *shpr* ("to number") that classical Hebrew regularly uses in reference to scribal activity. Clearly, this classical meaning does not suit the context ("and from Zebulon, those who carry the staff of a 'scribe'"), so many scholars postulate an older use of the term. Tsevat (107), for example, points to parallels involving *hq* ("to prescribe, decree," see below), the verb used in reference to Machir in the phrase immediately preceding the statement concerning Zebulon in Judges 5:14, and *mshl* ("to rule, govern") in Isaiah 14:5 and Ezekiel 19:11. He further connects Judges' use of *shpr* with Akkadian *shaparu* "to rule" and translates "and out of Zebulon, they that hold the scepter."

Finally, while the indictment of the tribe of Reuben in vv. 15b-16 (cf. Gen 49:3-4) clearly faults it along with Gilead, Dan, Asher, Zebulun, and Naphtali for abstaining from the battle with Sisera, the specifics of the accusation, which seem to involve two isolated idiomatic expressions, constitute a challenge to interpreters. The statement concerning Reuben begins with a rare noun, *pelagah*, derived from a verb meaning "to divide." Other than the two instances in Judges 5:15-16, the noun appears only in Job 20:17 where it refers to "streams" as "divisions," i.e., tributaries or branches, of a larger course of water. A related noun, *pelugah*, also appears only in 2 Chronicles 35:5, where it refers to a "division" of the Levitical priests. The martial context of Judges 5 suggests the translation "division (i.e., of an army)" in vv. 15-16. Military language continues in the final phrase of v. 15. RSV, NRSV, ESV, NAB, and NIV understand *hoqeq leb* as a synonym for the final phrase in v. 16 (*hiqre-leb*) and render both "searchings of heart," which would suggest that Reuben's failure to join the battle resulted from indecision. The verb *hqq/hqh* means "to cut, inscribe" and by extension "to decree," however. In fact, the related noun commonly refers to statutes, decrees, ordinances, and the like. Therefore, Crown prefers the more "literal" translation "commanders of the heart" and regards it a derisive expression with connotations similar to the American idiom "armchair quarterback." In contrast to the tribe of Isaachar, which acted on its intentions and followed Barak into battle "on foot" (i.e., by putting "boots on the ground"), Reuben stood on the sidelines.

The statement concerning Reuben becomes even more uncertain, however, in the first clause of v. 16, which accuses the tribe of resting "between the *mishpetayim*" in order to listen to the "hissing" of the flocks. The noun *mishpetayim* occurs only here, in the related passage in the blessing of Jacob (Gen 49:14), and in a possible interpolation based on Judges 5:16 found in Psalm 68:14. Both the ancient versions and modern scholarship have been unable to determine the meaning of the term. The tendency to rely on contextual clues complicates the issue since no single meaning yet proposed suits all three contexts equally. LXX translates "inheritance" (*kleros*) in Genesis 49:14 and Psalm 68:14. The dual Greek tradition of Judges 5:16 offers *digomias* "double burden" (LXX B) or resorts to mere transliteration of the Hebrew (LXX A). In addition to the traditional "sheepfolds" suggested by the context of Judges 5:16, the list of modern proposals includes (1) "saddlebags" suggested by the context of Genesis 49:14 and further supposed by LXX B of Judges 5:14 (e.g., Speiser, 367, following Saarisalo, 92); (2) "boundary" or "territory," which also suits the Genesis context and has the further advantage of a plausible etymology (either from *shft* "to judge" or from *shfh* "lip" and by extension "border"); (3) "trash heap" (etymologically related to Arabic *tafat*); (4) "fire-pit, hearth" (from Hebrew *shft* "to set, put [on fire]" with a purported Ugaritic cognate, *mtpdm* [so Albright 1950–1951, 22]); and (5) "loins, haunches" (understanding *shft* in the sense of "to set = to rest"; for discussions of the problem, see Lindars, 260–61; Butler, 119).

"Sheepfolds," the traditional translation of Judges 5:16, seems to suit the reference to the flocks that follows, but the precise connotations of this phrase are also unclear. The whole verse derides Reuben for preferring to sit (somewhere) listening to the sound of "the *sheriqot* for/of the flocks." The verbal root of the noun in question means "to hiss." A related and much more common noun, *shereqah*, "a derisive, mocking hiss," occurs regularly in the context of taunts (Jer 19:3; 25:9, 18; 29:18; 51:27; Mic 6:16; 2 Chr 29:8), a circumstance that raises the question as to whether "piping," the usual translation of the term in Judges 5:16, fully conveys its connotations. It is possible that, rather than invoking pastoral images of the shepherd's pipe, the statement mocks Reuben for preferring the (offensive, unpleasant?) sounds of animals to the cries of battle. In the end, of course, as with many of the ambiguities evident in Judges 5, any proposal will remain conjectural in the absence of additional clear evidence.

The other surprising feature of vv. 14-23, the description of the actual battle in vv. 20-22, stands out not only for its brevity (a mere three verses) but also for its content. Significantly, it emphasizes three moments: (1) the approach of the "kings of Canaan," (2) the turn of events when the stars caused it to rain, and (3) the flight of the panicked enemy (cf. Müller, 448). Reminiscent of the Exodus account of the crossing of the Red Sea and consonant with Israelite "holy war" traditions (cf. Ps 48:5-7), it attributes Israel's victory over Sisera to an eruption of the waters of chaos that rushed over Sisera's forces, putting them to rout. The text of vv. 20-22 does not even mention the activity of Israel's gathered forces and, even more surprising, omits any reference to YHWH whatsoever (cf. Fewell and Gunn, 400–402; Becker-Spörl; Echols; contrast Hauser 1992, 32–34). In themselves, then, vv. 20-22 leave the impression that they represent an ancient, perhaps even pre-Yahwistic tradition. The curse pronounced by the angel of YHWH against Meroz because it failed to come to YHWH's assistance ameliorates the omission.

**Two Women in Contrast (5:24-30).** Finally, the song turns to the actions of Sisera's nemesis, Jael, and Sisera's unnamed mother. In five lines of poetry devoted to each, the song paints a study in contrasts. Reduced to the barest of detail, the song celebrates Jael's decisive act of violence. Meanwhile, Sisera's mother, awaiting the return of her son from battle, grows concerned over his delay, ironically fearing that it may signify some mishap. Subtle undertones heighten the irony.

Jael, who offers Sisera milk instead of the water he requested, mimics maternal behavior. As in the narrative version, although much less explicitly, the song invokes the complex relationship between sex and violence. Under the force of Jael's blow, Sisera "bows down" and falls dead "between" (*ben*) Jael's "feet/legs" to "lie" there "devastated." All of the key terms in v. 27 can have sexual connotations. "Bowing down/crouching over" (*krʿ*) can refer to the sex act (cf. Job 31:10); "feet" (*regel*) is a common euphemism for genitalia in Hebrew (cf. Deut 28:57; 1 Sam 24:3; Isa 7:20; etc. and perhaps Isa 6:2 and Ruth 3:4, 7, 8); the expression "to lie (with)" (*shkb*) is also a euphemism for the sex act; and, in at least one passage (Jer 4:30), the term "devastated, despoiled, ruined" (*shadud*) connotes rape.

Meanwhile, Sisera's mother, Jael's counterpart, comforts herself with the idea that her son's delay may be due to the fact that, victorious over his enemies, he is pillaging, taking both material and human booty: "a maiden or two (*rcm rhmtym*, lit., "a womb, a pair of wombs") for every man; spoil of dyed stuff . . . ." As any mother might, she concludes the list of items that she imagines her beloved son to be pillaging with a gift for herself. "Of course," she persuades herself, "he tarries because he is getting something to bring his mother, dear boy." In fact, however, Sisera is not raping and pillaging; instead, he has been violently penetrated and despoiled (cf. Niditch 2008, 81).

## A Theology of History—Reprise

Two themes evident in the Deborah/Baraq/Sisera/Jael complex stand out theologically. Both narrative and poem portray the relationship between divine and human action, not in overt terms or mechanistically but implicitly or even mysteriously, with obvious emphasis on human initiative. Readers have already encountered this juxtaposition of human heroism and mysterious divine agency. Arguably, it constitutes a prominent subtext throughout the book. Ehud devises a stratagem and executes it; Jael sees an opportunity and seizes it. Both act autonomously, or at least they appear to do so.

In consonance with this emphasis on human initiative, both narrative and poem focus particular attention on the willingness or unwillingness to participate. Baraq's hesitancy and the abstention of the tribes of Reuben, Dan, and Asher contrast with the boldness of Zebulun, "a people that risked their lives to death" (v. 18), and the cunning courage of Jael. The angel of YHWH curses Meroz because "they did not come to the help of YHWH." Indeed, clues as to the literary history of the song, in particular, suggest that its rhetorical function prior to its incorporation in the book of Judges was to celebrate and motivate this willingness. Psalms 68:14 and 83:10-11 attest to the currency and power of this incident in the Israelite popular memory. No doubt, the editors/compilers of Judges appropriated it because of these connotations that reinforce the theme of Israelite incohesion, especially in the North (note esp. Judg 8; 9; 12:1-6; 15:9-13; 17–21; cf. Brettler 2002, 72, and Sweeney).

# Gideon

Judges 6–8

The account of the career of Gideon introduces a new compositional feature in the book of Judges, an element that becomes the norm as the book continues. To this point, the accounts of individual deliverers have been restricted to single incidents; the stories of Gideon, Jephthah, Samson, and even the "appended" narratives dealing with the Danite and Benjamite troubles, in contrast, constitute extended story cycles. Consequently, the central figures in these accounts present much more complex characters and, similarly, the religious, social, and political dynamics of the circumstances in which their stories transpire appear with greater clarity. Heretofore implicit literary and theological themes become explicit. For example, Gideon fulfills YHWH's specific command, consonant with the general instruction announced in the theological paradigm of the book (2:2), to "tear down" the altar of Baal, the first explicit reference to actual Israelite apostasy in the book. The editorial introductions to the stories of Ehud and Deborah indicate that YHWH had delivered Israel to its oppressors because Israel had done "evil in the sight of YHWH" (3:12; 4:1), without specifying the nature of this evil. The reader may assume Israelite infidelity, but neither the editorial frameworks of these stories nor the details of the events narrated in them explicitly depict such a circumstance. Similarly, while undertones of internal strife can already be heard in Judges 1 (see commentary above at "Growing Internal Disharmony") and the attention given, especially in the Song of Deborah, to the failure of certain tribes to join in battle against Sisera suggests disharmony within Israel, the outright conflict that will become the central issue by the end of the book of Judges surfaces openly in the Gideon cycle.

## Structure

The content and structure of the Gideon cycle already provides indications of this increased level of specificity and complexity. Framed by a somewhat expanded editorial introduction (6:1-6 + 6:7-10) and conclusion (8:28-35), the account of Gideon's career as judge unfolds in two blocks (cf. Amit, 233–36), consisting of four and five episodes, respectively. The first block deals with Gideon's call/commission and relative successes in combating idolatry within Israel and the enemies of Israel without; the second narrates a series of incidents involving the character of Gideon's leadership and the varieties of response to it from various segments of Israel. The first block already offers hints of inconsistencies and flaws at the core of Gideon's judgeship that come to the surface in the second block in Gideon's dalliance with aberrant religious practices and in the strife and contention he provokes. As a unit, the Gideon cycle depicts a complex figure, not a hero famed for one feat. Indeed, rabbinic tradition, noting these features of the story, considered Gideon one of the three "least worthy" of the judges along with Jephthah and Samson (Hamlin, 90; Sarna, 557). These downward trends will come to full bloom in the career of Gideon's son, the would-be king, Abimelech.

Introduction (6:1-6)
Supplement: The Prophet's Admonition (6:7-10)
    Block I: Gideon's Successes (6:11–7:25)
        Gideon's Call/Commission: Part 1 (6:11-24)
        Gideon and the Altars (6:25-32)
        Gideon's Call/Commission: Part 2 (6:33-40)
        Preparations for Battle (7:1-8)
        A Final Sign for Gideon (7:9-14)
        Triumph for YWHW and for Gideon! (7:15-25)
    Block II: Tensions and Conflict (8:1-27)
        Conflict with Ephraim (8:1-3)
        Conflict with Succoth and Penuel (8:4-9, 13-17)
        Gideon's Revenge (8:10-12, 18-21)
        Gideon Refuses the Crown but Makes an Ephod (8:22-27)
Conclusion (8:28-35)

## Introduction (6:1-6)

The editorial introduction in 6:1-6 (+7-10) includes the standard elements: an announcement that Israel "did evil in the sight of YHWH" and that, consequently, YHWH had "given them into the hand" of an enemy (v. 1); a description of Israel's suffering (vv. 2-5); and a report that Israel "cried out" to YHWH (v. 6). In comparison to previous such introductions, however, the second element stands out for its detail and the final element for the response it elicits from God, a response unique in the book of Judges.

Israel's enemies in this case, Midianites, Amalekites, and "sons of the East," were marauders from the wilderness regions to the south and southeast of Judah. Like Israel's history of interaction with the Kenites (see "Foreign Influence in the South and in the North" above), its relationship with the Midianites, who play a key role in the Gideon story (6:1-3, 6-7, 11, 13-14, 16, 33; 7:1-2, 7-8, 12-15, 23-25; 8:1, 3, 5, 12, 22, 26, 28; cf. 9:17), was apparently complex. Israelite tradition recognized the Midianites as the descendants of Abraham and his wife Keturah (Gen 25:1-2; 1 Chr 1:32). They lived in an area south-southeast of Edom on the Arabian Peninsula along the eastern shore of the Gulf of Aqaba. According to the biblical account, Israel encountered them there during its wanderings in the wilderness. Israel's sometimes cordial interactions with Midian may have reflected kinship ties, while, otherwise, rivalry prevailed. Zipporah, Moses' wife, was a Midianite (Exod 3:1), but Midian also joined in commissioning Balaam to curse Israel (Num 22:7) and was involved in Israel's sin at Baal-Peor (Num 25:15, 18; cf. Num 31:2-3, 7-9).

On the other hand, the biblical account of the relationship between the Israelites and the Amalekites, who lived in the Negev (Num 13:2) and were traditionally identified as descendants of Esau (Gen 36:12, 16; 1 Chr 1:35-36), portrays a history of perpetual animosity stretching from their first conflict before Israel reached Mt. Sinai (Exod 17:8-16; cf. Deut 25:17-29), through the careers of Saul (1 Sam 15) and David (2 Sam 1:1), and surviving in Israel's cultural memory well into the Persian period (Esth 3:1). The designation "sons of the East" is open to interpretation. In Genesis 29:1, the term refers to Laban's family in Haran, north-northeast of Israel, whereas Isaiah 11:14 seems to equate it with Edom, Moab, and Ammon, Israel's neighbors east of the Jordan, the likely referent here.

In a pattern that has repeated itself all over the world throughout the history of human settlement, these groups, living in regions relatively less suited for agriculture than Israelite territory, made a practice of raiding Israelite settlements after the harvests had been gathered, "destroying the produce of the land" and stealing livestock, leaving nothing "to live on" (v. 4; Heb. *mhyh*, a feminine noun derived from the root *hyh*, "to live, be alive"). Unable to defend their property, Israelite farmers resorted to hiding in the ravines (*minharot*, which RSV, NAS, and others translate "dens" and NRSV translates "hiding places," derives from a root that designates "rivers"), caves, and natural fortifications in the mountains.

Commentators have often called attention to the generic quality of the description of Israel's wrongdoing in the editorial introductions to the accounts of some of the judges. Some conclude that such subtleties betray the literary history of the book, arguing that the presence of such generic statements (Judg 3:12; 4:1; 6:1) alongside others that clearly specify Israel's wrongdoing as apostasy (Judg 1:11-13, 17, 19; 3:6) reflect at least two stages in the composition of the book (see introduction). Others argue that, in context, Judges 6:1, for example, which does not specify the nature of the "evil" that Israel committed, nonetheless clearly implies Israel's apostasy. The Gideon narrative represents an illuminating case study of how the book of Judges understands Israel's "evil-doing."

## Supplement: The Prophet's Admonition (6:7-10)

On one hand, nothing about the crisis it faced suggests any cause-effect relationship between Israel's wrongdoing and its sufferings at the hands of raiders. On the other, as the structural outline of the cycle already demonstrates, it narrates incidents that deal with two situations that prove to be symptomatic of "evils" at work in Israel at the time. While the theological interpretation offered by the editorial paradigm of Israel's history focuses on religious infidelity, the Gideon cycle gives at least equal weight and attention to the petty jealousies and strife incited by Gideon during his career as judge of Israel. In an apparent effort to assert the interpretation of Israel's history favored by the editors responsible for the final form of the book, they included the account, unique in the book of Judges, of the appearance of a "prophet man" (*'ish nabi'*), sent by God to announce the fundamental facts of the situation. In language familiar from the exodus and deuteronomic/deuteronomistic traditions in the Hebrew Bible, the prophet recounts the basis for Israel's relationship with its God (he delivered them from Egyptian bondage) and the foundation on which that relationship was to continue (loyalty and obedience to the God who delivered them) before delivering the brief accusation, "but you have not obeyed" (v. 10 b). Remarkably, in comparison to the typical prophetic pronouncement, neither an explicit diagnosis of the Midianite crisis confronting Israel as the result of this disobedience nor a concluding sentence ("therefore, thus says YHWH, 'thus and so will be the result'") accompanies this simple and straightforward charge. Its placement at the head of the Gideon cycle, however, explicates the otherwise ambiguous phrase "to do evil in YHWH's eyes" (v. 1) and effectively declares the cause-effect relationship between Israel's apostasy and disobedience on the one hand and its sufferings under Midianite oppression on the other.

## Block I: Gideon's Successes (6:11–7:25)

In striking contrast to the behaviors of the judges treated early in the book—Ehud, for example—Gideon proves, at first, a hesitant deliverer. The first block of material devoted to Gideon's career moves haltingly toward the comparably brief account of his major success, victory over Israel's oppressors. Whereas Ehud and others took decisive action when presented with the opportunity, Gideon obviously lacks the necessary confidence—in himself and apparently in God. YHWH must repeatedly provide confirmation of Gideon's commission and assurance of his success. Gideon's first act, the destruction of the altar to Baal in Ophrah undertaken under cover of darkness, brings him into a conflict with his neighbors that Gideon's father must resolve. Apparently, Gideon lacks the courage to defend himself. The sequence of events and the inner workings of Gideon's character they suggest sets the stage for his later surprising transmogrification from a hesitant hero into the virtual opposite.

### Gideon's Call/Commission: Part 1 (6:11-24)

Gideon, whose name means "hacker," first appears in the unusual tale that intermingles an angelic appearance, Gideon's commission to deliver Israel, and a cultic etiology. Ophrah, Gideon's city, must differ from the Ophrah listed as a Benjamite possession in Joshua 18:23 (1 Sam 13:17 provides no helpful information). The Abiezrites, Gideon's clan, are unknown outside the Gideon cycle. "Oak trees" (Hebrew singular *'elah/'elon*) often serve as sites of divine appearances or for other cultic activities. God appeared to Abraham at the "oaks of Mamre" (Gen 18:1); Jacob buried objects associated with idolatrous worship beneath the oak at Shechem (Gen 35:4); Deborah, Rebekah's nurse, was buried beneath the oak near Bethel (Gen 35:8); Joshua placed a copy of the Torah under the oak at the sanctuary in Shechem (Josh 24:25); the coronation of Abimelech, Gideon's son, took place at the oak in Shechem (Judg 9:6); the Abimelech account also refers to a "diviners oak" (Judg 9:37); the prophet from Bethel found the man of God from Judah sitting under an oak (1 Kgs 13:14); according to the account in 1 Chronicles (10:14), Saul and Jonathan were buried under an oak; and the prophets frequently refer to oaks as sites where idolatrous worship was practiced (Ezek 6:13; Hos 4:13).

Both the presence of the angel and the location of the appearance, then, heighten expectations that something of great significance will now transpire. The exchange between YHWH/the angel of YHWH and Gideon proceeds in a manner that seems to typify the common pattern of call or commissioning accounts in the Hebrew Bible (cf. Habel): YHWH or a representative appears to a human figure, identifies a need, and commissions the figure to take action to address the need; the one commissioned offers objections; YHWH or a representative promises that YHWH will "be with" the one commissioned and offers a confirming sign. Indeed, YHWH's promise ("I will be with you," *'ehyeh 'immak*), made verbatim otherwise only to Moses (Exod 3:12) and Joshua (Deut 31:23; Josh 1:5; 3:7), puts Gideon in lofty company in this regard (cf. Boling 1975, 132).

On closer inspection, however, this account departs from the standard pattern in several intriguing ways characterized by ironic juxtapositions and *non sequiturs*. The angel's appearance to Gideon when he is engaged in surreptitiously winnowing wheat inside a winepress for fear of Midianite marauders and the angel's greeting that identifies Gideon as a "mighty man of valor" (*gibbor hayil*), for example, introduce an ironic tone that will resound throughout the cycle. The farmer hiding in the winepress hardly suggests the figure of a hero. Gideon's response to the angel, which seems unaware of the prophet's message reported in vv. 8-10, however, demonstrates, if not courage, then at least a certain impertinence or even sarcasm. The angel does not identify the problem to be addressed; Gideon does so in an accusatory response that is unique among such call narratives. After Gideon brings up the Midianite problem, boldly implying that it results from YHWH's inattention, the angel responds in kind with his own sarcastic/ironic command for Gideon to "go in this *might of yours* to deliver Israel from the hand of Midian" (emphasis added, v. 14). Unlike the call accounts of Moses and Jeremiah, in which YHWH's response to their objections with a promise to be with them includes the offer of a confirmatory sign, Gideon must ask for such a sign.

At this point, a degree of incoherence compounds the irony and sarcasm of the text. Instead of immediately confirming the commission and the accompanying promise of divine presence with a sign, the angel assumes a passive role. Gideon takes the initiative, transforming the encounter into a quasi-cultic event, inviting comparison with Abraham's behavior at the oaks of Mamre when he entertained YHWH and his angels (?) unaware of their identities (Gen 18), and with Manoah, Samson's father, whose offer of hospitality became a sacrificial offering (Judg 13). Gideon elicits the angel's promise to remain while Gideon goes to prepare a "present" (v. 18, RSV).

Recalling the ironic use of the term *minhah* in the Ehud story (see "Ehud" above), where the interplay between connotations of "gift/tribute" and "sacrifice" help to convey the irony of the situation described, Gideon's choice of the term unwittingly anticipates the outcome of this encounter with the angel of YHWH. Despite the Massoretic pointing of the title "Lord/lord/sir" in v. 15 (*'adonay*), which produces the form of the term reserved in the Hebrew Bible for references to God, like Abraham and Manoah, Gideon does not recognize his dialogue partner as YHWH/the angel of YHWH until after the sign he has requested has been given (v. 22). When Gideon initially addresses the angelic figure (v. 13), the Masoretic text correctly has him employ *'adoni* ("sir"), the more generic form of the term.

The nature of the "present" Gideon offers his visitor confirms the conclusion that Gideon is not yet aware of the identity of the stranger. Unleavened wheat cakes (Exod 12:8, 15, 17, 18, 20, etc.; Lev 2:4, 5; 6:9; 7:12; 8:2, etc.) and goat meat (Exod 12:5; Lev 1:10; 3:12, etc.) were, indeed, commonly offered as sacrifices, but Gideon seems to have thought he was preparing a meal for his guest, not a sacrifice for YHWH. According to prescriptions throughout the Torah, unleavened bread meant for use in the cult was to be placed in a basket (*sal*; Exod 29:3, 23, 32; Lev 8:2; 26:31; Num 6:15). In fact, of a total of fifteen occurrences of *sal* in the Hebrew Bible, ten refer to baskets of unleavened bread. The term appears otherwise only here in the Gideon cycle and four times in relation to the baker in the story of Joseph's rise to power in Egypt. Judges 6:19 specifies, however, that Gideon put the *meat* in the basket. Furthermore, while bread and meat could serve as sacrificial elements, "broth" never appears in conjunction with sacrifice anywhere in the Hebrew Bible. Evidently, Gideon intended to offer hospitality to a guest. Ironically and inadvertently, however, he prepared the elements for a sacrificial offering.

Presented with the bread, meat, and broth, the messenger of YHWH converts them into the elements of a sacrificial offering, perhaps to fulfill Gideon's request for a sign (reading the incident as the continuation of the call narrative, see below) or perhaps to reveal his identity (reading the incident as central to the cultic etiology). Reminiscent of Elijah's preparations for the contest between YHWH and Baal on Mt. Carmel (1 Kgs 18:33-35), the messenger of YHWH instructs Gideon to pour (*shpk*, v. 20; the Kings account uses a synonym, *ytsq*, in v. 34 [English v. 33] to describe the pouring of water on Eliljah's sacrifice) the broth over the sacrificial items. Gideon recognizes the nature of the encounter, then, only when the messenger, touching the tip of his staff to the cakes and meat, ignites them and vanishes from sight.

In response to the accidental sacrifice and God's assurance that he would survive his encounter with the divine, Gideon constructed an altar. By the end of the account of Gideon's encounter with the angel of YHWH, therefore, the story departs from the typical focus of a call/commission narrative to take on the character of a cultic etiology relating the story of the foundation of the cultic site at Ophrah of the Abiezrites (v. 24).

Indeed, the occurrence of the ironic sacrifice on a "rock" (*tsur*) may obscure an ancient cultic reference. The Song of Moses employs the term *tsur* as a quasi-title for YHWH ("the One of the Rock/Mountain [Sinai?]"; Deut 32:30-31, 37-38; cf. 2 Sam 23:3; Isa 44:8; Pss 18:2, 47; 27:4-6; 61:3-5; see Albright 1968, 19, 21, 164) and a number of early Israelite theophoric names include it as the theophoric element (cf. Elizur, "my God is *Tsur*," Num 1:35; 2:10; 7:30, 35; 10:18; Zurishaddai, "My *Tsur* is Shaddai," Num 1:6; 2:12; 7:36, 41; 10:19; and Pedahzur, "*Tsur* has redeemed," Num 1:10; 2:20; 7:54, 59; 10:23; cf. Albertz, 97). Although knowledge concerning the earliest Israelite cultic practices is vague, the frequency of references to stone pillars, especially in the context of the establishment of cultic sites in the ancestral narratives (*matstsebot*, Gen 28:18, 22; 31:13, 45; 31:51-52; 35:14; later forbidden, see Lev 26:1; Deut 16:22) and the perhaps related injunction against building altars of "worked/hewn" (*gazit*, Exod 20:25) stone, may point to an early rationale for the establishment of cultic sites to commemorate encounters such as Jacob's at Bethel or Gideon's here using stones available on site as altars.

In any case, during the course of the transition to the cultic etiology, the objective of Gideon's call/commission narrative remains unfulfilled. Source critics argue with good reason that this combination of genres points to a redactional fusion of source materials that obscured both the original conclusion to the call narrative component and the full significance of the cultic etiology. Coupled with the appearance of yet another commissioning episode (vv. 33-39) in which, after receiving the Spirit of YHWH, Gideon seeks yet another sign, the aberrant and incomplete quality of the call narrative of Judges 6:11-24 functions in the final form of the text to characterize Gideon somewhat negatively. Gideon's failure to recognize his dialogue partner suggests his impertinence as an indicator that he was not taking seriously the implications of the angel's statements and accounts for the various departures from the standard pattern of commission/call narratives. Gideon becomes an inadvertent judge and an ironic cult founder.

## Gideon and the Altars (6:25-32)

The appearance of what seems to be a second account of the construction of the cultic site in Abiezrite territory (vv. 25-32), a doublet, heightens the source critic's impressions that the Gideon cycle combines once independent Gideon traditions. In context, the two stories are more significant for their respective emphases. The first altar episode, like the comparable account of Jacob's establishment of the cultic site at Bethel (Gen 18), revolves around the founder's unexpected encounter with the divine at a sacred site, an encounter that led him to establish an altar there. In the second account, by contrast, Gideon receives and fulfills a specific instruction to take aggressive action against the Baal cult already in place, to destroy the altar to Baal and the companion asherah, and to replace it with an altar to YHWH constructed of "stones laid in due order" (v. 26, RSV).

Again, irony runs throughout the story. YHWH gives detailed and specific instructions. With the second of his father's bulls, the seven-year-old one, Gideon is to destroy the Baal altar and to sacrifice the same bull on the new altar devoted to YHWH. The bull, according to every indication the animal most closely associated with Baal, would be instrumental in the destruction of the altar to Baal and would become the burnt offering to YHWH. Then Gideon, the "man of valor" (v. 12) who objected to the designation with the assertion that he was the least member of the weakest clan in Manasseh (v. 14), executed YHWH's instructions, to be sure, but only at night and only with the assistance of ten of his male servants. Gideon, the "man of valor," apparently hides from the townsfolk, relying on his father to defend him. Gideon the weak is the son of Joash, who evidently enjoys status and power sufficient to permit him to assert that anyone who acts on Baal's behalf "shall be put to death by morning" (v. 31). By virtue of his father's ingenious etymology (scholars are in general agreement that Jerubbaal probably means "Baal establishes," see Moore, 196), the "Hacker" (see McCann, 61), who destroys the altar "established" for the worship of Baal, receives an ironic new name, "Let Baal contend." Notably, the account fails to report the contest implied by the name (cf. the contest on Mt. Carmel recorded in 1 Kgs 18). Apparently, Gideon's opponents lack the courage to defy Joash. Baal remains silent.

## Gideon's Call/Commission: Part 2 (6:33-40)

The final episode recorded in Judges 6 (vv. 33-40), which functions on three planes of the narrative simultaneously, heightens the impression of either the incoherence or the complexity of the Gideon cycle. The alternatives depend on whether one views the material from a source-critical (analysis of the various original sources of the cycles), redaction-critical (analysis of the editorial combination of these sources), or narrative (analysis of the final form as a literary unit) perspective. These viewpoints are not, of course, mutually exclusive. First, the announcement of the invasion by the Midianites and their allies in v. 33 returns the storyline to the presenting problem identified in the editorial introduction and in Gideon's objection to the incognito messenger of YHWH, namely, Israel's sufferings under foreign oppression. After all, Gideon's commission as judge relates specifically to the task of delivering Israel from its oppressors, not to religious reform. Similarly, second, the report that YHWH's spirit took possession (*lbshh*, lit., "clothed," v. 34) of Gideon also returns to the main line of the plot. In this regard, the unit may be seen either as a resumption or a doublet of the call narrative. Finally, the focus of the passage, Gideon's request for a sign, even after being "clothed" by the spirit of YHWH, not only raises questions as to Gideon's motivations and objectives, but seems out of place since it would constitute a more fitting conclusion to the call narrative than the cultic etiology (vv. 18-24).

Taking the second of these issues, namely the question of placement, first, a number of observations indicate that vv. 36-40 would function better as a conclusion to the call narrative than they do in their present setting. As noted above ("Gideon's Call/Commission: Part 1"), nothing Gideon says or does prior to his unwitting sacrificial offering suggests that he knew he was making preparations for the wondrous consumption of the bread and meat as a burnt offering, despite the fact that he had asked for a sign (v. 17). Furthermore, Gideon's cautious approach to destroying the Baal altar and his second request for a sign suggest either that he did not take the lesson from the burnt offering, that he did not view it as a fulfillment of the original request for a sign, or that the cultic etiology displaced the original response to the request (vv. 36-40?) in the course of the redaction of the Gideon cycle. The wording of Gideon's request for the sign of the fleece, "If you will deliver Israel by my hand, as you have said" (v. 36), seems to refer directly to the angel's statement in the call narrative, "Go in this might of yours and deliver Israel." The significance of this allusion is difficult to assess, however, especially in view of the fact that the fleece account consistently refers to "God" and not to "(the angel of) YHWH" as does the call narrative.

Finally, the description of the possession of Gideon by God's spirit and the muster of Israelite forces seems to begin a narrative line that should lead, next, to a description of preparations for battle. Indeed, the logistics of events described in vv. 33-40 are unclear. Does the text mean to suggest, since the reference to the threshing floor (v. 37) indicates that Gideon is still at home, that the tribes responding to the muster came to Ophrah to join Gideon? Is the reader to imagine that the warriors assembled for battle milled around for the several days expended in the course of Gideon's twofold test (the day of the initial request, overnight, the day of the second request, overnight, the next morning, with departure the following morning [7:1])? In the Old Testament, the Israelite militia typically assembled on or near the field of battle (i.e., Josh 22:12; 1 Sam 17:2) as a practical matter. Indeed, the statement that warriors from the tribes of Asher, Zebulun, and Naphtali "went up to meet them" better suits such a situation. The verb *'lh*, "to go up," is a technical term in military contexts denoting the march into battle (i.e., Exod 13:18; Num 13:30, 31; Deut 1:21; Josh 8:1), just as the verb *qr'*, "to meet," often connotes military engagement (i.e., Judg 20:25, 31; 1 Sam 4:1; 1 Kgs 20:27). Furthermore, the third person plural masculine pronoun "them" must refer either to the Abiezrites and Manassites mentioned in vv. 34-35 or to the Midianite coalition mentioned in v. 33. If the expression in question is to be understood in the technical sense, i.e., "they marched out to engage [the Midianite coalition]," vv. 33-35 represent the introduction to the account of the battle or the preparations for it that should ensue immediately. Gideon's call for a sign interrupts the expected sequence. In sum, the role and placement of the sign of the fleece is probably the result of editorial activity, and has the effect of highlighting either Gideon's lack of perception or his reluctance, adumbrating the questions that will arise regarding Gideon's purposes and objectives.

Setting aside issues related to the literary history of the passage, the position of the fleece account in the current form of the text effectively amplifies the reader's growing inference that it depicts Gideon as much less than a paragon of faith and courage. Details of the story, both those included and those omitted, only add to the ambiguity of the portrayal. For example, although the cultic etiology may have been inserted into the call narrative, displacing the original account of the sign given Gideon, in context, his reference to a previous encounter with God (v. 37) can only be read as a reference to the call. In other words, it establishes that Gideon seeks a *second* sign. He has witnessed the wondrous consumption of his unwitting sacrifice, succeeded in demolishing an altar to Baal and destroying its Asherah, been "clothed" by the spirit of YHWH, and issued a call to arms that elicited willing response (in contrast to the response to Baraq's muster; cf. 5:16-17, 23). Nonetheless, he requires yet another indication that God has chosen him to deliver Israel. Othniel (3:10) and even Samson (14:6, 19; 15:14) immediately take action after being "clothed" by the spirit of YHWH, at the impulse and with the power of the divine spirit. Gideon and Jephthah pause to seek the assurance of a sign or a vow (11:29), respectively.

Gideon is not in good company. Not only does the account implicitly compare him to Jephthah but Gideon's own words reveal something of his attitude. Stating his request that the sign of the fleece be repeated under new conditions, Gideon beseeches God's permission to stage just one more "test" (*nsh*). While he stops just short of specifying that he asks for what is tantamount to a test of God himself, the care with which he words the petition reveals his awareness of the dangerous area he has entered. In addition to the explicit plea for patience, the Hebrew employs the cohortatives and, twice, the polite particle *na'* used by inferiors speaking to their superiors as an acknowledgment of the power imbalance and as a sign of submission. The Bible takes a strong and clear position regarding "testing" God. While YHWH often tests both individuals (Gen 22:1) and the whole people of Israel (Exod 15:25; 16:4; 20:20; Deut 8:2), the Bible expressly prohibits the contrary (Deut 6:16) and reports the negative outcomes of several violations of the prohibition (Exod 17:2, 17; Num 14:22). Gideon dares to put God to the test and even to say so—not once, not twice, but three times.

Not surprisingly, perhaps, commentators have offered explanations of Gideon's actions regarding the fleece that tend to mitigate the affrontery of Gideon's bold and persistent doubt. Klein (55), for example, suggests that Gideon calls for the second demonstration because the first test only confirmed the expectation that, under normal conditions, fleece would retain moisture absorbed overnight while dew deposited on the ground would be soaked into the soil. The second test, on the other hand, produced a result contrary to normal expectations. Presumably, Gideon either realized the inconclusive nature of the first assay only after it had been conducted or he viewed it as a "control" sample. As Beck (37) has pointed out, however, the account emphasizes the quantity of moisture absorbed by the fleece, namely, enough to fill a "bowl" (v. 38, *sefel*, a term that occurs only here and in Judg 5:25, where the accent seems to be on the vessel's size) so that even the first test produces a significant result. Beck's suggestion that Gideon's intention is to stage a demonstration of YHWH's might in matters related to agriculture, comparable again in some respects to the contest on Mt. Carmel, assumes an audience for the demonstration. Yet the text does not even hint that members of Israel's assembled militia witness the events described. In fact, the swift response of the tribes to Gideon's summons implies their willingness to follow Gideon and their confidence in his role as deliverer, not their doubt. In other words, judging from both explicit and implicit indicators in the text, Gideon seems to be the sole audience of the fleece demonstrations. Gideon elicits evidence that God truly intends for him to be the instrument of Israel's deliverance because Gideon himself is not yet fully convinced. Indeed, Gideon's failure to acknowledge the import of the second test along with the subsequent report of still another sign given Gideon (7:13-15) intimate that, even after this second sign, Gideon continues to doubt.

**Preparations for Battle (7:1-8)**
Judges 7 opens with the notice that, finally, Gideon and the Israelite militia "rise early," presumably a day after the second sign of the fleece, to march to the staging area for the expected battle. While modern understanding of the geography presumed in the comment is incomplete, the proper names mentioned here already contribute significantly to the story based solely on their associations or etymologies. Some commentators regard the parenthetical identification of Jerubbaal as Gideon, the protagonist of the cycle, which seems redundant after 6:31-32, as further evidence (see above on the meaning of the name, Jerubbaal) that the tradition has linked the once distinct figures of Gideon and Jerubbaal, perhaps in order to incorporate the account of Abimelech, Jerubbaal's son, into the Gideon cycle (cf. Guillaume, 52, and see further below). "Harod," the name of the spring where the Israelite militia camped the night before battle, involves paronomasia, or wordplay, on the Hebrew term translated "trembling" in v. 3 (cf. McCann, 66), and "Moreh," the name of the hill near the Midianite encampment, can be understood as a form of the Hebrew term for "teacher." Together, the place names suggest, quite ironically, that the "trembling/fearful" Israelite army will be the Midianites' "teachers" in the upcoming conflict.

Despite the announcement that Israel has marched out to engage in battle, however, Judges 7 delays the account of the battle itself still further by inserting reports dealing with the counterintuitive reduction of the Israelite militia to a select 300 warriors and with yet another sign for Gideon that God will use him as the instrument for delivering Israel from Midianite oppression. In tandem, these two accounts not only postpone the actual battle report even more but also develop an element often manifest in relation to the Holy War theme in the Hebrew Bible, namely, the assertion and demonstration that the enemy, the victory, and the spoils all belong to YHWH, not to Israel or its leadership. At the same time, once introduced, the conventions of Holy War become part of the ideological backgrounds against which the portrayal of Gideon the unconvinced shifts, at first subtly, toward a depiction of Gideon the self-aggrandizer.

Before Gideon can launch the engagement with the Midianite coalition, YHWH instructs Gideon to diminish the fighting force. The reasons stated are clear and characteristic of Old Testament Holy War ideology. Deuteronomy 20:1-8, the only declaration of the principles of Holy War in the Hebrew Bible, outlines the key ideas. Foremost is the assertion that Israel can fight without fear, supremely confident in success, "for YHWH your God is the one going with you, to fight for you against your enemies, to deliver you" (v. 4). Furthermore, since YHWH does the fighting and Israel need not rely on its own might, it should take unusual measures regarding the constitution of its army. The fearful, those who have built houses but have not yet occupied them, those who have planted vineyards but have not yet harvested them, and those who are newly married should be dismissed from service (vv. 5-9). Finally, again since YHWH fights against and defeats his enemies, and, since in cases involving Israel's near neighbors they represent a syncretistic threat to Israel, prisoners of war and the spoils of battle alike are subject to the ban. They must be destroyed. (For a more detailed discussion of this charter for Israel's conduct of Holy War, see Biddle 2003, 313–20.)

While, seen against the backgrounds of Israel's Holy War tradition, the motivation for YHWH's instructions to Gideon to take measures to reduce the size of the militia are clear, the logic of the procedure itself defies explanation. YHWH wants it to be unmistakable to Gideon and Israel that YHWH has delivered his people, that they have not won the victory to ensue by their own might, saying "my own hand has delivered me." Similar expressions abound in the Gideon cycle and serve as a marker of the course of events and as something of a guide to Gideon's mindset along the way. The cycle's opening statement of circumstances describes them as the result of YHWH giving Israel "into the hands" of the Midianite coalition (6:1, 2). The anonymous prophet recalls when it was otherwise, when YHWH delivered the Israelites "from the hand of the Egyptians" (6:9). Gideon objects to the positive language of the angel's greeting. Gideon asserts that it does not comport with the obvious evidence and that, in fact, YHWH has abandoned his people "into the hands" of their enemies (6:13). Later, Gideon seeks and receives assurances that, in fact, YHWH intends to deliver Israel by his, Gideon's, hand (6:36, 37). Now, however, just before the battle, YHWH directs Gideon to take measures specifically designed to guard against any impression that deliverance comes by any means other than YHWH's intervention. Does the sequence of references to the "hand" as a symbol of power, either to oppress or to deliver, imply that YHWH has recognized in Gideon's need for assurance the seed of egocentrism?

In any case, YHWH prescribes a series of "tests" as means for reducing the Israelite fighting force to a size that will render it almost impotent against the coalition forces it will soon engage. First, in accord with the prescriptions outlined in Deuteronomy 20:9, Gideon is to dismiss any who are afraid. Just over two-thirds of those who responded to the muster return home, leaving a force of 10,000. Then YHWH devises an unusual test involving the manner in which the remaining men drink water from the nearby stream.

The precise behaviors distinguished in this test are unclear, as is the underlying rationale. YHWH envisions that some of the men will "bow down on [their] knees" (i.e., they will "kneel") to drink while others will "lap water with his tongue, as a dog laps" (v. 5) or "lap, putting their hands to their mouths" (v. 6). It is not possible to drink from a stream while remaining erect. One must either bring the water to one's mouth, which requires kneeling, or bring one's mouth to the water, which requires kneeling or even prostrating oneself on the ground. Thus, the reference to those who kneel, taken by itself, does not constitute a distinction and could refer to either procedure. "Lapping with the tongue, like a dog" seems to describe the act of lying on the bank and drinking directly from the stream with one's face to the water; "lapping, putting one's hands to one's mouth," on the other hand, which, in fact, is obviously not the way dogs drink, describes bringing the water to one's mouth. The apparent contradiction between lapping "with the tongue" and "putting one's hands to one's mouth" has led scholars to view the phrase "with their hands to their mouths" in v. 6 as a scribal gloss (Budde, 58; cf. Guillaume, 46, and Moore, 202, who comments that lapping and drinking from the hand "are precisely the two different ways of drinking which are here distinguished").

The rationale for this procedure is equally unclear. Presumably, the behaviors in question indicate something significant about the character of the men being chosen for battle. Assuming, regardless of the difficulties inherent in vv. 5 and 6, that the two options involved one posture that was more upright, several interpretations are possible. Klein (57), for example, argues that the men's posture itself is the issue: God chose those who remained upright, like men, while they drank, rather than lapping like dogs. As indicated in the discussion above, it is unclear, however, whether the "lappers" or the "kneelers" assumed the more upright posture. Guillaume focuses rather on the attitudes reflected in the postures but finds the evidence ambiguous. Were those who remained more upright demonstrating vigilance or timidity? Were those who adopted a more prone posture evidencing a sense of security or foolhardy inattention to their surroundings (Guillaume, 46; cf. Amit 1999, 258–60; Soggin 1981, 137)?

Regardless of the precise nature of the actions described in vv. 5-7, the resultant reduction of the fighting force available to Gideon would seem to set the stage for YHWH's victory of the enemy. Indeed, despite yet another series of ambiguities in the first half of the verse, the comment in v. 8 heightens the expectation that the account of the battle will ensue immediately. The narrator reports that Gideon has YHWH's handpicked force of 300, whom he "strengthened (encouraged)," and that the Midianite camp was located just below in the valley. Gideon has the high ground.

The final comment in the account of Gideon's preparations for battle (v. 8) presents yet another difficulty. The Hebrew syntax of the verse allows for two translations of the initial clause: "They took the provisions of the people in their hand and their trumpets" or "The people took provisions in their hand and their trumpets." The former reflects the word order of the Hebrew but raises the question of the referent of the pronouns (presumably the 300). The latter is at least possible but still leaves open the question of whether "the people" refers to all the assembled Israelites or only the 300. The continuation of the verse is thornier. The syntax of the phrase "and every man of Israel (= each individual Israelite)," which involves a so-called "direct object marker," would seem to indicate that it constitutes the third in the sequence of objects of the verb "to take" in the preceding clause, i.e., "they took provisions, trumpets, and every Israelite." Furthermore, it is unusual for the object to precede the related verb in Hebrew prose, a circumstance that argues against construing this phrase with the predicate "he sent." Besides, this grouping produces the redundant "and every Israelite he sent each to his tent." These difficulties seem to have motivated the translators of the RSV and the NRSV to emend *tsedah*, the term for "provisions," to *kad*, the term for "jar" that appears in vv. 16, 19 and 20, although there is no supporting manuscript or versional evidence. Apparently, then, v. 8a reports that the bulk of the assembled militia packed up provisions and trumpets (?) and that Gideon then sent them, each and every one, back home. The phrase "to his tent," which could be understood to mean that they remained bivouacked nearby, functions as an idiom for "back home" in 1 Kings 12:16. Later in Judges 7, Gideon issues a second call for the militia to assemble (vv. 23-24), which would have been unnecessary had he not previously dismissed them. The comment may be meant to emphasize that Gideon went into battle against the Midianites with only the force of 300 men, that is, without the possibility of ready reinforcement.

## A Final Sign for Gideon (7:9-14)

Readers of Judges have good reason to expect that Gideon and his elite force will now mount their attack. God has twice provided Gideon with signs that God is with him, Israel has responded without hesitation to Gideon's call to assemble, and God has "handpicked" the warriors who will constitute the attack unit. Indeed, v. 9 reports that, immediately after this selection process, God instructed Gideon to attack the Midianite encampment. Notably, however, God does not assume that Gideon has the necessary confidence and instead volunteers a third confirmation that God is with Gideon. The account reports Gideon, accompanied by his aide-de-camp, Purah, sneaking into the Midianite encampment by night. There they overhear one Midianite guard recounting to a comrade the content and interpretation of a dream: a barley loaf, representing "Gideon, the son of Joash, an Israelite," that rolled into camp demolishing a tent portends Gideon's defeat of the Midianite hosts. Along the way, this report provides details concerning the magnitude of the task awaiting Gideon and his band of 300. Employing several stock similes, the narrator describes the size of the enemy force as resembling a locust horde, an image of both size and destructive power (cf. Judg 6:5; Ps 105:34; Jer 46:23; Joel 1:4; 2:25; Nah 3:15, 17), or the sands of the sea (cf. Gen 22:17; 32:12; 41:49; Josh 11:4; 1 Sam 13:5; 2 Sam 17:11, etc.). Finally, Gideon seems convinced that God has indeed commissioned him for this task, that "God has given the host of Midian into [Israel's] hand." The dream of a Midianite warrior accomplishes what the wondrous consumption of the burnt offering (6:21), possession by the spirit of YHWH (6:34), and the twofold sign of the fleece (6:36-40) could not.

## Triumph for YHWH and for Gideon! (7:15-25)

In fact, a subtle transformation in Gideon's attitude may be observed as events unfold subsequent to this ironic encounter with the Midianite dreamer. The text presents a number of inconsistencies and improbabilities. Several commentators point out that Gideon's warriors need a third hand to smash the jars while blowing the trumpet and suspect that two sources have been intertwined here (cf. Budde, 61; Soggin, 146). Furthermore, it is difficult to envision how Gideon is supposed to have coordinated the "attack" if his 300 troops were stationed around the "outskirts" of the Midianite forces that occupied an entire valley. Despite these difficulties, the general thrust remains clear. On the one hand, the tactics employed in the actual "attack," which apparently follows immediately upon Gideon's return from overhearing the dream, continue the Holy War theme introduced in the selection process. The Israelite "special forces" rely on YHWH to amplify the effects of their deception and surprise. Armed chiefly, if not indeed solely, with torches concealed in pottery jars and horns, they surround the Midianite encampment and, on Gideon's signal, simultaneously break the jars exposing the light of the torches within, and sound their horns. Since, presumably in ancient times as in more recent history, a bugler implied a military unit, the sudden bugling of 300 horns and the accompanying outburst of light would not only startle the sleeping Midianites but would also elicit the impression that they were surrounded by a force 300 units strong. In the resulting disarray and confusion, the coalition forces lost the "command and control" necessary for fighting effectiveness. The ancient equivalent of "friendly fire" in the "haze of war" only multiplied the chaos and terror (v. 22).

On the other hand, several elements of the battle account and the subsequent report of the "mop-up" action at least suggest that Gideon begins at this point to undergo a transformation in his attitudes, "moving from fear to self-assertion" (McCann, 67). For example, since the text reports no divine instruction concerning the conduct of the exercise, Gideon apparently takes the initiative to plan ("he divided the three hundred," v. 16) and lead ("Look at me . . . do as I do," v. 17) the incursion in the Midianite camp. To be sure, the ridiculous tactics Gideon employs comport with the Holy War tradition's tendency to emphasize the fact that any victory won by such improbable methods must have been by virtue of YHWH's intervention. With a newfound boldness, Gideon finds the courage to foray virtually unarmed and supported only by 300 similarly equipped warriors into the teeth of the enemy force. By themselves, Gideon's initiative and his uncharacteristic bravery are innocuous or perhaps even praiseworthy. But twice he claims for himself or allows others to attribute to him equal billing with YHWH, as it were: he instructs his special forces at the key moment to yell, "For YHWH and for Gideon!" (v. 18), and, when the moment comes, in fact, they cry out, "A sword for YHWH and for Gideon" (v. 20). These compound battle cries are unique in the Old Testament. Only Gideon is elevated to such status. In fact, they skirt the boundaries of propriety in the context of Israelite Holy War ideology: YHWH alone is Israel's leader, victor in battle, and object of devotion and praise. These subtle indications of Gideon's late-blossoming (over-)confidence presage Gideon's subsequent egocentrism and apparent disregard for fundamental tenets of Israelite Holy War, a disregard that culminates in idolatry.

For the moment, however, Gideon's strategy succeeds, setting the Midianite army in disarray and putting them to flight (v. 22). In order to execute the "mop-up" phase of the engagement, Gideon must recall the men he had earlier dismissed (v. 24; cf. 6:35; Zebulun is omitted in the second muster), adding to the number the Ephraimites whom he charges with taking control of the fords across the Jordan and its tributaries and cutting off the Midianites' retreat back to the south (v. 24). Apparently, Gideon intends to execute a "pincer" maneuver, trapping the fleeing Midianites between the pursuing forces of the northern and Transjordanian tribes and the Ephraimite forces positioned at transit points farther to the south. The strategy succeeds. Ephraimite forces capture and kill two of the Midianite chieftains, Oreb (Hebrew for "raven") and Zeeb (Hebrew for "wolf"), bringing their heads to Gideon as evidence of their victory. The tradition of this Ephraimite victory also made its way into Israel's prophetic (Isa 10:26; cf. 9:4) and liturgical (Ps 83:9-12) literature, although, notably, none of these texts refer either to Ephraim or Gideon. Instead, they attribute the defeat of the Midianites solely to YHWH.

## Block II: Tensions and Conflict (8:1-27)

The apparent shift in Gideon's attitude from reticence, even fear, to bold confidence noteworthy in the progression of events recorded in Judges 7 extends into a new sphere in the events recorded in Judges 8. The Gideon of Judges 6–7 seems at times humble and uncertain to the point of inaction. Despite the direct call of God and several indications of God's presence with him in the undertaking before him, Gideon repeatedly seeks yet further assurance that God has truly chosen him for the task and that God intends to bless him with success. The axis of relationship shifts temporarily in Judges 8 to Gideon's dealings not with God but with segments of his own people and with his enemies. While the narrator(s)/editor(s) of the Gideon cycle do not provide readers explicit editorial guidance as to how events recorded here should be understood, the focus can hardly be mistaken. The cautious, timid Gideon of the fleece episode becomes zealous for his own reputation. Even though he ultimately rejects an offer to accept Israel's crown as its first king, he violates the primary commandment of the Mosaic covenant in an act of self-aggrandizement that, reading canonically, recalls Aaron's error (Exod 32) and anticipates Jeroboam's (1 Kgs 12:26-33). Taken together, Gideon's relationships with groups within Israel, his vindictive treatment of his enemies, his refusal of kingship, and his presumptuous abuse of power in creating a religious icon constitute a narrative examination of issues that persistently beleaguer Israel's leaders.

Judges 8 divides readily into nine units grouped in three uneven sequences. The first three deal with Gideon's confrontations with groups of fellow Israelites (Ephraim, vv. 1-3; Succoth, vv. 4-7; Penuel, vv. 8-9).

Following the account of Gideon's successful capture of the Midianite kings, Zebah and Zalmunna ("Sacrifice" and "Protection Withheld"; see Soggin, 149, and Hamlin, 98), and defeat of the remnant of Midian's forces (vv. 10-12), two episodes relate Gideon's exaction of vengeance on his opposition, both domestic (Succoth and Penuel, vv. 13-16) and foreign (Zebah and Zalmunna, vv. 18-22). The Gideon cycle culminates in Gideon's ambivalent refusal of the throne coupled with his creation of a heterodox religious symbol (vv. 22-27), which serves to set the stage for a complex unit summarizing Gideon's career as judge and transitioning to the story of his son, Abimelech, who will manifest his father's worst traits.

## Conflict with Ephraim (8:1-3)

The chapter opens with the comment that the Ephraimites "contended (*yrybwn*) vigorously with [Gideon]," an allusion to Gideon's other name, Jerubaal, that signals the dominant theme of this section. Centuries and cultural differences obscure the details of the social and political dynamics underlying the Ephraimites' displeasure with Gideon's conduct of the campaign against the Midianite coalition. It is tempting to speculate that, as elsewhere in the book of Judges (cf. 5:14, 17, which notes that Gilead, a constituent of Manasseh, refrained from joining in support of Deborah; 9:1-57, the account of Abimelech's "monarchy" at Shechem, which was originally in Manasseh and later in Ephraim; and the report of a similar overt conflict between Gilead and Ephraiam in 12:1-6; see Kingsbury, esp. 133–34), this account reflects some historical tension between the closely related northern tribes of Manasseh (cf. 6:15) and Ephraim. Whatever the historical case may have been, from a literary perspective, the conflict between Ephraim and Gideon functions to introduce the conflict theme into the Gideon cycle, to foreshadow similar conflicts to come later, and thus to introduce the theme as it appears in the book overall. As Amit (1999, 243) notes, in fact, the Judges material dealing with Israel's contentious and ultimately failed leadership material concentrates on the Transjordanian tribes, much as the book of Joshua views those tribes as fertile ground for heterodox religious practices (cf. Biddle 1998, 194–95, 199, 200).

Returning to the passage at hand, apparently, either the Ephraimites resented the lost opportunity for glory and plunder or they considered the fact that Gideon omitted them from the initial muster, which included only the tribes of Manasseh, Asher, Zebulun, and Naphtali (6:35; cf. 7:23, which omits Zebulun), an insult to their reputation as warriors. Gideon's response suggests that he recognized both of these possibilities. First, he flatters them with the comparison of their superior "gleanings" to his own clan's inferior harvest (v. 2), noting that they have already captured the Midianite military leaders Oreb and Zeeb (and implying that he has not yet captured the Midianite kings he pursues). Second, this recognition of their success also reminds them that he had not overlooked them entirely in the call to arms, since he gave them the significant responsibility for sealing the crossing of the Jordan, which would have provided the enemy its best route of escape (7:24). Gideon's strategy for placating the Ephraimites succeeds.

**Conflict with Succoth and Penuel (8:4-9, 13-17)**
More important, however, it demonstrates Gideon's capacity for inspiring resistance to his leadership and contrasts with his subsequent dealings with his opponents. These elements appear in full bloom in the episodes that follow, namely, Gideon's encounters with the inhabitants of the city of Succoth (east of the Jordan and north of the Jabbok in the territory of Gad) and nearby Penuel (cf. Jacob's journey to encounter Esau) recorded in vv. 4-9 and 13-17, respectively. As with the previous account, the sociopolitical dynamics of these encounters are far from transparent to modern readers. As Niditch (2008, 104) points out, these incidents compare in some respects to the near-encounter between David and Nabal. In both cases, a charismatic leader of an armed band asks someone for provisions for his followers, is harshly rebuffed, and threatens to exact retribution for the slight. It is not clear in either case that those who refuse to grant the request have violated any social requirement, or even expectation, that would justify the reactions of the rebuffed. To be sure, Nabal explicitly insults David, and the leaders of Succoth suggest that Gideon must first earn their allegiance, at least implying their doubts as to his worthiness. Even though David suffers the most obvious affront, however, Abigail's speech makes it clear that the revenge he intends to take on Nabal would be tantamount to shedding innocent blood (*dam hinnam*, 1 Sam 25:31; note David's tacit agreement, v 33).

In other words, while both Gideon and David may have justifiably felt insulted, the harm done to their honor certainly did not merit lethal responses. In fact, Gideon, at least, holds others to a standard he did not himself meet. Whereas he repeatedly demanded evidence that God was with him, Gideon responds to the people from Succoth and Penuel, who desire evidence that he deserves their support (cf. MacCann, 69), selfishly, peevishly, and viciously. Because the cities of Succoth and Penuel refused his request, Gideon threatens to "thresh [their] flesh with thorns (*'et-qotse*) of the wilderness and with briars (*'et-habbarqanim*; the phrase may allude to the name *baraq*)" or to "tear down [their] tower" (vv. 7, 9), respectively. Indeed, after capturing the Midianite kings, Zebah and Zalmunna, Gideon makes good on his threat. In a calculated and methodical manner, he captures a young man from Succoth, interrogates him to learn the names of seventy of Succoth's leading citizens, reminds the people of Succoth of their insult, and carries out his threat. He not only demolishes Penuel's tower, as he had threatened, but also viciously "kills the men of the city."

**Gideon's Revenge (8:10-12, 18-21)**
Layered within these accounts of Gideon's vengeful treatment of his fellow Israelites is the account of his treatment of his foreign opponents (vv. 10-12, 18-21), an account that only confirms Gideon's egotism, petulance, and ruthlessness. As before with the Midianites, Gideon takes his enemy by surprise, panicking the enemy army; the leader of the enemy forces flees the field of battle; the Israelites pursue, capture, and execute the enemy leader. In the case at hand, Zebah and Zalmunna and the remnant of the "army of the people of the east" retreat to Karkor, a city in Transjordanian Gilead, east of Gideon's home in Ophrah and of the area around Moreh and Harod, the site of the battle recorded in Judges. From nearby Succoth, Gideon and his band of 300 warriors approach Karkor via the trade route farther to the east, circuiting to attack unexpectedly from the flank. After returning to Succoth and Penuel to exact revenge, Gideon executes Zebah and Zalmunna, not, as one might expect, in fulfillment of the requirements of Holy War (cf. 1 Sam 15) nor even as a penalty for their aggression against Israel, but as an act of personal revenge and for personal profit (v. 21).

As is true of the psychosocial dynamics of the exchange between Gideon and the leadership of Succoth, the interaction between Gideon and the Midianite kings seems to involve a level of communication that is nearly inaccessible to a modern Western reader. Gideon's initial question to the Midianite kings (v. 18) may already hint at a subtext. Although translators often render *'efo*, the interrogative pronoun employed here as "where" (cf. RSV, ESV, JPS, NAB), four observations suggest another option followed by several (ASV, KJV, NAS, NIV, TNK). First, Zebah and Zalmunna will have had no reason to move the bodies of the men killed at Tabor from Tabor. Gideon could have safely assumed that he knew their whereabouts. Second, the text offers no indication as to why Gideon would have been especially interested in the fates of these men. This reference is the sole mention of Tabor and its inhabitants in the Gideon account. Third, and most significant, the response by Zebah and Zalmunna does not, in fact, answer the question concerning the location of the bodies. Finally, in a secondary meaning, *'efo* can sometimes better be rendered "of what sort" (see Gen

27:33, 37; 43:11; 2 Kgs 10:10; Job 9:24; 19:6; 24:25; Prov 6:3; Isa 22:1; cf. Exod 33:16; Judg 9:38; Isa 49:21; Job 19:23).

Indeed, the assumption that Gideon's question served his intention to acquire information that would enable him to deduce the identities of the deceased ("Of what sort were the men you killed?"—i.e., "Describe the men you killed") avoids all the difficulties of the translation "where." The question focuses, then, not on the location of the bodies but on the identification of the victims. The question itself reveals the grounds for Gideon's interest in the fatalities at Tabor; aware that his brothers were among the combatants there, he naturally seeks to gain information about their fates. Finally, the response of the Midianite rulers presupposes a question seeking identifying information: "What sort of men were they?" "Like you, Gideon, they seemed to be royalty."

Therefore, the account of this episode fulfills a dual function. On one hand, it solidifies the portrayal of Gideon as vengeful, petty, and increasingly egocentric. By his own admission (v. 19), he had not originally planned to execute the Midianite kings, but the conclusion that they have killed his full brothers motivates him to take personal revenge. On the other hand, however, it also introduces a new theme in the story of Gideon, namely, the issue of Gideon as a potential king. As is characteristic of Hebrew storytelling, the narrative of the exchange between Gideon and the Midianite kings refrains from supplying subjective detail concerning the thoughts and motivations of the actors. Zebah and Zalmunna may have offered honest evaluations of the bearing and manner of their victims at Tabor and of Gideon; alternatively, they may have made the comparison in Gideon's favor in an attempt to ingratiate themselves with him. In either case, Gideon's reaction reveals his self-understanding. Without hesitation, he concludes that men of royal stature among the Israelite combatants, presumably captured on the battlefield and taken to Tabor somewhat to the north to be executed, must have been his brothers. In other words, Gideon took it as a given that his family had an obvious air of regality.

As quickly as the account insinuates that Gideon's sense of himself has changed radically since he described himself as the least member of the least clan and tribe in Israel (6:15), it interjects a note of ambivalence, however. Jether's fearful reticence to execute Zebah and Zalmunna on Gideon's orders recalls the earlier, less than regal, cowering behaviors of his hesitant father (i.e., 6:11, 27; 7:10). The reaction of the Midianite kings, who essentially taunt Gideon, challenging him not to rely on the youth but to do his own killing, both accentuates the transformation Gideon has undergone since his initial encounter with the angel of God and undermines the notion that Gideon's family, namely his brothers and his sons, are innately royal.

### Gideon Refuses the Crown but Makes an Ephod (8:22-27)

Before the complex summary comment on his judgeship, the story of Gideon proper draws to an end, then, with a final narrative episode that epitomizes the growing sense of ambiguity associated with Gideon's character and thus prepares for the further development of the themes of egocentric spitefulness and petty arrogance evident in the story of Gideon's son, Abimelech. Together, this concluding episode and summary assessment of Gideon's career raise the question of Gideon's status among the judges.

The narrative episode relates the interaction between Gideon and the people of Israel concerning the people's suggestion that Gideon become their king. At first glance, Gideon's response to the suggestion seems to embody the theological orthodoxy associated with the position stated in the interaction between the prophet Samuel and God concerning Israel's request to be given a king (1 Sam 8:6-9) and to reflect Gideon's proper humility before God. Yet, the summary assessment of his career indicates that the tendencies toward self-aggrandizement Gideon began to demonstrate after engaging the Midianites continue to appear in Gideon's later life. Gideon's household of seventy sons by his many wives, in itself a mark of wealth, power, and status, rivals the households of Israel's most celebrated kings, David and Solomon. Moreover, the concluding observation that the Israelites failed to remain loyal to Gideon's household after his death presupposes a dynastic principle characteristic of the institution of the monarchy but contradictory to charismatic judgeship (cf. the remark concerning Samuel's sons in 1 Sam 8:1-3). Finally, Gideon's refusal of the crown notwithstanding, he named one of his sons Abimelech, "My Father Is King." One could argue that the text portrays a figure who effectively reigned as king, regardless of whether he bore the title.

In one respect, Gideon certainly resembles Israel's kings as described in the Deuteronomistic History: whether intentionally or inadvertently, he promoted idolatry. Perhaps to commemorate their victory over the Midianites/Ishmaelites (cf. v. 24 and the account of the sale of Joseph into slavery, which also equates Midianites and Ishmaelites, Gen 37:25-28), Gideon collects one earring from each of the Israelites who have taken booty from their defeated enemies (the text is silent on the possibility that they have violated the principles of Holy War in so doing), garnering roughly nine pounds of gold, not including the plunder taken from the Midianite kings and their camels (v. 26b; that is, the plunder that Gideon seized personally), in order to make from them an "ephod." While the term sometimes refers to a type of garment (cf. Exod 28:4; 1 Sam 2:18; 2 Sam 6:14) or to a device used in divination (cf. 1 Sam 23:6-12), it seems to denote a type of religious statuary here. Gideon's act of creating it and installing it in his hometown of Ophrah recalls Aaron's conduct in creating the golden calf (Exod 32) and, relatedly, Jeroboam's establishment of shrines in Dan and Bethel (1 Kgs 12:26-33). As a result, "all Israel," including Gideon and his family, committed idolatry. In the end, the Gideon who destroyed the cult site of Baal (6:25-27) replaces it with an idol image of his own making.

## Conclusion (8:28-35)

Finally, two incidental features of the summary assessment that concludes the Gideon cycle merit comment with regard to the transition to the story of Gideon's son, Abimelech, Israel's first (self-styled) king. From a structural standpoint, the transitional character of vv. 28-35 is evident in the manner in which references to Abimelech (vv. 29-31, 35?) have been interwoven into a formulaic (and rather positive) summary assessment of Gideon's career (vv. 28, 32-34; cf. Moore, 234). The summary assessment includes the expected elements: the report that the enemy was defeated/subdued and that, consequently, Israel enjoyed "rest" for a certain period (v. 28), the report of the judge's death and burial (v. 32), and the report that the people of Israel then once again committed apostasy (vv. 33-34). The reference to Israel's disloyalty to Gideon's house in v. 35 stands out as an unexpected promonarchial sentiment and because of its reference to Gideon as Jerubbaal, the name that normally appears in contexts associated, ironically, either with Gideon's destruction of the Baal cult in Orphah or with Abimelech his overly ambitious son. In other words, the very name echoes the issues raised by the content of v. 35 and suggests that v. 35 is more closely related to the Abimelech material in vv. 29-31 than to the summary assessment.

From the standpoint of family dynamics, the characterization of Abimelech in vv. 30-31 raises intriguing possibilities. While this material is as devoid of overt characterization of impulses, drives, and thoughts as any in the Hebrew Scriptures, the information that Abimelech was one of Gideon's seventy sons and that his mother was a concubine from Shechem may ominously portend things to come. The text categorizes Abimelech's mother as Gideon's *pilegesh*, a term that describes a status that is not entirely clear to researchers. Etymology offers no guidance since the term, which is not Semitic, has uncertain origins (Egyptian? Philistine?). Theories concerning how the status differed from that of wife focus on the fact that, in texts set in

Israel's earliest times, it seems to denote a wife who does not live with her husband. Proponents of these theories characterize these relationships as patrilocal versus virilocal (that is, a *pilegesh* is a wife who remains in her father's house after marriage; see Bal, 81–86) or natolocal (that is, the woman remains in the community where she was born, see Jost, 297) marriages. Others propose that the term means "a legal wife of secondary rank" (cf. Exum 1993, 177). Jost (296) points out that, regardless of the anthropological and sociological backgrounds of the institution, the Old Testament employs the term chiefly in the context of royal polygyny (2 Sam 3:7; 21:11; 5:13-16; 15:16; 16:21; 19:6; 20:3; 1 Chr 3:9; 1 Kgs 11:3; Cant 6:8f.; Esth 2:14; 2 Chr 11:21). Besides being yet another indication of the royal undercurrent running throughout Judges 8:18-35, the status of Abimelech's mother may have implications for Abimelech's status (what became of Jether, Gideon's firstborn?) and may help to account for the tensions evident later between Abimelech and the leadership of Shechem, his mother's (and presumably his) hometown. These and other observations lead Hauser (1979, 299) to posit that Gideon made a treaty with Shechem sealed by his marriage to a Shechemite and ruled there after delivering Shechem from Midianite oppression. Indeed, Abimelech's resentment toward his family anticipates the attitude of Jephthah, the son of a prostitute, toward his half-brothers, and Abimelech's presumption of the status of heir to his father's role; it also adumbrates the behaviors of Absalom, the son of David and a foreign wife.

At any rate, the transition to the Abimelech materials provides the occasion for the reader to pause for a summary assessment of Gideon's character and career. Although the voice of the narrator remains substantially silent, Gideon's behaviors seem to outline a clear trend. As events unfold, the reticent, even fearful Gideon encountered at the beginning of the cycle devoted to him becomes increasingly self-centered, his primary concern becomes his own reputation, and his devotion to the unadulterated worship of YHWH gives way to a dangerous flirtation with idolatry. Paused before the story of Abimelech is about to begin, one wonders whether the catastrophe of Abimelech's career represents punishment for Gideon's idolatry, as Amit (1999, 41) characterizes it, for example, or the extension and maturation of the tendencies of the father in the life of the son—or whether, in this case as in many others recorded in Scripture (cf. again, David and Absalom), the two options constitute sides of a coin. Regardless, apart from Aaron as a representative of the priesthood, Gideon stands as the first (in canonical order) of Israel's leaders to exhibit the tendencies that will prove to be Israel's fatal flaw, at least in the deuteronomistic scheme of Israel's history.

# Abimelech

Judges 9

While the Gideon story portrays an arc in the character development of the protagonist from hesitance to egocentrism, the story of his son, Abimelech, paints a consistently negative picture. The son will exceed the father in vengeful lust for power. Three overlapping themes unfold: the illegitimacy of (royal) power based on violence alone, the crime of infidelity to family and to legitimate authority expressed dually in Abimelech's fratricide and Shechem's disloyalty to the house of Gideon/Jerubbaal, and the certainty of ironic retribution.

Students of the Deuteronomistic History have long puzzled over the apparently contradictory attitudes it expresses toward the legitimacy of the Israelite monarchy (see, for example, Gerbrandt, McKenzie, and Nelson 1981 and 2005, among many others) and, particularly, the contribution of the book of Judges to its overall portrayal of the institution. On the one hand, passages such as 1 Samuel 8 and 10 resonate with Gideon's sentiment that YHWH is Israel's proper king (8:23) and seem to indicate that, in the Deuteronomists' eyes, the monarchy's fundamental flaw doomed it from the outset. On the other hand, periodic assertions of the model character of Judean kings such as David (1 Kgs 3:14; 9:4; 11:4, 6, 33, 38; 14:8, etc.) and Josiah (2 Kgs 22:1-2; 23:24-25) seem consonant with the assessment made several times toward the end of the book of Judges that anarchy and lawlessness characterized the pre-monarchial period "when Israel had no king and everyone did what was right in their own eyes" (17:6; 18:1; 19:1; 21:25). Little wonder, then, that commentators turn to the Abimelech story for evidence as to how the book of Judges and, more broadly, the Deuteronomistic History assess the institution of monarchy.

To be sure, both the editors who produced the book of Judges, presumably during the late monarchial and exilic periods, and later readers aware of the canonical context of the book will have recognized or will recognize, respectively, the many parallels that Abimelech's career manifests with events in Israel's history such as Absalom's grab for power (2 Sam 14–18), Jehu's unwarranted annihilation of the Omrides (2 Kgs 9–10), and Athaliah's attempt to seize the throne in Jerusalem by exterminating the Davidic dynasty (2 Kgs 11). Nonetheless, careful attention to the development and interrelationship of the three themes elaborated in the account of Abimelech's career do not support the claim that it represents a commentary on monarchy, per se. Instead, it exemplifies the more limited principle that authority established on shaky foundations will crumble from the foundation upward.

## Structure

The account unfolds in seven episodes: Abimelech's fratricidal power grab (vv. 1-6), Jotham's parable (vv. 7-15) and its interpretation (vv. 16-21), Shechem's jealousy and rebellion (vv. 22-29), Abimelech's siege of Shechem (vv. 30-41) and vengeance on it (vv. 42-49), and divine retribution (vv. 50-57). An overarching structure underscores the third of the major themes in the account, namely, the ironic symmetry of retribution (Boogaart, 47):

|  | **Revolt against the house of Jerubaal** | **Revolt against Abimelech** |
| --- | --- | --- |
| Comes to Shechem | v. 1a | v. 26a |
| Issue of kinship | vv. 1b-3a | v. 26a |
| Conspiracy | vv. 2-3a | vv. 28-29 |
| Question of ties | v. 2b | v. 28 |
| Trust conspirator | v. 3b | v. 26b |
| Execution of rulers | v. 5 | vv. 30-42 |

This symmetry culminates when Abimelech, who had assassinated seventy of his father's sons "on one stone" (9:5), dies as the result of one stone hurled by a solitary woman (9:53). An executioner's chopping block constitutes a shaky foundation for a royal house indeed.

## Abimelech's Fratricidal Power Grab (9:1-6)

The conclusion to the Gideon story introduces Abimelech with only the most basic information concerning his status as the son of Gideon's concubine from Shechem, leaving the reader to surmise regarding the significance of this information. Likewise, the initial episode in the story of his brief career provides only meager information concerning the circumstances surrounding Abimelech's play for power in Shechem. It is entirely unclear, for example, how Gideon's seventy sons, who were from Ophrah and apparently continued to maintain residence in their ancestral home, would have become the rulers of Shechem (cf. Guillaume, 56). The extent of Abimelech's ill-gotten power is also unclear. Moore (239) considers it most likely that Abimelech became the king of Shechem only, since, as a Canaanite city, it would have probably conformed to the city-state model of government characteristic of Canaanite culture. Notably, the text does not suggest that any element of Israel recognized his authority, a circumstance that may have bearing on the question of whether the book of Judges and the larger Deuteronomistic History regarded the Abimelech affair as an illustration of the flaws inherent specifically in the *Israelite* monarchy.

Despite the scarcity of detail regarding Abimelech himself, and the political circumstances surrounding the beginning of his career, the opening section of the account offers several unmistakable clues as to the central concerns of the narrator. Frequent specifications of family relationships divide participants into two kinship groups with Abimelech figuratively in the middle (cf. Niditch 2008, 115). On the one side are Abimelech's half-brothers, the seventy sons of Gideon/Jerubbaal, and on the other are Abimelech's maternal kin, the population of Shechem. Judging from other biblical traditions concerning Shechem (Gen 33:19; Josh 24:32), archaeological evidence (see Stager), and references to "the house of Baalberith" and other cultic sites and objects at Shechem (v. 6), Abimelech seems to have sided with his Canaanite heritage instead of taking up his father's early opposition to Baalism (cf. 6:25-32; see Lewis; cf. also Moore, 239). As Burney (267) has observed, although Abimelech was half Canaanite by birth, he seems to have been wholly Canaanite by tribal customs.

What motivates Abimelech's animosity toward his half-brothers? While, consistent with Israelite narrative technique, the account refrains from providing subjective information about its characters, three clues suggest that Abimelech sought to avenge a perceived slight related to his status as the son of a concubine. First, as noted above, the narrator takes pains to point out Abimelech's unique status in Gideon's family. Second, although the state of scholarly understanding of the *pilegesh* role obscures the full implications of this information (see further, Stone 1995a, 193–94), in the larger context of the book of Judges, the dynamics between Abimelech and his Ophrahite half-brothers recall those between Jephthah, Gilead's son by a harlot, and Gilead's "legitimate" sons. When Jephthah's half-brothers call on him to assist them in their defense against the Ammonites, he reminds them that they expelled him from his paternal heritage and demands that, if he succeeds against the Ammonites, they acknowledge him as their superior, their "head" (*rosh*; Judg 11:19). The comment that Abimelech hired a mercenary band of "worthless and reckless fellows" (*'anashim reqim ufohazim*, v. 4; cf. *'anashim reqim*, 11:3; see Jost, 180) underscores the comparison between Abimelech and Jephthah. The overall context suggests, then, that Abimelech, the son of the Shechemite concubine, may have acted out of a similar resentment toward his "legitimate" half-brothers (see Amit 1999, 102). Third, the language describing the survival (*ytr*, "to remain," 9:5) of Jotham, the youngest son of Gideon/Jerubbaal, involves an ironic reference to Jether (*ytr*, which can also mean "preeminence"), the oldest son of Gideon/Jerubbaal mentioned in the account of the execution of Zebah and Zalmunna (8:20). The recurrence of the tri-literal root calls attention to the fact that the family of Gideon/Jerubbaal has now been decimated, his princely brothers dead at the hands of the Midianite kings, and his seventy sons, headed by the "preeminent" Jether, reduced to the one "survivor."

Thus, the first episode in the sordid story of Abimelech's career plots the course of its development and outlines a principle that will manifest itself repeatedly in Israel's history. Fundamentally, Abimelech rebels against his family (cf. Steinberg, 57), eliminating all the rivals in his father's family. Founded on violence and jealousy, his authority will prove to be illegitimate and unsustainable. He was a usurper, not a judge (cf. Niditch 2008, 115, and McCann, 72), and certainly not a legitimate king.

In fact, this understanding of the Abimelech story raises questions as to its function as commentary on the institution of kingship. Rather than illustrating the dangers and flaws inherent in monarchy per se, it may better be understood as an illustration of the faulty character of authority built on aggression and raw power, a theme that runs throughout the history of the Israelite, but not the Judean, monarchy. According to the Deuteronomistic History, David chose life as a fugitive rather than act against Saul, YHWH's anointed (1 Sam 24:6, 10; 26:9, 11, 16, 23; 2 Sam 1:14, 16). In contrast, the succession of apostate northern kings included eight who usurped the throne by regicide (see 1 Kgs 15:27-29; 16:9-12, 16-19; 2 Kgs 15:7, 14, 25, 30). Jezreel, the name of Hosea's firstborn (Hos 1:4-5), constituted a warning against the dynasty founded in the valley of Jezreel by King Jehu (2 Kgs 9:22, 27), who, like Abimelech, eliminated all his rivals, including the seventy sons of Ahab (2 Kgs 10:1). According to the books of Kings, only one such episode threatened the Davidic succession in the south, the nearly successful attempt made by Athaliah, who may have been the daughter of the notorious northern king, Ahab (cf. 2 Kgs 8:26-27), to eradicate the royal household in Jerusalem (2 Kgs 11).

## Jotham's Parable (9:7-15)

In the place of a narrative voice commenting on the significance of Abimelech's behavior and the Shechemites' decision to make him their king, the account includes Jotham's parable about the trees' choice of a king and his explication of it. He speaks to the inhabitants of Shechem from atop Mt. Gerizim, where Deuteronomy reports that the people pronounced the blessings of the covenant in Moses' day. His parable, which elaborates a motif common in the world's folklore (note Thompson's motifs J411.7 and J461.1; see Niditch 2008, 116) and which also made its way into one medieval manuscript of Aesop's fables (Vat 777, 14th century; see Guillaume, 57–64), functions both as Jotham's assessment of events and his forecast of their outcome.

On its face, the parable permits a number of interpretations. The olive tree, the fig tree, and the vine all refuse the throne because they do not want to abandon the productive roles they already fulfill in order to assume the arboreal throne. In contrast, the "bramble" (*'aṭar*), whose response points to its functions as the source of shade and fuel, is willing. The implication may involve the relative merits of the candidate ultimately willing to accept the appointment, the fourth on the list. Otherwise, the verb that the plants employ to describe the function of the ruler, *nw'*, "to sway" (vv. 9, 11, 13), refers elsewhere to the staggering of the drunkard (Ps 107:27, Isa 24:20; etc.), the wandering of the fugitive or the lost (Gen 4:12; Num 32:13; etc.), the tottering of an object (Isa 6:4; 7:2; etc.), or the shaking of a person's head or some other body part (1 Sam 1:13; 2 Kgs 19:21). Obviously, the plants do not view the role of king with particular regard. The parable can be interpreted, then, as the criticism that the monarchy pales in significance in comparison with productive roles, that it is best held by someone who does not otherwise make any real contribution.

Alternatively, Amit (1999, 108) points out that, contrary to the sequence of events in Shechem's choice of Abimelech, "The parable does not describe a bramble [that] offers itself for kingship and whose offer is accepted by the trees, but the opposite: the trees approach the bramble and anoint him despite his threats and warnings." Therefore, she concludes, the point of the parable is that the choice should not have been left to the trees alone (that is, the people should defer to God's choice for their king). The bramble's statement, however, raises the question of whether the other trees act "in good faith" (*be'emet*, v. 15) and offers alternative consequences: refuge in its shade or wildfire, the scourge of forests. Apparently, the bramble, as the fourth on the list of candidates, suspects rightly that the other trees regard it a makeshift prospect for the throne and have no intention to grant it full allegiance and respect. Niditch (2008, 116) argues, therefore, that the parable suggests the need for good faith and mutuality if monarchy is to succeed.

### Jotham's Interpretation (9:16-21)

Jotham's interpretation hinges, in fact, on the notion of "good faith and integrity (v. 16, *tamim*, from a verbal root meaning "to be complete," and thus connoting "wholeness, completeness, integrity, sincerity"). Jotham relates it not to the transaction between Abimelech and the Shechemites but to the Shechemites dealings with the legacy and household of Gideon/Jerubbaal. Indeed, Jotham relegates Abimelech to third-party status. For him, the Shechemites committed the chief act of bad faith. Despite the fact that his father, Gideon/Jerubbaal, had fought in their defense, delivering them from Midianite oppression, they have "risen up against" (*qamtem 'al*, v. 18) their champion's household. Jotham accuses the Shechemites, and not Abimelech (cf. v. 5), of killing his brothers. Although this may reflect a variant tradition, it is probably consistent with Jotham's dismissal of Abimelech's importance. Abimelech may have committed the act, but he did so as Shechem's agent with Shechemite financing. In a final slight confirming the reader's suspicions that internecine jealousies and status disputes motivated Abimelech from the outset, Jotham describes him as the son of Jerubbaal's "maidservant" (*'amah*, v. 18). Jotham concludes his explication of the parable by applying the bramble's alternatives to the relationship between Abimelech and his Shechemite subjects. His statement takes the form of a conditional paired blessing and curse. If they have acted in good faith *with Gideon and his household*, then he wishes for them a prosperous relationship with Abimelech; if they have not (and he has already indicated his conclusion that they have not), then he invokes a conflagration with Abimelech as its source and with both parties as the fuel.

### The Usurper Usurped (9:22-29)

People who can be persuaded to be disloyal once can be persuaded again. Usurpers have no claim to loyalty. If usurpation succeeds once, it will succeed again. Sooner or later, others may well do to the usurper what he has done. Indeed, after the passage of four apparently uneventful years, God sends "an evil spirit" to spark animosities between Abimelech and the

Shechemites, animosities that the account recorded in vv. 22-29 suggests were innate in the relationship. Parallels with the relationship between Saul and David are unmistakable: In both instances, God accelerates and exacerbates the inevitable outcome of the consequences of an individual's behavior by igniting the fuel already present in the situation. In both cases, this fuel consists of mistrust and jealousy.

The Judges account reports events in this episode in a curious order. Following the summary characterization in vv. 23-24, the narrative records the Shechemites' act of rebellion (v. 25) before introducing the usurper (v. 26), depicting the context in which the decision to renounce Abimelech took place (v. 27), and, finally, reporting the usurper's argument that they should shift their allegiance (v. 28). This curious arrangement calls attention to other oddities in the continuation of the account of Abimelech's relationship with Shechem. First, after Abimelech's victory over Gaal and the rebels at Shechem, his apparent restoration of control over the city, and his return to his home in nearby Arumah (modern *Hirbet 'el-'Orme*, 8 km southeast of Shechem; see Fritz, 130), renewed hostilities culminate in another attack on the city and its destruction (contrast v. 41 and vv. 42-45). Second, the comment that "it was told Abimelech" repeated in vv. 25 and 42 may be an example of the type of narrative resumption that biblical editors employ to facilitate the interpolation of insertions and parenthetical observations suggesting that v. 42 may once have followed directly after v. 25. Third, Zebul's role and Abimelech's residence outside Shechem suggest a vassal relationship rather than Abimelech's direct rule over Shechem and raise the question of whether the materials concerning Abimelech represent a collection of variant traditions. Finally, nothing in the account indicates a motivation for Abimelech's attack on Thebez (vv. 50-54), an observation that underscores the possibility that the extended account does not represent a literary unity but a composite of disparate traditions. A number of scholars conclude from these and similar observations that the entire Gaal episode (vv. 26-41) represents an insertion (Fritz, 129–30; cf. Niditch 2008, 118) culminating in the restoration of Abimelech's dominion over Shechem and demonstrating that rebellion against the king does not succeed (Fritz, 138).

While certainly plausible, even this insertion hypothesis fails to account for the unusual order that remains in vv. 26-29 (the Shechemites place their confidence in Gaal and celebrate before he makes the case for their shift in allegiance). The intent of this curious arrangement may have been to focus attention on Gaal's delayed appeal for the Shechemites' allegiance. Whereas Abimelech based his argument on kinship ties, Gaal emphasizes the concept of servitude, obliquely affirming Jotham's characterization of Abimelech.

Gaal's three successive rhetorical questions hinge on the central issue of status. The first inquires as to the identity of Abimelech relative to the Shechemites. Does Abimelech hold status that justifies serving him? The second question implies an answer to the first. Is it not true that, before usurping authority, both Jerubbaal and his deputy Zebul were inferior in status, that both had once been servants of "the men of Hamor" (cf. Gen 33:19; 34:2; Josh 24:32)? Gaal implicitly echoes Jotham's assertion that Abimelech's mother was Gideon/Jerubbaal's Shechemite servant (9:18) and that, as the son of a Shechemite servant, Abimelech himself was born into servitude. The final question ("So why should we serve him?") implies its answer: "Indeed, we Shechemites should not accept the ignominy of servitude to our former servant!" How the mighty has fallen! First, Jotham, Gideon's surviving "legitimate" son, effectively demotes the son of Gideon's *pilegesh*, who became the ruler of Shechem through violent usurpation, to the status of the son of a servant. Now, Gaal, ironically identified as "the son of Ebed (Heb. "servant")," has rhetorically reassigned Abimelech himself to his former state. In the Shechemites' viewpoint, apparently, status is even more important than kinship. (For a contrasting interpretation, see Boling 1963, who concludes that the issue is Abimelech's mixed ancestry and that Gaal argues for serving the full-blooded Shechemite).

## Abimelech Suppresses the Rebels: Part 1 (9:30-41)

Abimelech, at home in nearby Arumah, would have known nothing of the rebellious sentiment growing in Shechem were it not for Zebul, whom he had presumably appointed governor of the city. In a manner similar to the actions of Hushai, David's spy at Absalom's "court" (2 Sam 15-17; cf. Niditch 2008, 117), Zebul played the key role in Abimelech's successful suppression of the rebellion. First, Zebul informed Abimelech of the situation and advised him to take reprisal. The translations reflect some confusion regarding the text of v. 31, which reports that Zebul sent messengers to Abimelech *betarmah*, a *hapax legomena* in the Hebrew Bible (i.e., a word that appears only once). Some translations (JPS, TNK) read it as the preposition *be* ("in") plus the otherwise unattested place name, Tormah, apparently understanding it as an alternative for "Arumah." Others make this understanding explicit by translating "in Arumah" (NAB, NRSV, RSV). The Old Latin version translates uniquely "with gifts" (= Heb. *bitrumot*). The more likely translation, given the atmospherics of this episode involving ambush, treachery, and deceit, takes the phrase as the preposition plus a noun derived from the verbal root *rmh* ("to deceive") and translates "in secret" or the equivalent (ASV, ESV, KJV, NAS, NIV; cf. Niditch, 113). Zebul acted without alerting Gaal and his allies to the danger they faced.

Second, when Abimelech had taken Zebul's advice and surrounded Shechem undetected with a force divided into four companies, Zebul delayed Gaal's response by offering a patently false interpretation of Gaal's detection of Abimelech's forces (v. 36). Abimelech and his forces were advancing against the city at dawn (v. 33), when mountain shadows can easily be mistaken for men and vice versa. Gaal's hesitation no doubt cost him in terms of preparedness.

Third, when the growing daylight confirmed Gaal's original fears, Zebul goaded Gaal to take the field of battle, challenging him to back his boasts with action (v. 38). Zebul's idiomatic taunt, "Where is your mouth now?" is the rough equivalent in contemporary American English of expressions such as "put up or shut up" or "you talk big, but can you back it up."

Finally, although, according to v. 40, Abimelech chased a fleeing Gaal away, wounding many of Gaal's supporters in the ensuing fight, v. 41 reports that Zebul expelled and banished Gaal and his relatives from Shechem. Indeed, the account of the battle itself is remarkably brief and inconclusive. Verses 42-49 report a second attack against Shechem, as noted above, vv. 25 and 41 form a "narrative resumption," and v. 41 seems to envision Abimelech at home in Arumah while Zebul deals with Gaal. These observations together with the brevity of the account in v. 40 suggest that vv. 30-40 and vv. 42-49 may represent a doublet—alternative traditions concerning the fate of the rebels at Shechem.

## Abimelech Supresses the Rebels: Parts 2 and 3 (9:42-49)

The combination of the two reports into a single account of Abimelech's dual retributions against Shechem produces a story that underscores Abimelech's ruthlessness. As the text stands, Abimelech followed his attack on Gaal and his supporters with another attack the next day targeting the populace of Shechem generally and the aristocracy (the inhabitants of the "Tower of Shechem") in particular. Learning that the men of the city planned to work in their fields outside the protection afforded by the city walls, Abimelech, still hungry for retribution, prepared a sophisticated ambush. He divided his forces into thirds, personally commanding one group, which he positioned at the gates of the city to prevent the Shechemites who had left the city from retreating to its protection. Cut off from the rear, these farmers would then have been largely defenseless against the two companies attacking from the opposite direction. With the male workforce decimated in the fight outside the city walls, the population inside the walls, presumably mostly older men, women, and children, presented Abimelech no significant military resistance. Typically, the account of the engagement omits important details. The major challenge for Abimelech would have been the city walls and any fortifications incorporated into them. If, however, he sprung his attack while the city gates were open to permit the workers to exit, he may have been able simply to enter the city without breeching the city walls. In any case, v. 45 reports summarily that, in a daylong battle, Abimelech seized the city, killed its population, razed it, and sowed it with salt to render it infertile henceforth.

Meanwhile, the aristocracy, "all the lords of the Tower of Shechem (*ba'ale migdal-shekem*)," have sought refuge in the fortification associated with the temple of El-berith, probably the same structure Judges 10:4 calls "the temple of Baal-berith." Members of this segment of Shechemite society, the "lords of Shechem (*ba'ale shekem*)," were Abimelech's first supporters in Shechem (10:2-3), the financiers of his fighting force (10:4) and, therefore, of the assassination of Gideon's seventy sons (10:5). They have replicated their disloyalty to Gideon and his household in their disloyalty to Abimelech just as Jotham had predicted that they would. In a further ironic fulfillment of Jotham's curse, Abimelech angrily sparks the conflagration that will consume them all, "about a thousand men and women" (v. 49).

Gideon's career manifested his capacity for inciting conflict and his propensity for revenge. The son exceeded the father by several orders of magnitude.

## The Outcome of Disloyalty (9:50-57)

The text leaves it to the reader to surmise the motivation for Abimelech's attack on Thebez (perhaps the modern Tubas, 11 miles northeast of Shechem). It may have been a satellite of Shechem and would therefore have been implicated in Shechem's rebellion against Abimelech's authority. Abimelech's attack would then have been a continuation of his effort to subdue the insurrection. Alternatively, the verb *lkd*, "to capture," in v. 50 suggests that Abimelech was on a campaign of conquest and expansion. Regardless, the omission of such background information reveals the report's primary interest, namely the outcome of Abimelech's aggression. As ultimately the people of Shechem did, the people of Thebez react to Abimelech's attack by retreating to the protection of their city's tower fortification (v. 51). In turn, as he had at Shechem, Abimelech sets fire to the tower to burn its inhabitants out, or up.

Unlike his campaign against Shechem, however, his attack on Thebez proved his undoing. A "certain woman" (Heb. "one woman"), from her vantage point high above in the tower, threw a millstone, presumably of the household variety used for grinding small quantities of grain in the kitchen (the ancient equivalent, both in purpose and size, of a food processor), mortally striking Abimelech in the head (v. 53). Fearing dishonor to his reputation should it be said that he died at the hands of a woman, Abimelech commanded his armor-bearer to kill him with the sword (v. 54). Thus, the account of Abimelech's career ends anticlimactically. Seeing that Abimelech has died, the Israelites comprising Abimelech's army simply abandoned the attack and returned home (v. 55).

Although the account relates this event with extreme economy, it abounds in allusions that connect it with other sections of Abimelech's story, other accounts in the book of Judges, and other narratives in the Hebrew Bible. Several scholars (Boogart, 51; Janzen 1987) have called attention, for example, to the ironic use of the phrase "one woman" (v. 53), comparing it to Abimelech's offer of "one man" rule (v. 2), the assassination of Gideon's seventy sons "on one stone" (v. 18), and the approach of "one company" (*rosh 'ehad*, lit., "one head") of Abimelech's forces (v. 37). Outside the Abimelech story, the phrase also resonates with references to Gideon's defeat of the Midianites as though they were "one man" (Judg 6:16; cf. Boogart, 51) and repeated references, in themselves ironic, to the Israelite tribes acting "as one man" as they exacted retribution on the tribe of Benjamin (Judg 20:1, 8, 11). In the Abimelech story, as in the tale of the near-eradication of one tribe of Israel by the other eleven, "oneness" ironically signifies disharmony, disunity, and disintegration. Similarly, the manner of Abimelech's death recalls the ignominious deaths of Sisera at the hands of Jael (4:21), of Saul at the point of his armor-bearer's sword (1 Sam 31:4, although by his own hand), and of Uriah as the result of David's treachery (2 Sam 11:21; cf. Bal, 217–18). The parallels liken Abimelech to Israel's enemy; to its first failed king, known for his disloyalty to the covenant and to his son-in-law, David; and to David himself, whose disloyalty extended to adultery and murder. Conversely, the anonymous woman of Thebez parallels Jael, Israel's deliverer.

The account of the usurper, Abimelech, ends with the editorial assessment (vv. 56-57) that links the end of Abimelech's career with its beginning. In accordance with the curse Jotham had invoked on both Abimelech and the Shechemites (cf. Fritz, 132–33), who had both been disloyal to Gideon/Jerubbaal, God brought the seed of disloyalty—distrust, jealousy, and treachery—to full and destructive fruition. Fratridice cannot be the foundation for authentic leadership.

# Jephthah

Judges 10–12

Judges 10–12 constitutes a complex of materials dealing with the troubled and troubling career of the Gileadite judge Jephthah. It divides quite neatly into ten units. Framed by lists of the "minor judges" (10:1-5 and 12:7-15) and introduced by a restatement of the book's historical framework (10:6-16) coupled with the Gileadite leadership's statement of their need for a military commander (10:17-18), the core of the complex consists of six units of uneven length. They divide into two groups of three units that roughly parallel one another. The first three of the core units relate Jephthah's various negotiations with the major parties involved in his career: with the Gileadites, he negotiates the terms of his leadership (11:1-11); with the Ammonites, he vindicates Israel's claim to the disputed Transjordanian territories (11:12-28); with God, he bargains for success (11:29-31). Although the sequence does not correspond to the first set (ABC—BCA), each of the units in the second set recounts the outcome related to Jephthah's negotiations: he defeats the Ammonites (11:32-33); he fulfills his vow, at great cost (11:34-40); indeed, he leads the Gileadites, but in a virtual civil war against the Ephraimites (12:16).

Several features of the block of materials in Judges 10–12, located roughly at the midpoint of the book, indicate that it fulfills a key function in determining the overall shape of the "plot" of the deuteronomistic book of Judges. Two lists of so-called "minor judges" (10:1-5; 12:[7]8-15), which appear as interludes in the book otherwise characterized by narratives, frame the story of Jephthah at the core of the block. They mark the career of Jephthah as somehow central to the course of events recorded in Judges, not just as the middle of the book. Similarly, the editors' application of the paradigmatic framework in 10:6-16 diverges significantly from the standard in ways that highlight the aberrant character of the situation in which Jephthah's career unfolds. Finally, in a manner somewhat reminiscent of the tale of Abimelech's rise to power through a political bargain, the transition from the restatement of the paradigm to the account of Jephthah's career proper sets the stage for the Gileadites' selection of Jephthah as their leader (*rosh*, lit., "head"). The resemblance to Abimelech subtly casts a shadow on Jephthah's legitimacy based on political negotiations rather than God's call. With such beginnings, the horrible end of Jephthah's career comes as no surprise.

## The "Minor Judges" (10:1-5; 12:[7]8-15)

The brief lists of "minor judges" in Judges 10:1-5 and 12:(7)8-15 have occasioned significant debate in modern scholarship. They are notable for their formulaic brevity. Each entry names the individual, asserts that he "judged Israel" for a specific period of time (ranging from seven to twenty-three years), and indicates the judge's burial place. Despite the impression given by the statements that these individuals "judged Israel," the lists associate them with localities (Shamir in Ephraim; Kamon in Gilead, Bethlehem; Aijalon in Zebulun; Pirathon in Ephraim) rather than pan-Israel. Moreover, the lists attribute no specific accomplishments to these individuals. Instead, comments concerning the size of the families of three of the "minor judges" apparently intend to indicate that they were wealthy and influential. Jair's thirty sons each had his own means of transportation and ruled one of a league of thirty cities; Ibzan not only had thirty sons but also thirty daughters and thirty daughters-in-law; Abdon's prosperity persisted into a third generation—he had forty sons and thirty grandsons, each riding his own ass.

Modern scholarship debates the historical significance of these figures. Unlike the treatment of "major" judges in the book, these lists do not describe the military feats of champions who delivered (*ysh'*) Israel from its enemies. Instead, the intimation of their wealth and status together with the lengthy periods of their activity and the designation of that activity as "judging" (*shft*) have often been taken as evidence that these individuals fulfilled a more legal and administrative function than did Ehud and Gideon. In the middle of the twentieth century, for example, Noth (1966) hypothesized based on these lists and other evidence in the Hebrew Bible that, before the monarchy, Israel constituted itself as a loosely confederated tribal league or "amphictiony," a model of organization known from ancient Greece (e.g., Anthela and Delphi). Noth's model postulates that the tribes of Israel would have shared allegiance to and responsibility for the central sanctuary housing the ark of the covenant, would have acknowledged a common legal and ethical code, would have been obligated to provide mutual defense, and would have recognized the authority of a leader of the amphictiony in matters pertaining to the alliance. According to Noth's model, the "minor judges" (*shft*) would have been such amphictionic officials, to be distinguished from *ad hoc* military champions (*ysh'*). In terms not of the political history of Israel but of the composition history of the book of Judges, Richter saw the distinction between "deliverers" and "judges" as a clue to the existence of a "book of saviors" (*Retterbuch*) that contained the Ehud, Deborah, Gideon, Jephthah, and Samson accounts and that was expanded at some point into the book of Judges by the addition of the materials in Judges 1 and 2, the deuteronomistic framework material, the lists of "minor judges," and the Danite materials that conclude the book (Judg 16–21; see introduction).

Although Noth's hypothesis produces a neat, coherent model of Israel's political organization during the period prior to the monarchy, it suffers from a number of deficiencies (for a concise review and critique of the discussion, see Lemche). As a rule, both the major and the minor judges acted as local figures, not leaders of all Israel. Furthermore, the accounts of their activity do not link them to locations associated with the ark of the covenant. Since they were regional figures, nothing excludes the possibility that the careers of some of the judges overlapped (cf. Hauser 1975, 194–96). Finally, the texts do not reveal the precise nature of the function envisioned by the term *shft*, "to judge." The legal and administrative connotations of the English term notwithstanding, the total silence of the lists of "minor judges" regarding the details of their activity provides no real data. While the book never assigns the title "judge" to the "major" judges, it does describe their activity with the verb "to judge" (3:10; 4:4; 15:20; cf. Mullen, 189). In fact, the book clearly describes the activity of Deborah, "a prophetess . . . who judged Israel" (4:4), to whom "the people of Israel came for judgment (4:5; *mishpat*, a noun form of the root *shft*), in a fashion that cannot be construed to refer to an administrative *office*. Even the deuteronomistic framework, which employs the title, emphasizes the charismatic nature of the role; that is, it does not envision an institution but a function.

Furthermore, the book of Judges may not draw the distinction between "major" and "minor" judges as sharply as Noth, Richter, and others conclude. Just as the text refers to the "deliverers" Othniel, Deborah, and Samson as "judges," Judges 10:1 calls the "judge" Tola a "deliverer." The account of Jephthah's career ends (12:7) with a summary statement that follows the pattern of the entries for the minor judges and that, in fact, begins the second list. Indeed, certain literary features of the lists do not evoke the impression that their primary function is to convey precise historical information about the activities of these figures. Paranomasia, "wordplay," figures prominently, as in the play on the name "Jair," which resembles Hebrew words for "donkey" and "village." Jair owned thirty of each (10:4). In some cases, such as the observation that Elon was buried in Aiyalon, the wordplay implies a truncated etiology (cf. Guillaume, 120–21). In comparison to other literary treatments of the significance of an individual's name (i.e., the importance of laughter and play in the life of Isaac [Heb. "he laughed"]) and other place-name etiologies (i.e., Jacob's naming of Bethel, Gen 28), the components of the lists of minor judges lack detail, elaboration, and plot. It is as though they represent the point of a story that goes untold.

In sum, the terms "judge" and "deliverer" can best be understood as virtual synonyms in the book of Judges. The interchange probably indicates stylistic preferences. The narratives preserve the diction of a source or sources. The framework, and perhaps the lists of "minor" judges, on the other hand, exhibit the style of the editors. Nonetheless, the major contribution of the lists of minor judges to the book of Judges in its final form is to "frame" the Jephthah story as a critical juncture in the overarching story (Mullen, 201). In addition to drawing attention to the material so framed, the lists may also offer subtle commentary on Jephthah's behavior and ultimate degree of success. The large families of the "minor" judges not only ironically recall Jerubbaal's seventy ill-fated sons, victims of fratricide, but also contrast with Jephthah's sacrifice of his only child, a daughter (cf. Hauser 1975, 197–99). Unlike Abdon, the last of the "minor" judges listed, Jephthah will have no grandsons. Similarly, the stability implied by the lengthy judgeships of Tola (twenty-three years) and Jair (twenty-two years) that precede Jephthah contrast with the relatively brief judgeships that follow (six, seven, ten, and eight years, respectively). The career of Jephthah marks a turning point.

## The Framework Statement (10:6-16)

Signs that the story of Jephthah constitutes a pivotal juncture in the book of Judges continue to appear in the unique statement of the paradigmatic historical framework of the book (10:6-16). Hamlin (110–11) has pointed out that the editors charge Israel with seven cases of apostasy (the Baals, the Ashtaroth, the Syrian gods, the Sidonian gods, the Moabite gods, the Ammonite gods, and the Philistine gods; v. 6) despite the fact that seven times YHWH had delivered them from oppression (Egyptian, Amorite, Ammonite, Philistine, Sidonian, Amalekite, and Maonite, v. 11). This heptad may signal that the cycle of sin and deliverance has reached a climactic point. Indeed, Israel's seven-fold apostasy prompts YHWH's initial refusal to deliver an eighth time (v. 13). Significantly, this announcement appears in the climactic last of three "prophetic messages" in the book of Judges (cf. 2:2 and 6:10). The message suggests that perhaps the gods that the Israelites have chosen instead of YHWH will save them (v. 14; cf. Jer 2:28). Uniquely in the book of Judges, the people actually confess their sin, first in response to Ammonite oppression (v. 9) and then in response to YHWH's initial refusal to deliver (v. 15). Moreover, v. 16, the only record in the book of Israel actually reforming its behavior, constitutes a final unique feature of the passage, highlighting the character of the situation facing Israel in this moment.

The fact that YHWH ultimately acted to deliver Israel from Ammonite oppression despite his stated refusal to do so raises a number of questions. In the immediate context, YHWH's refusal to deliver hangs over the accounts of Jephthah, Samson, Micah, the Danites, and the outrage at Gibeah that follow, presaging the declining state of affairs they depict (cf. Mullen, 199–200). In the broader context of the Deuteronomistic History (Joshua through 2 Kings), the fact that, presumably after only a few generations since settling in the land, Israel's cycle of sin has already pushed YHWH's patience near the breaking point serves the Deuteronomists' overarching interest in a theodicy of history. If, having seven times forgiven Israel's seven apostasies, YHWH delivered yet once more, Israel can level no accusation of impatience against God hundreds of years later when, having forgiven seventy times seven, YHWH delivers Israel into the hands of the Babylonians.

With a view to the story of Jephthah in particular, YHWH's behavior contrary to his statement that he would no longer deliver Israel contrasts ironically with Jephthah's steadfast determination to carry out an unwise and rash vow. YHWH's failure, in a sense, to keep his word points to a profound insight into the character of the biblical God. The God of Israel enters into authentic relationship with people (Fretheim, 13–22). That is, while not capricious or wavering in character, the God of Israel adapts in response to altered behavior (cf. Jer 18:7-10; see Biddle 2004, 247–65). Josiah's faithfulness gains a temporary reprieve from even the categorical sentence pronounced against his grossly idolatrous ancestor, Manasseh (cf. 2 Kgs 23). The entire prophetic enterprise depends on the notion that, if truly successful in persuading the audience to modify its behavior, the prophetic message, the divine word of warning, will not, in fact, come to pass. Paradoxically, warnings and threats become realities only if the prophetic message fails in its mission (see Biddle 2007, 154–66).

Indeed, the description of the dynamics of YHWH's activity (v. 16) illustrates this insight. The syntax of the sequence of two clauses in v. 16 and the idiom describing YHWH's reaction suggests just this sort of response to changed behavior. Biblical Hebrew presses a single conjunction (*wa-*) to many purposes so that it can be rendered by the English "and," "but," "therefore," "then," or "consequently," to name only a few options. Israel "put away the foreign gods . . . and served YHWH; and/then/consequently [YHWH]" reacted. Israel's repentance and reformed behavior motivated YHWH to abandon, at least temporarily, the original determination to refrain from delivering Israel from its Ammonite oppressors. What, however, was the character of that response? The versions render *tqsr nfshw b'ml ysr'l* (lit., "his self/life became short with/over the trouble/toil/misery of Israel"), the idiom that denotes YHWH's reaction, variously: "his soul was grieved for the misery of Israel" (KJV, ASV); "he became indignant over the misery of Israel" (RSV); "he could not bear the miseries of Israel" (TNK, NAS, NIV); "and he became impatient over the misery of Israel" (ESV). The idiom belongs to a family of expressions. In biblical Hebrew, a short *nose*, which Hebrew thought associated with anger, connotes a "short temper" (Prov 14:17); a short *hand*, impotence (Num 11:23; 2 Kgs 19:26 [= Isa 37:27]; Isa 50:2; 59:1); a short *spirit* (*ruah*), either a shortage of courage (Exod 6:9) or of patience (Job 21:4; Prov 14:29 [where the parallel expression *'erek 'appayim*, "long of nose," an idiom for "patient," suggests a contrast between patience and a quick temper"]; Mic 2:7). The shortage of "self" mentioned in Judges 10:16 can connote a lack of courage (Num 21:4), a lack of patience (Zech 11:8), or a lack of resistance/endurance in the sense of "to become worn down" (Judg 16:16). Thus, YHWH "lost patience" with Israel's suffering; it "wore him down" so that he could no longer refrain from intervening on Israel's behalf despite his earlier declaration to the contrary.

## Gilead Seeks a Leader (10:17-18)

Accounts of the beginnings of the careers of the judges exhibit no fixed pattern. Despite the framework's assertion that God periodically "raised up judges" (2:16), the stories themselves report a wide variety of ways in which the judges came to take up the role. The framework's phraseology, modified by the substitution of "deliverer" for "judge," describes the beginning of the careers of Othniel and Ehud (3:9, 15). The brief report concerning the activity of Shamgar concludes with the comment that "he, too, delivered Israel" (3:31). The first list of minor judges asserts simply that each of these figures "arose to deliver" (10:1, 3), while the second list abbreviates the statement further to declare only that the figures "judged" (12:8, 9, 11, 13). Deborah relays God's command to Barak that he engage Sisera in battle (4:6-7), although the text does not detail how she received the information. Messengers commission Gideon (6:14) and, indirectly, Samson (13:3-5), to their tasks.

One can describe the beginning of Jephthah's career as judge, however, as the inverse of Abimelech's. Whereas Abimelech, the outcast son of Jerubbaal and later the head of a band of brigands, approached the leadership of Shechem offering to assume authority, the leadership of Gilead approached Jephthah, an outcast son and the head of a band of brigands, asking him to take command. The text attributes no overt role to God in either case. God's spirit comes upon Jephthah (11:29), to be sure, but only after the Gileadites commission him and he negotiates terms with them (11:1-11) and after his failed diplomatic overture to the Ammonites (11:12-28). The similarities between Abimelech and Jephthah highlight the warning note sounded by this odd reversal in the proper order of things. Who should choose Israel's leaders? Is God's function to be no more than ratifying the people's decision after the fact? Even before the account of Jephthah's work begins, the tone set by YHWH's initial refusal to deliver Israel yet again and by the Gileadite's usurpation of a divine prerogative establishes an ominous background for Jephthah's career.

## Jephthah Negotiates Terms with the Gileadites (11:1-11)

With an economy typical of Hebrew narrative, the story pivots from the Gileadites' recognition of their need for a leader in the face of Ammonite aggression to introduce Jephthah (*yiftah*, "He (God) opens"), soon to be the Gileadites' choice for the task. The text provides only the most pertinent information. The Gileadites turned to Jephthah because of his reputation as a warrior who, like Esau (Gen 32:7; 33:1; cf. 27:40) and Abimelech (Judg 9:4, see the commentary above) before him and David (1 Sam 22:2) after him, had assembled a band of brigands. Apparently, all four of these leaders and their bands made their livelihood as "social bandits," "peasant outlaws whom the lord and state regard as criminals, but who remain within peasant society, and are considered by their people as heroes, as champions, avengers, fighters for justice, perhaps even leaders of liberation, and in any case as men to be admired, helped and supported" (Hobsbawm, 20). Conveniently,

Jephthah was not only a successful bandit who could be expected to succeed against the Ammonites but also himself a Gileadite.

At the same time, Jephthah's parentage complicated his candidacy for leadership. Indeed, the account quickly appends to the information concerning these two key characteristics (Jephthah's ancestry and his occupation) a pair of qualifying statements. The precise significance of the fact that "Gilead was the father of Jephthah" is unclear. According to Numbers 26:29-30, Gilead, the son of Machir and grandson of Manasseh, had six sons (Iezer, Helek, Asriel, Shechem, Shamida, and Hepher). Jephthah is not listed. Scholars theorize that the genealogies of the Gileadites and the Machirites, like many biblical genealogies (cf., for example, the competing lineages attributed to Shechem, sometimes described as the son of the Canaanite Hamor and sometimes as the son of Gilead), express sociological relations between people groups at certain points in Israel's early history rather than lines of descent in the strict sense (for summaries of recent study of biblical genealogies, see Levin, 230–34; Bustenay, and Wilson). Nonetheless, Judges 11:1 takes pains to assert that, while Jephthah indeed descended from Gilead, his mother was an *'ishshah zonah*, a "harlot," a circumstance that complicated his pedigree.

Everything unfolds from these two factors. In a manner that recalls circumstances involved in the Abimelech affair, Jephthah's half-brothers, jealous for their patronymy, expelled him from the household and stripped him of his inheritance because he was the son of an *'ishshah 'acheret*, "another/a different/a strange woman." Undoubtedly, this family history created the understandable animosity Jephthah expresses in v. 7. Without home or means, Jephthah withdrew to the land of Tob (perhaps the site of the modern Taiyibeh, east of Edrei; cf. Maisler, 83) a location otherwise known only from 2 Samuel 10:6-8, where it is associated with Beth-rehob, Zobah, and Maacah. These Aramaean (Syrian) cities in the northern Transjordan reportedly supplied mercenaries to the Ammonites in their resistance against David. Absalom later fled to Geshur, an Aramaean city-state in the same region, where his maternal grandfather was king. As an outcast, Jephthah attracted others like him: outlaws, outcasts, "worthless fellows." Given the likely location of Tob in the region, Gilead, claimed throughout the biblical period both by Israel and specifically by the tribes of Reuben, Gad, and half-Manasseh, Jephthah and his band would probably have conducted raids against the Ammonites to the south and the Syrians to the north. His success against these groups would have likely contributed to his reputation back home in Gilead. Parallels with David's activity during his period as a fugitive from Saul (see 1 Sam 27:8-12), when, ostensibly mercenaries in the employ of the Philistine king Achish, he and his band engaged primarily in raids targeting Israel's enemies, the Amalekites, bolstering his reputation in Israel (see 1 Sam 28:26–30:31), are self-evident.

The stage is set, then, for the ensuing discussions between Jephthah and the leaders of Gilead. Prompted by Ammonite aggression, the Gileadites send an embassy to Jephthah in Tob asking him to return home and assume command of Gilead's defense (v. 6). On the surface, the talks seem straightforward and transparent. In response to the invitation to assume leadership of the Gileadite resistance to the Ammonites, Jephthah understandably expresses bitterness that the people who expelled him from his paternal home now turn to him for assistance in their time of distress. The Gileadite leadership apparently counters Jephthah's resentment by sweetening the deal. Whereas they had originally offered Jephthah the opportunity to be their military leader (*qatsin*, cf. Josh 10:24; Isa 22:3; Dan 11:19; and perhaps Prov 6:7), they meet Jephthah's reticence with the proposal that he become "the head (*rosh*) of all the inhabitants of Gilead," a status that would presumably include civil as well as military authority (see Willis, 34–35). Jephthah accepts the offer, returns with the elders of Gilead, and enters into a formal agreement with Gilead at Mizpah.

Closer inspection of the exchange, however, reveals a range of subtleties that may indicate a subtext. First, as their eagerness to choose a leader already intimates (Judg 10:17-18), the Gileadites' counteroffer, which does not address the objection Jephthah raises, reflects their awareness that they cannot refute his justifiable accusations. Their strategy relies on appeasement rather than honest reconciliation. In short, from their perspective, the goal of the negotiations is to obtain Jephthah's services, not to mend the relationship. The issue is the cost. Although the specific connotations of the terms "leader" (v. 6) and "head" (v. 8) are unclear (they appear as parallels in Mic 3:1, 9, for example), the addition of the phrase "of all the inhabitants of Gilead" in their second statement emphasizes the scope of the position the Gileadites offer Jephthah. They are desperate enough to offer the highest office.

Second, as has already been observed, the Gileadites act on their own initiative, apparently without even consulting the deity. Jephthah, who introduces an unexpected element of contingency in so doing, involves YHWH in the matter only in his strange acceptance of the Gileadite offer. Instead of simply agreeing to assume leadership over all Gilead, Jephthah links his assumption of that role to whether YHWH gives him success in the campaign against the Ammonites. Does he mean to accept the position of military leader but to distinguish it from the higher office? Does he imply that the Gileadites do not have the authority to bestow this office, that instead only YHWH can do so (cf. Brensinger, 133)? The text offers no commentary explaining Jephthah's motivations and rationale. Jephthah's overall attitude toward his kinsfolk, however, strongly suggests that he acts and speaks out of mistrust of the Gileadites and their motives. By predicating the assumption of office on God-given success in battle, Jephthah may have sought to establish his authority on a demonstration of God's approbation in order to preclude the Gileadites from reverting to their previous attitudes once the crisis has passed. In other words, Jephthah elevates the transaction above the realm of an agreement between human parties, probably because he does not trust his human partners in the agreement.

Finally, even though Jephthah seems to accept the position only conditionally, the account of the episode concludes with the report that, after the Gileadites invoke YHWH as witness to their intention to keep the agreement, Jephthah returns with the Gileadites to "speak all his words before YHWH at Mizpah." Problems and possibilities abound here. First, the specific location of the Mizpah mentioned here is uncertain. The Bible refers to up to six locations by the name Mizpah ("lookout, watchpost, watchtower"), three of which obviously have no relevance to the Jephthah story: (1) a site in the plains of Judah (Josh 15:37-41), a region near Mt. Hermon (Josh 11:3), and a city in Moab (1 Sam 22:3).

On the other hand, the name Mizpah refers to two, perhaps three, other locations that may relate directly to the Jephthah story. At the first, Mizpah in Gilead ("hill of witness"), Jacob and Laban covenanted to part company permanently, invoking the place names in reference to the rock pile ("this heap is a witness") and the pillar ("may YHWH watch between you and me") they established there as evidence of the surety of the agreement (Gen 31:44-54). The Genesis account's themes of witness, the names Gilead and Mizpah, and the invocation of YHWH as guarantor clearly echo in Judges 11:9-11. The parallels serve to suggest that the kinds of tensions that characterized the relationship between Jacob and Laban also mark the relationship between Jephthah and the Gileadites. Judges 11:29, which puzzles interpreters because it reports a journey that does not play any obvious role in the narrative, also refers to Gilead and Mizpah and may function to underscore the association with Jacob and Laban. At the second, Mizpah in Benjamin, which became the provisional Judean capital and cultic center after the destruction of Jerusalem in 586/587 BCE (2 Kgs 25:23; Jer 40:6-8), the prophet Samuel held cultic gatherings (1 Sam 7) and installed Saul as Israel's first king (1 Sam 10:17-27). Indeed, Judges 11:9-11 makes several suggestive verbal and thematic allusions to the account of the installation of Saul.

Obviously, both instances involve the selection of a leader motivated by the people's interest, not undertaken on God's instruction. The expression "before YHWH" in both accounts (Judg 11:11; 1 Sam 10:17, 25) marks the events narrated as cultic occasions. The statement that Jephthah "spoke all his words before YHWH at Mizpah" (v. 11) suggests that he solemnized the agreement he had reached with the Gileadites concerning the terms of his leadership with God as witness and guarantor (cf. v. 10); similarly, Samuel "told the people the policy (*mishpat*) governing the monarchy and wrote it in a book and placed it before YHWH" (1 Sam 10:25). The account manifests additional parallels between Jephthah and Saul. Jephthah's selection transpired in the context of Gilead's strife with the Ammonites, with whom he sought to negotiate terms (11:12-28); in his first act as king, Saul defended the inhabitants of Jabeshgilead from the aggression of Nahash the Ammonite, but only after the city had failed to negotiate surrender terms (1 Sam 11:1-11).

Clues that Jephthah's troubled leadership, begun in the wrong way and for the wrong reasons, will end in trouble accumulate. As was the case with Abimelech, long before the crisis, the signs of the crumbling foundation of Jephthah's status point to ultimate collapse. In the context of the Deuteronomistic History, allusions to events at Mizpah and Jabeshgilead anticipate the beginning of Saul's ill-fated reign.

## Jephthah's Failed Embassy to the Ammonites (11:12-28)

Now installed as Gilead's "commander and head," Jephthah first seeks to convince the Ammonites to discontinue their encroachment into Gilead. An exchange of messages between Jephthah and the anonymous Ammonite king begins with Jephthah's question concerning the Ammonites' justification for their attacks (v. 12). The Ammonites respond with the assertion that Israelites seized the territory in question in the conquest and the request that Israel return control of the area to Ammon—its rightful owner in their view. Jephthah's second communication constitutes a lengthy refutation of the Ammonites' position. It hinges on four arguments. First, Jephthah rejects, as a matter of fact, Ammon's legal claim to the territory in a detailed account of Israel's conquest of the region between the Arnon and the Jabbok (vv. 15-22). Jephthah portrays Israel's actions as a justifiable reaction to the unprovoked animosity exhibited by Sihon, the *Amorite* (i.e., not *Ammonite*) king of Heshbon. The version of the episode attested in multiple biblical texts (Num 21:24; Deut 2:18-23; Josh 12:2; 13:10; contrast Josh 13:25) specifies that, although God "gave Sihon and his land" to the Israelites

(2:31), God prohibited Moses and the Israelites from "approaching the land of the Ammonites" south of the Jabbok (2:37). That is, Jephthah emphasizes that the portion of Gilead taken in the conquest was Amorite territory, not Ammonite. Second, Jephthah interprets Israel's success against Sihon theologically (vv. 23-24). In a manner consistent with the strand of biblical thought manifest most notably in Deuteronomy 32:8-9 (see Biddle 2003, 474–75), Jephthah suggests that, just as by granting Israel success against Sihon Israel's God had given it Sihon's territory as a possession, the Ammonites should be content with the heritage that their god, Chemosh, has given them. Third, Jephthah offers the experience of the Ammonites' neighbor, the Moabites, as a warning. He invokes the precedent of Balak, the Moabite king who, motivated by fear of the Israelites (Num 22:2-4), engaged the prophet Balaam to curse Israel only to learn that the prophet could not bring a curse on Israel whom YHWH had already blessed (Num 24:1-9). Against the background of the Numbers account, Jephthah's apparently straightforward question assumes the character of a taunt: "Now, are you better than Balak (who feared Israel and whose efforts to curse only resulted in blessing)?" (v. 25). Fourth, since Ammon had asserted no claim to the territory during the three centuries of Israelite occupation, Jephthah argues either that the Ammonite king's predecessors tacitly recognized Israel's claims to the territory or that any such claim had, in any case, long since lapsed (v. 26).

Jephthah concludes from this quite sophisticated legal argumentation that the Ammonite aggression is wholly unjustified and states his willingness to trust the disposition of the case to YHWH, "the judge" (v. 27; cf. Gen 18:25, the only other passage in the Hebrew Bible to identify God with this definite noun). Indeed, the entirety of Jephthah's case, which borrows heavily from parallel passages in Numbers 20–22 and Deuteronomy 1–2, sounds more like the reasoning of a scribe or a lawyer than of an outcast and a brigand. Noting a nexus of complicated literary dependencies on the Numbers and Deuteronomy accounts, Täubler (1958, 290) described the unit as "a tractate that originated in the scribal school." The Judges text replicates verbatim major sections of the Torah (cf. Judg 11:17, Num 20:14, and Deut 1:30; Judg 11:18 and Num 21:4, 11, and 13; Judg 11:19, Num 20:21, and Deut 2:26-27; Judg 11:20, Num 21:23, and Deut 2:30, 32; Judg 11:21 and Deut 2:33; Judg 11:21-22 and Num 21:24-25; Judg 11:25 and Num 22:2, 4, 10, and 11). The details of the literary process undertaken to produce the Judges text have the potential to yield fascinating information concerning the editing of biblical texts and, perhaps, the historical and social setting of this process, though these are concerns that lie outside the interests of a literary and theological commentary. Nonetheless, the observation that the book places the words of this scholarly tractate in the mouth of Jephthah as his first official act, just before the account of events that culminate in the sacrifice of his daughter—arguably the pivotal episode in the biblical story of Jephthah—calls for reflection. What picture of Jephthah does it help to paint?

No other judge makes a similar effort to negotiate terms with an enemy of Israel or seeks to offer a legal justification for offering resistance. Together with his extended and nuanced negotiation of terms before accepting leadership over Gilead, Jephthah's diplomatic approach to the Ammonite problem reinforces the assessment of Jephthah's character implied by his negotiations with the Gileadites. Common to both conversations is a curiosity, even a suspicion, of the motivations of the other party, understandable given Jephthah's family history and Israel's history of relations with Ammon. Does this suspicion of others' motives reflect a healthy sense of caution or an unhealthy insecurity, comparable in many ways to Gideon's lack of confidence and Abimelech's animosity toward elements of his family? The two negotiations also share a legal atmosphere involving witnesses, agreements, legal argumentation, and precedents, and ultimately invoking God as guarantor (vv. 11-12) and judge (v. 27). Evidently, Jephthah's caution (or insecurity) manifests itself in a concern for studied decision-making. The Jephthah of Judges 11:1-28 does not act precipitously; he analyzes and deliberates. Finally, both discussions reflect tension between human initiative and divine direction. The Gileadites enlist Jephthah, apparently without first even consulting YHWH. According to the arrangement of the narrative elements in Judges 11, Jephthah contemplates YHWH's role in the conflict with the Ammonites as a hypothetical possibility (v. 9) and then invokes YHWH as the court of last appeal in the controversy with Ammon over property rights (v. 27); the first indication that YHWH will, indeed, endorse Jephthah's mission appears only in v. 29. Immediately thereafter, the text reports Jephthah's vow.

## The Spirit, the Vow, and the Victory (11:29-33)

Not surprisingly, the Ammonites disregard Jephthah's well-argued case for Israel's claim to Gileadite territory, its admonition to learn from the case of Balak, and its warning that Jephthah intends to put the case to the test before YHWH, "the Judge." The surprise involves the sequence of events that culminate in Jephthah's victory over the Ammonites (vv. 32-33). The text reports that the "Spirit of YHWH came upon Jephthah" only after the

Gileadites had sought him out, after he had negotiated the terms under which he would assume leadership, and after he had attempted to dissuade the Ammonites from their aggression. Furthermore, Jephthah makes his vow to YHWH *after* the Spirit had come upon him. The sequence alone raises three important issues: What is the relationship between Gileadite initiative and divine prerogative? What is the degree of Jephthah's confidence in YHWH's presence? And what is the precise intent of Jephthah's vow?

Several commentators on this passage note the peculiarity that Jephthah alone among the judges discussed in the book comes to (authentic, contrast Abimelech) leadership primarily through a human process of selection. As Brensinger (135) observes, at least at first, apparently, "God has nothing to do with it." Unfortunately, the editors provide only contextual clues as to how to interpret this feature of the Jephthah account. The most intriguing of these clues appears in the editorial statement (10:6-16) that, in response to Israel's confession, repentance, and reform, YHWH relents after eighteen years of Ammonite oppression concerning his decision no longer to deliver Israel from its enemies. Now, in similar fashion, YHWH reacts to the Gileadites' initiative in selecting Jephthah as their leader by endorsing their choice. The relationship between human actions and divine responses involved here recalls YHWH's reaction to the birth of Ishmael (Gen 17). YHWH's intention all along had been to fulfill the promise of progeny through a child born to Abraham and Sarah. Because this promise had included any and all of Abraham's descendants, YHWH was willing, however, to extend the promise to Ishmael while continuing toward the original objective (cf. Gen 17:17-21). The context, especially the sequence of events, intimates that Jephthah was Gilead's, not God's, choice even though God was willing, finally (reluctantly?), to endorse the selection.

If YHWH lacks enthusiasm for Jephthah's judgeship, Jephthah seems in turn to lack confidence in YHWH's support. The tension between the bestowal of the divine Spirit and Jephthah's subsequent vow cannot be overlooked (cf. Neef, 211). If YHWH has bestowed his Spirit upon Jephthah, why does Jephthah feel it necessary to elicit YHWH's cooperation with the promise of a sacrifice? From the outset, Jephthah's attitudes concerning God's support for Gilead's cause against the Ammonites and particularly for Jephthah's leadership betray his doubt. He offers to assume leadership of Gilead "if YHWH gives [the Ammonites] over to me" (11:9); despite the apparent confidence he expresses to the Ammonites that the Divine Judge will rule in favor of Gilead (v. 27), he reacts to the gift of the divine Spirit with yet another "if you [YHWH] give the Ammonites into my hand" (v. 30; cf. Trible, 61).

Clues that God and Jephthah do not have full confidence in one another, as it were, set the stage for the most troubling aspect of Jephthah's career. The fact that Jephthah felt it necessary or advisable to make a vow in order to try to assure God's support in the struggle against the Ammonites already raises questions about Jephthah's attitude. In addition, however, the wording of his vow creates a circumstance in which Jephthah confronts the consequences of his attempts to secure what God has already given. The full implications of his vow become evident after his victory over the Ammonites. It need only be observed here that the apodosis, the "then" statement, of Jephthah's vow is ambiguous in Hebrew. It can be translated "whoever comes out the doors of my house" (RSV, NRSV) or "whatever comes out" (ASV, JPS, KJV, NAS, NIV, TNK). In essence, the Hebrew allows for the possibility that, whether he intended it or not, Jephthah may be met by either an animal or a human being. Either he intentionally vowed to make a human sacrifice in exchange for victory over the Ammonites, or he spoke so carelessly that his statement included the possibility. Again, the text does not offer direct insight into Jephthah's mind and the interpreter must rely on contextual clues. In support of the view that Jephthah knew very well what his vow might entail, some have observed that the most likely scenario for greeting a hero returning from victory on the battlefield would have been a human welcoming party. Indeed, in ancient Israel, such homecomings were typically occasions for the women to celebrate the hero's exploits (Exod 15:20-21; Judg 5:3; 1 Sam 18:6) so that Jephthah would likely have anticipated that the women of his hometown, probably including his daughter, would greet him on his return. Furthermore, Jephthah has already demonstrated a precise and skillful "legal" mind in his negotiations with the Ammonites. He can be expected to have stated his vow with equal clarity and precision (cf. Neef, 214). Others argue that Jephthah could have as easily expected to be met by a domestic animal, but admit that the imprecision of his promise left open the possibility that it would also apply to human beings.

In the context of lengthy negotiations and unnecessary vows, the report of Jephthah's victory over the Ammonites (vv. 32-33) stands as a remarkably concise and straightforward statement. One might expect it to be the climax of the Jephthah story. The brevity of the account frustrates that expectation, however. Instead, the matter of Jephthah's homecoming constitutes the major complication of Jephthah's preparations for conflict with the Ammonites.

## Jephthah's Daughter (11:34-40)

The account of Jephthah's victorious homecoming to Mizpah after subduing the Ammonites has bewildered and troubled readers, interpreters, and scholars like perhaps no other text in the Bible. Superficially, it seems straightforward enough. Jephthah's unnamed daughter welcomed him home with a celebration of his victory (v. 34). Since she was the first person he encountered, he immediately recognized the implications of his vow (v. 35). The daughter affirmed the necessity of fulfilling the vow, asking only that the execution of the vow be delayed for two months so that she and her companions could journey into the mountains to "mourn [her] virginity" (vv. 36-37). Jephthah acceded to her request (v. 38). When the two months had passed, the daughter returned and the father fulfilled the vow. The passage concludes by underscoring the daughter's virginity and identifying this episode as the foundation of an otherwise unknown annual commemoration of Jephthah's daughter and her sacrifice (v. 40).

Yet, despite the superficial simplicity of the account, the text abounds in tantalizing subtleties and ambiguities. It portrays Jephthah's homecoming celebration as a private affair, for example. Only the daughter of the victorious general, not a jubilant crowd, waits to greet him. Does this element of the story suggest that the Gileadites, who once openly despised Jephthah, had still not fully embraced him? The text takes pains to establish the fact that Jephthah had only one child (v. 34), an unnamed daughter of an unmentioned mother, an ironic circumstance given Jepthah's family history. Jephthah's outcry when his daughter comes to welcome him home (v. 35) very nearly blames her for his "trouble (*'kr*)." Feminist critics, in particular, note in horror not only this hint at Jephthah's attitude but also the daughter's stoic acceptance of her fate as if the text views a father's sacrifice of his only daughter as unobjectionable. The cumulative silence of Jephthah, his daughter, and the editor appalls and perplexes. Furthermore, the emphasis on the daughter's virginity, both in the daughter's request and in the etiology of her annual commemoration, overshadows the more fundamental element of this tragic situation, namely, human sacrifice. In fact, as is often noted, the text never depicts or describes the central act of the story, always employing instead a circumlocution (e.g., "he did to her the vow he had vowed," v. 39). Does the text intentionally obscure the central reality? The feature that plays the most important role in interpreting the account, of course, involves the text's silence with regard to YHWH's view of events, a silence that hangs over the entire Jephthah story. YHWH did not choose Jephthah; YHWH did not solicit the vow. Does YHWH affirm it?

Obviously, the notion of a father sacrificing his own daughter to the God of Israel offends. Understandably, the incident, narrated with this range of subtleties, ambiguities and silences, has occasioned a wide range of interpretations. A tradition of biblical interpretation that views the judges, like the patriarchs, the prophets, and the apostles, as heroes of the faith and therefore as models of faith and obedience, lauded Jephthah and his daughter as stalwarts of obedience (see Liptzin, 393–94). Even at great cost, as this interpretation argues, Jephthah kept his word to God, and his daughter acquiesced. Each, therefore, exemplifies fidelity for all believers after them. This interpretation overlooks the moral obstacle at the center of the story, however. Does the requirement to fulfill a vow outweigh the value of a human life?

Recent biblical scholarship takes a more realistic view, aware that biblical characters exhibit human shortcomings that are not to be understood as models for behavior (e.g., David's adultery and murder to cover it up, 2 Sam 11). In the absence of positive assertions, it is sometimes difficult to assess whether the biblical author approved or disapproved of a character's actions. Neef has identified seven major alternative positions advocated by interpreters in the effort to grapple directly with the difficulties in the story.

1. Jephthah did not, in fact, sacrifice his daughter; instead, she remained a lifelong virgin. Support for this position includes the ambiguity of Jephthah's vow (v. 31b), i.e., that he did not mean to include the possibility of human sacrifice; the fact that the text does not actually report a sacrifice; the emphasis on the daughter's virginity; and the fact that the Bible nowhere condemns Jephthah for human sacrifice.

2. Jephthah's vow demonstrated his lack of faith, and the fulfillment of the vow only compounded his error. Proponents of this reading call attention to the tension between the bestowal of the divine Spirit and Jephthah's therefore unnecessary vow. From this perspective, Jephthah's vow takes on the character of bargaining, representing the third instance in which Jephthah seeks to negotiate the outcome he desires. This reading finds additional support in the selfish tone of Jephthah's lament upon encountering his daughter.

3. An interesting ancient interpretation found in a Latin manuscript of uncertain date and provenance (Kisch, xxxix:11), notable for its positive portrayal of Jephthah's daughter (it gives her a name, "Seila," attributes to her a prayer of lament, and makes her a much more active figure in the episode, generally), regards the circumstance that "Seila" met the conditions of Jephthah's vow not as happenstance but as the work of God. Angered by

the reckless imprecision of Jephthah's vow, which could have applied to anything or anyone Jephthah may have met at his homecoming and which, therefore, inherently risked insulting God (Pseudo-Philo contemplates that it could well have been a dog), God arranged the encounter such that Jephthah paid for his implicit insult.

4. As might be expected, recent feminist biblical criticism sees the account as testimony to the patriarchal objectification of women, describing the incident as the sacrifice of Jephthah's daughter not to God but to patriarchy. Fuchs (35) argues, for example, that the ambiguities and omissions in the account serve ". . . as a kind of apology, a subtle justification of Jephthah's behavior. By suppressing details about the sacrifice, the narrator makes it possible for us to deny that the sacrifice has even taken place. Though the tragedy is ultimately the daughter's, it is Jephthah who is presented as the tragic victim of circumstances."

5. Noting Jephthah's propensity to bargain, the fact that Jephthah could have anticipated that his only daughter would likely be the first to greet him upon his return, and the biblical prohibition against child sacrifice (Lev 18:21; 20:2; Deut 12:31; 18:10), some have suggested that Jephthah intentionally phrased his vow in a manner that would result in the very dilemma that eventuated. In other words, he made a vow that he knew he could not fulfill without violating the Torah. His vow constituted a sly effort to avoid payment.

6. A psychoanalytical interpretation of the episode views the daughter, the first person to meet returning Jephthah, as a substitute for the mother, the first person one meets in life. Her "death" represents the eradication of Jephthah's "feminine" element so that he can become a pure warrior.

7. Finally, post-modernist and deconstructionist critics argue for reading the story of Jephthah's daughter as an "absurdity" as evidenced by the multiplicity and variety of interpretations. The account resists reduction to a single statement of meaning; it points to the absurdity of all the institutions and the worldview inherent in the situation narrated; it underscores the ultimate ambiguity, the absurdity, of language itself.

Neef's categorization of interpretations can be supplemented by at least four other significant recent approaches.

1. Römer (1998) argues that the story of Jephthah's vow and the sacrifice of his daughter was inserted into the Jephthah cycle much later than the original (deuteronomistic) composition of the book of Judges, probably well into the Hellenistic period. He notes a number of phenomena that point to

the secondary character of the vow/sacrifice material. Verses 29 and 32a appear to be a literary resumption of the kind that often marks an insertion. The subsequent unit (12:1-6) seems entirely unaware of the incident. Finally, the contradiction concerning Jephthah's hometown (Mizpah, 11:34; Zaphon, 12:1) indicates the presence of two literary strands. Römer concludes that a redactor composed vv. 30-31 for their present context to create tension between bestowal of the Spirit and the vow. In support of the post-deuteronomistic, Hellenistic dating for the vow/sacrifice material, Römer points to the deuteronomists' treatment of a near parallel involving Saul and his son Jonathan (cf. 1 Sam 12:11) in which the people have no difficulty discerning the priority of the prohibition against human sacrifice over the necessity of keeping a vow. In contrast, as proponents of other interpretations have also observed, the Jephthah story remains strangely silent on the morality of human sacrifice. Finally, Römer calls attention to parallels not primarily with the sacrifice of Isaac but with the Hellenistic legend of Iphigenia. Contrary to the former, an episode that features God as instigator, provider, and protector, and similar to the latter, God is absent in the Jephthah story. The tone of both the Jephthah story and the Iphigenia legend is fatalistic. A vow once spoken must be fulfilled, even if with tragic consequences.

2. Some interpreters have focused on the etiological character of the story of Jephthah's daughter and theorized as to the nature of the ritual mentioned in the conclusion. Obviously, in the absence of any other evidence, although both are possible, neither of these creative interpretations can be evaluated beyond the test of plausibility. Day (esp. 60) has reconstructed a four-day menarche ritual. As a rite of passage, the onset of menses marks the "death" of the girl and the "birth" of the woman.

3. Böhler (329–30) has argued, instead, that Jephthah's daughter represents "Daughter Jerusalem" and has correlated the four days of the ritual with the four days scattered across the Jewish festal calendar that commemorate the fall of Jerusalem.

4. Finally, representative of a major trend in recent studies of the book of Judges that emphasize the decline of cultural values in Israel as the book progresses (i.e., the increasing inter-tribal disharmony, the downward trend in the treatment of women, etc.), Michael Smith (289) has argued that Jephthah constitutes a parade example of the growing failure of kinship bonds that begins with Abimelech and culminates in the near-eradication of a whole tribe of Israel. In support of this reading of Jephthah's actions as the low point of family values in the book of Judges, Smith has called attention to the chiastic structure involving the size of the judges families (Gideon,

seventy sons; Jair, thirty sons, thirty cities, and thirty asses; Jephthah, one daughter; Ibzan, thirty sons, thirty daughters, and thirty daughters-in-law; and Abdon, seventy sons and grandsons; thus 70/30/1/30/70).

Since the story of Jephthah's daughter exemplifies the significant premium that Hebrew narrative style places on brevity and suggestive, even provocative, ambiguity, interpreters must pay careful attention to contextual clues and especially to any explicit indicators the narrator has chosen to provide. The immediate context of the story, for example, shapes the reader's expectations of Jephthah. Jephthath's default mode of dealing with challenges is through negotiation and bargaining. Further, as already noted, three sequences of unusual relational transactions parallel one another. The Israelites' repentance motivates God's change of heart; the Gileadites' effort to enlist Jephthah elicits only his conditional acceptance of the commission; Jephthah reacts to God's endorsement of the selection through a vow. In the aggregate, this conditionality produces a dual effect. On one hand, it accentuates an otherwise subtle but theologically significant theme in the book of Judges, namely that, in the Jephthah cycle, God reacts to human decisions and actions. Indeed, in the Jephthah cycle God only reacts to human initiative; at no point does God manifestly direct the course of affairs. The reader can only wonder whether Jephthah would have been God's choice; an attentive reader will wonder, too, whether God was involved in any way in the vow and the sacrifice.

Furthermore, this arrangement highlights Jephthah's insecurity. He cannot accept the Gileadite overture at face value and in good faith; he cannot trust in the presence of God's Spirit as evidence of God's approval and support. Thus, against its immediate context, Jephthah's unsolicited vow appears to have been entirely unnecessary. Just as he need not have bargained with the Gileadites for something they were already prepared to give him unconditionally, and in fact did so before the condition was met, Jephthah need not have bargained for the divine assistance already promised in the bestowal of the divine Spirit (cf. Trible, 60).

The redundant vow was also supremely unwise. Jephthah's imprecise wording, out of character for the "legal mind" evident in the negotiations with the Ammonites, has already been noted. He could have vowed anything he chose, specifically excluding human beings and especially his daughter, but he spoke too quickly, ill advisedly, rashly. Jephthah even voices this assessment of the vow, in retrospect, when he laments to his daughter that he has "opened his mouth to YHWH" (v. 35). In light of the rarity of such evaluative statements in Hebrew narrative, Jephthah's carries considerable weight. A rare idiom in the Hebrew Bible, "to open (*ptsh*) the mouth" refers elsewhere either to ravenous consumption (Gen 4:11; Num 16:30; Deut 11:6; Ps 22:14; Ezek 2:8) or to false or foolhardy speech (Job 35:16; Ps 66:14; Isa 10:14; Lam 2:16; 3:46), the usage evident here. The connotation might be expressed best in English by idioms such as "I opened my big mouth" or "I spoke too soon."

Two issues emerge then, that resonate in the canon beyond the book of Judges: the optional, even unnecessary, nature of vows and the problem presented by two conflicting obligations. Interestingly, although not a topic that the Bible treats extensively or systematically, other texts dealing with vows focus precisely on these two issues. Jacob's vow at Bethel (Gen 28:20-22), consonant with his character and reminiscent of Jephthah's vow, attempts to strike a bargain with God for the prosperity and protection that God had already graciously promised Abraham and all his descendants (Gen 12:1-3), specifically Jacob himself (Gen 28:13-15). It gains him nothing, but it does provide confirmation that Jacob is a deal maker, much like Jephthah. While warning that one must "keep what passes from [one's] lips and do according to [one's] vow to YHWH" because "YHWH will surely expect it," the admonition in Deuteronomy 23:22-24 (23:21-23 Eng) centers on the reminder that vows are not mandatory (cf. Eccl 5:3-4). Related, Proverbs 20:25 observes that, "It is a snare for a man to say rashly (Heb. *l'*, "to talk wildly") 'It is holy,' and to reflect only after making his vows." In perhaps the closest parallel to Jephthah's vow, Saul's army recognized the moral dilemma inherent in keeping the terms of the curse Saul had pressed upon them (1 Sam 14:24) as he invoked the name of YHWH in an oath (1 Sam 14:39, 44), even if it meant killing an innocent who had been unaware of the obligation (1 Sam 14:45).

In the end, the story of the sacrifice of Jephthah's daughter may well pose more questions than it answers. Chief among these questions, however, are two that continue to have relevance: Must one keep a vow that should never have been made in the first place (see Biddle 2003, 353–54)? What, if anything, outweighs the value of a human life?

## Conflict: Jephthah and Ephraim (12:1-6)

The Jephthah story shifts abruptly from trouble within Jephthah's family to conclude with an account of turmoil within Israel. Several features of this passage amplify the jarring effect of the sudden transition. Above all, one would expect some acknowledgment of the tragedy that has just transpired, but the incident involving the Ephraimites betrays no knowledge of Jephthah's vow or his daughter. Zaphon (lit., "north"), a word that serves in the Hebrew Bible to designate the cardinal direction (e.g., Exod 26:20), a mythic location (e.g., Job 37:22; Ps 48:3), and a locality, probably refers here to the city in northern Gad also mentioned in Joshua 13:27. If so, it conflicts with earlier statements locating Jephthah's home in Mizpah, a city in the southern hills of Ephraim. Similarly, v. 2 presumes that Jephthah called Ephraim to arms in the conflict with the Ammonites, although Judges 10 records no such call (cf. 10:9). Source and redaction critics understandably take these phenomena as evidence that a process of literary growth produced the Jephthah cycle. The literary result, however, is a jolting conclusion to a jolting career.

Although Judges 12:1-6 reveals no hint of the difficulties Jephthah has brought on himself through his efforts to bargain with God, it continues the motif of Jephthah as failed negotiator. As with the Ammonites, his attempt to explain his actions to the Ephraimites fails entirely, evoking only a taunt in response. In retrospect, the impression one gains from the careful argumentation Jephthah forwards in the exchange with the Ammonites proves misleading. In his negotiations with the Gileadites concerning their offer to install him as leader, Jephthah sets conditions that ultimately do not influence the outcome. The Ammonites respond with silence to his justification for Gileadite control of disputed territory in the Transjordan. He bargains with YHWH for something YHWH has already decided to grant, indeed, has already confirmed through the bestowal of the Spirit. The vow ultimately proves to be flawed not only with regard to the motivation for it but also in its very terms. Now Jephthah's diplomacy fails even within Israel, only exacerbating existing inter-tribal tensions and resulting in civil war.

Overtones of these inter-tribal tensions resound throughout the unit. It narrates the third incident in the book of Judges involving the Ephraimites and the fords of the Jordan that mark the boundary between the Ephraimites and the Transjordanian tribes. The sequence of these three incidents inscribes a downward arc in Ephraim's relations within Israel. In the first, in response to Ehud's summons, the Ephraimites hold the fords of the Jordan against fugitive Moabites (3:28-29). In the second, the Ephraimites upbraid Gideon because he did not invite them to join in his campaign against Midian, even though he had tasked them with holding the fords of the Jordan where they had, in fact, succeeded in capturing two fugitive Midianite princes. Now, the Gileadites seize the fords of the Jordan "against the Ephraimites" (v. 4) who have once again taken umbrage at Jephthah's supposed failure to include them in his campaign against the Ammonites. Judges 12:1-6 illustrates that "nothing but trouble comes from Ephraim!" (Guillaume, 154). The taunt the Ephraimites level at the Gileadites and the reference to the dialectical pronunciations of the word "shibboleth/sibboleth" point to the regional rivalries underlying and fueling mounting tensions. Ultimately, they erupt in open civil warfare and 42,000 Ephraimite fatalities (v. 6).

To the extent that the Jephthah cycle represents the midpoint of the book of Judges, both in terms of its length and as indicated by the framing structure and other aspects discussed above, it offers the opportunity to reflect on the downward trends evident to this point in the book. In addition to the increasingly contentious behavior of the Ephraimites, the characters of the judges themselves exhibit a tendency toward the negative. Barak's need for Deborah's support, Gideon's hesitance, and now Jephthah's propensity for manipulative bargaining all manifest a clear negative direction. Whereas Caleb readily granted the request for sources of water made by his daughter, Achsah, Deborah fulfilled the role of judge, and Jael ultimately vanquished Israel's foe, the book acknowledges by name no other woman besides Delilah. Indeed, beginning with Jephthah's daughter, and with the exception of Samson's unnamed mother, women figure only as victims or villains. Family grudges motivate Abimelech's grab for power and Jephthah's lack of confidence. Gideon, who inaugurates his career as judge by destroying the Baal altar in his hometown, ends his career with the manufacture of an ephod; Jephthah's quasi-pious vow results in human sacrifice. What lies ahead? Does the midpoint also mark the turning point, or will the trends continue inexorably toward decay?

# Samson

Judges 13–16

The cycle of materials devoted to the career of Samson, perhaps Israel's most famed judge, presents interpreters with a number of problems involving its literary structure and compositional history, the degree and nature of unity it exhibits, and, related to the first two questions, its dominant theme. Interpreters generally agree that the editors have structured the cycle as two largely parallel sequences (chs. 14–15; 16*) with a prefixed birth/call narrative (ch. 13). The brief account in Judges 16:1-3 appears as a miniature version of the plot and theme shared by the two major sequences of material (for convenient surveys of interpretations of the Samson cycle, see Matthews 1989 and Craig). The two major cycles elaborate Samson's encounters with dangerous women (Samson's Philistine wife, a harlot, Delilah), trickery and mischief of various kinds (the riddle, the foxes, the city gate), betrayal (the Philistine wife's disclosure of the solution to the riddle, Delilah's disclosure of the secret of Samson's strength), revenge (Samson burns the Philistine's crops, kills 1,000 with the jawbone of an ass, collapses the temple), and God's response to Samson's plea for assistance (15:18-19; 16:28-30; see, for example, Exum 1981).

## The Character of the Cycle and of Its Central Figures

Pointing not only to the duplication in the development of the plot in Judges 14:1–15:20 and in Judges 16:4-31 but also to features such as the duplication of the comment concerning the duration of Samson's judgeship (15:20; 16:31), some commentators view the Samson cycle as a conglomeration of similar but originally independent Samson traditions held together in their present form only by the person of the hero. Some argue, further, that the brief anecdote concerning the harlot in Gaza, which stands between the lengthier treatments of Samson's adventures in Timnah and in the Valley of Sorek and which represents the least-developed Samson tradition, supports the notion that the stories about Samson and his three women represent individual realizations of a common pattern. In this view, much like those surrounding the American folk figure, Johnny Appleseed, the various Samson tales will have "emerged from a separate traditioning community or circle, each remembering Samson stories for its own reasons and in its own way" (cf. Wharton, 64).

Interpreters who view the Samson cycle as a collection of Samson tales united around the Samson figure do not seek a unifying theme in Judges 13–16 apart from the characterization of its hero. This approach has resulted in a wide range of proposals concerning the nature of the Samson figure. His name (*shimshon*, if derived from *shemesh*, "sun") suggests origins as a solar hero (see Segert, 459–60; Margalith 1986a, 227–28). For some, he exemplifies the trickster figure familiar in folk literature; more specifically, given the centrality of the insider/outsider, us/them (i.e., Israelite/Philistine) dynamic of the account, he typifies the "social bandit" (cf. Crenshaw, 78–81; Weitzman; Niditch 2008, 154). Others point to Samson's similarity to the "wild man" figure known in many literatures of the world, especially in the ancient Near Eastern characterization of Enkidu, counterpart of Gilgamesh. Like Enkidu, Samson is a hairy, strong master of wild beasts who sometimes resides in the wild and eats wild honey but whom women can tame (see Mobley). In contrast to these interpretations of Samson against ancient Near Eastern backgrounds, Margalith has championed the view that Samson's Danite heritage masks a cultural relationship with the Greek Danaoi and that, in fact, the Heracles legends were the model and source for the Samson stories. In a series of articles (1985; 1986a; 1986b; and 1987), Margalith calls attention to commonalities between the two superheroes, one a Danite and the other descended from Perseus the Danaid. Females entrapped both. Both had a mighty club, killed a lion barehanded, carried city-gates on their shoulders, and were involved with pillars, for example.

Instead of a focus on episodic elements and motifs, attention to overarching structural and thematic features of the cycle, especially when the prefixed call/birth narrative is taken into account, produces another series of interpretations. While, read alone, the two cycles that recount Samson's exploits resemble folk legends about the hero's feats of trickery and daring, read together with the call/birth narrative, certain features of the account of Samson's career suggest an editorial agenda embodied in the shaping of the whole. Commentators differ, however, even with regard to the central theme of this editorial agenda. Crenshaw, for example, points to the conflict between loyalty to family and people and attraction to exotic women evident in Samson's life and reads the cycle as an account driven by the theme of filial devotion versus sexual desire. Others take their cue from the broad context of the Samson cycle in the Deuteronomistic History. Emmrich and Brooks, for example, call attention to parallels between the Bible's depictions of Samson and of Saul, including a number of parallels in the two birth narratives, their opposition to the Philistines, the use of the unique phrase "and the Spirit of YHWH rushed upon him" in reference to both (Judg 14:6, 19; 15:14; 1 Sam 10:6, 10; 11:6), and the fact that both commit suicide. Indeed, some scholars speculate that the birth narrative now associated with Samson once belonged to the Saul tradition (see Brooks, 20–21).

Although no reading can claim consensus support, perhaps the plurality of interpreters read the Samson story through the lens of the requirement that the divine messenger imposed on Samson's mother and on Samson himself in the announcement of Samson's birth. According to this interpretive scheme, this divine announcement sets the hero apart from the other judges and demands a theological interpretation of Samson's career. Indeed, the central feature of the announcement, the Nazirite requirement made of Samson's mother even before Samson's birth and applicable to Samson from the womb, is unique not only in the book of Judges but in the whole Hebrew Bible. As the cycle unfolds, one component of Nazirite status, unshorn hair, becomes pivotal, unifying the concluding sequence of events in Samson's life with the beginning. Similarly, the activity of the Spirit of God, first reported in Judges 13:35, relates Samson's violent reaction to Philistine subterfuge (14:6, 19) to his Nazirite beginnings. Finally, given the reticence of Hebrew storytelling to offer such commentary, the narrator's aside reporting that Samson's parents were unaware of YHWH's intention to utilize Samson's undesirable dalliance with a Philistine woman as "an occasion against the Philistines" (14:4) forcefully extends the theological umbrella of the birth narrative over the tales of Samson's adventuresome career. As the commentary below will illustrate, however, even those who agree that Samson's Nazirite status functions as the (editorially imposed) key to the cycle disagree as to the precise significance of this theme (see also Niditch 1990, 612).

## Samson's Birth Narrative (Judg 13)

The anecdotal character of the narrative units that comprise Judges 14–16 seems to support the view that the Samson material originated as tales about a rugged, even wild, "frontier" mischief-maker celebrated for harassing Israel's ancient Philistine foe. On the other hand, elements of editorial shaping and framing such as the birth narrative and interspersed narratorial comments justify reading the cycle as a whole and in relation to an editorial program. Did the editors responsible for the current form of the collection intend to depict Samson's career as shaped by his breech of the vow so that Samson continues the downward trend evident to this point in the book of Judges (so, influentially, Blenkinsopp, esp. 65). Alternatively, do peculiarities in the phrasing of the references to the Nazirite vow in the birth narrative reflect concessions the editors have made to the content of the legendary material, concessions that effectively absolve Samson of any infraction against his Nazirite status?

Following the typical editorial comment in 13:1 setting the life of Samson in the context of the historical and theological scheme that frames the book of Judges, the birth narrative begins in typical Hebrew narrative fashion: "Now there was a certain man of Zorah . . ." (v. 2). The account that follows divides neatly into three major sections: vv. 3-10, the appearance (*r'h*, v. 3) and reappearance (*r'h*, v. 10) of the messenger of YHWH to the unnamed woman; vv. 11-18, an exchange between Manoah and the messenger involving Manoah's four requests and the messengers' responses; and vv. 19-23, the account of Manoah offering (*lqh*, v. 19) his guest a meal that YHWH accepts (*lqh*, v. 23) as a burnt offering, confirming for Manoah (v. 16b) the woman's perception (v. 6) that the messenger represented YHWH (cf. Exum 1980, 44–45).

## Genre as a Clue to the Focus of the Account

Although scholars often consider Judges 13 as an example of the birth announcement genre, it manifests a number of characteristics that suggest rather that it constitutes an amalgamation of formal features derived also from the call account and the cultic etiology. Richter (141), for example, lists five motifs common to birth narratives in the Hebrew Bible: (1) birth to a barren woman (cf. 1 Sam 1; Gen 18:11-15); (2) the promise of a son (cf. Gen 18); (3) hospitality extended to the incognito deity (cf. Gen 18; Judg 6); (4) the recognition of the visitor's identity (cf. Gen 18; Judg 6); and (5) the response of fear at the moment of recognition (cf. Judg 6). The fact that Richter also finds several commonalities between Judges 13, a birth narrative, and Judges 6, a call/cultic etiology narrative (see "Gideon's Call/Commission: Part 1" above; Böhme seems to have first noted the relationship between Judges 6 and 13, which is widely acknowledged although variously interpreted), already points, however, to the composite character of Judges 13 from a formal perspective. This composite character will merit further discussion shortly.

Before examining the composite nature of Judges 13, the fact that it also constitutes a peculiar realization of the pattern in respect to several of the individual items on Richter's list deserves attention. First, the unit devotes little energy to the promised child as the fulfillment of the barren woman's hopes for a child. Instead, as the structural analysis of the unit indicates, it manifests primary interest in the messenger (cf. Exum 1980, 46) and his message. The paired appearances of the messenger in the first section frame the messenger's announcement to the woman, her report of the event to her husband, Manoah, and his prayer asking YHWH to send the messenger again with further instructions concerning the boy to be born. Only the second of Manoah's four requests to the messenger deal with the boy (v. 12, "What is the boy to do?"). The other three involve the messenger, specifically his identity (v. 11, "Are you the man who spoke to this woman?"; v. 15, "Let us feed you"; v. 17, "What is your name?"). The third and concluding section focuses entirely on Manoah's recognition of the identity of the messenger and his wife's inference concerning the significance of the messenger's appearance.

Second, this recognition motif and its companion, the fear response, do not belong, in fact, to the birth announcement genre. At no point in Genesis 18:1-16, the text Richter cites as a parallel, does it become clear that either Abraham or Sarah have recognized their visitors as divine. There is no manifest moment of recognition. Furthermore, the debate between Abraham and YHWH concerning the fate of any possible righteous persons in Sodom and Gomorrah that follows, in which Abraham obviously knows the identity of his dialogue partner, belongs to a new unit. In any case, neither Sarah, who laughs aloud at the audacity of her guest's prediction, nor Abraham, who boldly challenges YHWH to "do what is just" in the subsequent unit (Gen 18:25), react in fear to their visitor. In the only other case of a birth announcement recorded in the Hebrew Bible, Hagar responds to the recognition that she has encountered a divine messenger by naming YHWH "El Roi, for," she says, "you are a God of seeing." The account functions incidentally as a place-name etiology.

These and other observations, especially concerning the affinities between Judges 13 and the narrative of Gideon's call—affinities that are closer in many ways than the relationship between Judges 13 and other birth announcements in the Hebrew Bible—have led many scholars to conclude that the editors of the Samson cycle crafted Judges 13 on the model of Judges 6 (see, for example, Stipp, 346–48). Others object that Judges 13 does not employ motifs such as the request for a sign and the fire-wonder reported in Judges 6. They argue that proponents of the notion that Judges

13 depends literarily on Judges 6 must explain these omissions (see, for example, Kegler, 105, and Exum 1980).

The extensive series of often-verbatim verbal parallels and similar plot elements listed below, which notably concentrate in 6:18-24 || 13:15-23, clearly establishes that the two texts stand in a relationship to one another that invites definition.

| | |
|---|---|
| Host detains guest for meal | 6:18; 13:15 |
| Guest converts meal into sacrifice | 6:21; 13:19 |
| *minhah*—"grain" or "offering" | 6:18; 13:19 |
| *gedi 'izzim*—"goat kid" | 6:19; 13:15, 18 |
| *ml'k h'lhym*—"messenger of the God" | 6:20; 13:6, 9 |
| *tswr*—the "rock" altar of sacrifice | 6:21 (cf. *sela'*, v. 20); 13:19 |
| messenger vanishes | 6:21; 13:20-21 |
| *ki-mala'k YHWH hu*—the recognition formula | 6:21; 13:21 |
| assurance of survival | 6:23; 13:23 |

Furthermore, the motif of the meal-turned-sacrifice appears only in these two texts in the Hebrew Bible and does not seem to be integral to either the call narrative or the birth announcement genres. The similarities between the two passages probably cannot, therefore, be attributed to some common background tradition or genre. In the narrative of Gideon's call, the motif constitutes the sign that God often gives the one commissioned to confirm God's presence and assistance in fulfilling the task (compare Moses' staff that becomes a serpent, Exod 4:1-5; regarding the call genre, see Habel), to be sure, but it appears in this function uniquely in Gideon's call. In the announcement of Samson's birth, on the other hand, it serves primarily to answer Manoah's questions regarding the identity of the messenger. Again, however, no similar motif appears in other birth announcements in the Hebrew Bible.

Finally, even the birth announcement's omission of elements from the Gideon account supports the dependence of Judges 13 on Judges 6 and suggests the editors' motivation for constructing the linkage. To suit the new context, the editors of Judges 13 transformed Gideon's request for a sign into Manoah's request for the reappearance of the messenger. Manoah's doubts about the identity of the messenger and the validity of his message corresponds to Gideon's doubts about the validity of his call. Similarly, although the Gideon text culminates in a cultic etiology and the Samson text does not, the appropriation of the former as the model for the latter accounts for the omission. Many commentators, especially in an earlier era, have speculated that even the Samson story derives from an ancient cult legend (see, for example, Cook, 376; Gese, 43; Gressmann, 240–41; Kübel, 226–27; and von Rad, 333). As argued in the analysis of Judges 6 above (see "Gideon's Call/Commission: Part 1"), however, from a generic perspective, the composite nature of Gideon's call already represents the adaptation and insertion of a cultic etiology into a non-cultic context. Explaining the establishment of an otherwise unknown cultic site plays no significant role in Gideon's call and has even lesser importance in the announcement of Samson's birth. Stipp (347) argues, therefore, that the cultic dimension disappears in Samson's birth narrative because it constitutes a reworking of a reworking and has no purpose in the new context. In fact, the editors responsible for Judges 13 had such little interest in cultic concerns that twice they even thoughtlessly referred to the "rock" where Manoah placed the grain (Manaoh's *minhah*; see Segert, 460) and the goat as "the altar" (v. 20), assuming "facts not in evidence," as it were.

Regardless of the question of literary dependency, the functions of the meal/sacrifice sections of both passages and the significance of the similarities in the literary context of the book merit consideration. In both contexts, the meal-turned-sacrifice serves to confirm the authority of the messenger and, hence, the validity of his message (Gideon's call, Samson's birth and Nazirite status, respectively). That is to say that the recognition scene and its accoutrements in the announcement of Samson's birth deal with Manoah's doubts (and presumably, by extension, the reader's) about the messenger or, more aptly, about his message. It is the focus of the account.

### The Focal Issue, Then: Samson, the Nazirite
Given the denouement of the Samson story, this focus on the identity of the messenger and therefore the validity of his message marks its contents as key not only for a reading of Judges 13 but also for the whole Samson cycle. The messenger does not simply announce the birth of a son to a barren couple but designates this son to a special dual status—Nazirite and deliverer. Consequently, any reading of the Samson cycle must evaluate Samson's behaviors in terms of their fidelity to his Nazirite obligations and his career in terms of the degree to which he succeeded in delivering Israel from the Philistines. Chisholm (157) has conveniently summarized the three possible options for interpreting the significance of Samson's Nazirite identity as follows:

First, Samson's situation should be interpreted in light of Numbers 6:1-21 in its entirety. All the rules listed there would apply in his case. Second, only the Nazirite regulations specifically referred to in the angel's instructions were applicable in Samson's case, namely, those pertaining to cutting one's hair and to drinking the fruit of the vine. The rule pertaining to contact with a corpse did not apply because of the special circumstances of Samson's Nazirite calling. Third, Samson's Nazirite status differed from the situation described in Numbers 6. In Samson's case the only rule pertained to the cutting of his hair.

The data that can constitute a basis for deciding the question derive from the wording of the statements concerning Samson's Nazirite status in the birth announcement and an analysis of Samson's behaviors allegedly proscribed by the Nazirite vow.

Several recent studies of the birth announcement have noted interesting dynamics involved in the statement and restatements of the obligations imposed on Samson—and his mother (see esp. Exum 1980 and Reinhartz). The original message contains two identical announcements of the impending birth of a son (italicized below) each followed by a prescription, first for the mother and then for the son. Notably, the messenger instructs the mother to abstain from alcohol and carefully to observe food restrictions, two expectations of the Nazirite, but does not proscribe cutting her hair or contact with corpses, two other key components of the Nazirite scheme. Furthermore, the messenger's instructions for the boy specify only that he is to remain unshorn. Later, Samson will not, in fact, strictly abstain from alcohol or from unclean (or at least objectionable) foods. Quite possibly, the editors responsible for Judges 13 tailored the messenger's statement of Samson's obligations to suit the traditional materials concerning Samson's exploits already at hand. If so, Samson's fidelity to his Nazirite status can only be measured by the criterion of his hair, the only restriction explicitly imposed on him.

> Look, you are barren and have not given birth,
>     but *you will conceive and bear a son.*
> Now, take care and do not drink wine or strong drink
>     and do not eat anything unclean.
>
> For, look, *you will conceive and bear a son,*
>     and no razor shall touch his head
> for the boy will be a Nazirite of God from the womb,

and he will begin to deliver Israel from the hand of the Philistines. (13:3-5)

Significantly, when the woman reports the conversation to her husband, she modifies the message by omitting any specific expectation of the boy along with the reference to the boy's role as deliverer, and by supplementing the expression "for the boy will be a Nazirite of God from the womb" with the phrase "until the day of his death." Exum (1980, 49) points out that, in the woman's account, this phrase, ominous in prospect, replaces the reference to Samson's role as deliver. She considers the substitution a "subtle hint that death will prevent Samson from completing the task. Samson does, in fact, only *begin* to deliver Israel." Ironically, the anonymous woman, in analogy to the anonymous messenger, makes a prophetic statement (Reinhartz, 31–32), subtly linking Samson's Nazirite hair, his role as deliverer, and his death, when "the dead he killed in his death were more than those he killed in his life" (16:30). Remarkably, in the messenger's second appearance, he responds to Manoah's question about the boy's "way of life" (v. 12) by restating only the requirements set for Manoah's wife; that is, he avoids the question, leaving Manoah, and the reader, to wonder about the details of this "way of life."

Stipp takes another approach to the problem of the precise nature of Samson's Nazirite status, subjecting the episodes in Samson's career that allegedly constitute violations of the Nazirite vow to critical review. He notes that Samson does not, in fact, cut his own hair and therefore does not violate that element of the vow. The announcement of Samson's birth entirely omits reference to contact with corpses as prohibited the Nazirite by the regulations in Numbers 6:2-21, raising the question as to whether the messenger invokes that provision of the Nazirite regulation by association or intentionally omits it in view of Samson's role as deliverer. In any case, Stipp observes that, in priestly diction, the noun *nefesh* utilized in Numbers 6 never refers to a dead animal, for which priestly material exclusively employs the term *nebelah*. Consequently, Samson cannot be charged with damaging his Nazirite status through contact with the cadaver of a lion or the jawbone of an ass. Samson's alcohol consumption remains a violation of the Nazirite regulations as stated in Numbers 6 but not, as Stipp also notes, as stated by the messenger in Judges 13.

In sum, then, based on the anecdotal character of the materials in Judges 14–16, the evidence that editors modeled elements of Judges 13 on elements of Gideon's call narrative, the formal departures from the birth announcement genre that focus attention on the identity of the messenger and the validity of his message, and the unusual dynamics evident in the account's treatment of the Nazirite obligations placed on Samson and his mother, Judges 13 was probably composed specifically to introduce a preexisting collection of Samson narratives or as part of their combination. In order to facilitate a theological interpretation of Samson's career, the editors responsible for this customized introduction reinterpreted the wild man's strength-giving hair as the mark of a "Nazirite of God" (13:5, 7); it was sacred but not magical. The details of Samson's behavior as recorded in the existing anecdotes required, however, that the obligations of the Nazirite be tailored. Furthermore, the sophisticated restatements of the messenger's announcement subtly foreshadow the end of the story and of Samson's life.

Even if this interpretation acquits Samson of charges that he repeatedly violates his Nazirite vow, questions still remain concerning Samson's attitudes, motivations, and character. The final form of the cycle assumes Samson's awareness of his Nazirite status and the importance of his uncut hair, but it *does not* make it clear whether he knows that he has been chosen as a "deliverer." His mother omits that information in her report to Manoah (did she ever relate it to Samson?), and Samson only acts against the Philistines in reprisal for personal affronts (cf. Chisholm, 154–55). Indeed, the narrator intimates that, while Samson's interests may have been amorous, God was behind the scenes "seeking an opportunity against the Philistines" (14:4). Samson seems much more the mischief-maker than the deliver. Although he does not violate his Nazirite status by cutting his hair, he does endanger it, his strength, and God's purposes by revealing the truth about it to a woman who has clearly demonstrated a willingness to betray him. Is he arrogant or naïve? What is God up to behind the scenes?

Judges 13 ends with two brief comments, one (v. 24) reporting the birth, naming, and maturation of the boy Samson, blessed by the Lord, and another (v. 25) stating that Samson's charismatic gift began to manifest itself while he was in Mahaneh-Dan ("the encampment of Dan"), "between Zorah and Eshtaol." As with other biblical heroes such as Moses, Samuel, and even Jesus, the Bible omits detailed accounts of Samson's upbringing. The geographical detail in the second statement marks it as an inclusion with the final statement in the Samson cycle (16:31) that reports Samson's burial in his father's tomb, somewhere "between Zorah and Esthaol." Just as Samson's activity as "deliverer" began when the Spirit of YHWH "began to stir" him there, he was buried there when it was ended.

## Samson's Adventures in Timnah (Judg 14:1–15:20)

In two acts (14:1-20 and 15:1-20), the book of Judges narrates Samson's adventures among the Philistines in Timnah. The first extended episode in Samson's career quickly frustrates any expectation that a reader may have developed for this divinely foretold and divinely empowered "deliverer." Unlike Moses and Samuel, Samson does not embark on a mission in response to God's direction. Instead, the account of Samson's career begins as a human story of lust, betrayal, and revenge. It unfolds on this level as a continuation of Samson's love affair. On another level, however, God works through Samson's human motivations and behaviors. As the narrator indicates both explicitly (14:4) and implicitly (15:11-13), even the human actors in these events do not recognize that God intends to take advantage of Samson's appetite-driven impulsiveness. In fact, the Judeans consider Samson's behavior reckless and dangerous. Without the benefit of the narrator's privileged knowledge, the reader, too, might well find it difficult to see Samson as a deliverer of Israel.

### Samson in Timnah: Act I (Judg 14)

Structurally, frequent comments that Samson, or in one case his father, "went down" (*yrd*, vv. 1, 5, 7, 10, and 19) or "returned" (*shwb*, v. 8) somewhere (Timnah, vv. 1, 5, 7, 8, 10; Ashkelon, v. 19) drive the plot. First, Samson "went down to Timnah, and at Timnah he saw one of the daughters of the Philistines" (14:1). Infatuated with the Timnite, Samson enlists his father to arrange a marriage. Together with his parents, he then "went down" to Timnah again to arrange the marriage. Incidentally, he secretly kills a lion in the vineyards near Timnah on the way. Later, returning to "take" the Timnite as his wife (v. 8), Samson eats honey from its carcass and shares some of it with his parents, telling no one of the honey's origins. Joined by his father ("and his father went down," v. 10), Samson hosts a seven-day wedding celebration during which he poses a "riddle" concerning the lion and the honey as a challenge to the young Philistine men who are guests at the party. His wife betrays him by wheedling the answer from him and revealing it to her compatriots. He exacts revenge of a sort and returns to his parental home in anger. Apparently thinking that Samson has abandoned his new bride (cf. 15:2), her father gives her in marriage to Samson's best man, setting the stage for the second act of Samson's adventures in Timnah. Events that began with Samson "going down" to Timnah come to a temporary pause when Samson "goes up" to his father's home (v. 19).

**Prelude to a Wedding (14:1-9).** Read on this level, the story of Samson's adventures in Timnah bears all the marks of a tale of the mischievous and mighty folk hero. Samson's egocentric motivations, not his sense of duty as Israel's deliver, account for all his behaviors. His interest in the Timnite outweighs any stricture against intermarriage with non-Israelites (Exod 34:16; Deut 7:3) and the respect due his parent's wishes. Marriage to a Philistine woman seems to conflict with Samson's role as divinely designated deliverer. In terms of plot development, the incident involving the lion reported in the awkwardly repetitive vv. 5-9 functions primarily as a device to facilitate the "riddle" at the marriage feast, the plot complication that makes the story worth telling. Even the sequence of events narrated in vv. 5-9 suggests that the incident offers nothing of intrinsic significance. Samson and his parents "go down" to Timnah (v. 5); after killing the lion, Samson (alone?) "goes down" to the woman (v. 7); some time passes before Samson "returns to take her" (v. 8). These repeated trips do not further the plot apart from delaying the story's progress in order to give time for the colony of bees to take up residence in the lion carcass and produce honey. Further, this encounter with the lion becomes the first incident in which the divine Spirit empowers the deliverer's feat of strength. One might expect that the deliverer's first such act would be directed against Israel's enemies. Instead, on its face, it is little more than a showy display of prowess. In context, however, it provides the indispensible background for the riddle.

Incidentally, while Samson's father obviously acquiesces and arranges the marriage (cf. vv. 5, 10), the fact that he does so provides little information concerning the background of marital customs in ancient Israel. The common and reasonable assumption based on comparative anthropological and sociological considerations that, in a patriarchal culture such as ancient Israel's, the parents of the prospective bride and groom will have arranged marriages, actually finds little direct support in Scripture. Apart from arranged royal marriages (cf. 1 Kgs 9:16; 11:19; 16:31; 2 Kgs 8:18; etc.), which were more a political than a family institution, the Bible offers no evidence that arranged marriages were the norm in ancient Israel. Furthermore, Samson's marriage to the Timnite is one of two instances recorded in the Hebrew Bible in which, even though the groom's father negotiated the terms of the marriage, the prospective groom first chose his bride (cf. Shechem in Gen 34:1-4). Of course, neither prospective bride seems to have had a say in the matter, on the other hand.

**The Marriage Feast and the "Riddle" (14:10-14).** The marriage celebration (he has already "taken" the woman as his wife [v. 8]; his guests and the narrator refer to her as Samson's wife [vv. 15, 16]), or, more specifically, the "riddle" Samson poses to his thirty Philistine guests and its solution constitute the heart of the first act in the drama of Samson's adventures in Timnah. Because the seven-day celebration takes place in the bride's hometown, the Philistines supply thirty groomsmen (v. 11). The text offers no explanation of the significance of the number, although the fact that the people contribute these thirty young men "when [they] saw" Samson suggests a motive. One might speculate that they reacted to the Israelite's imposing physical appearance. If so, the detail may imply that, in the Philistines' assessment, Samson had the strength of thirty men. In any case, the account shows no interest in describing the festivities but rushes immediately to relate Samson's challenge to his guests. Again, however, the account provides no indication of Samson's motives for staging the contest. Some scholars have pointed to parallels in Hellenistic poetry competitions (Margalith 1986a, 229; Yadin, 418–19), an observation that has implications primarily for dating the composition. With respect to a literary interpretation of the account, the notion of a contest of wits also has the advantage of explaining the "proverbial" character of the Philistines' response to Samson's saying and of Samson's counter-response. Presumably, Samson, the mighty lion killer, seeks an opportunity to demonstrate not just his physical prowess but also his superior wit (v. 11; see Camp and Fontaine, 135; cf. the queen of Sheba's test of Solomon's reputed wisdom involving *hidot* or "hard questions," RSV).

The "riddle" itself continues to puzzle interpreters as much as it puzzled the Philistines. First, despite the common English translation of the term *hidah* as "riddle," the rare term (with only nine occurrences in the Hebrew Bible apart from the eight instances here in Judg 14) does not, in fact, seem to refer to a "riddle." None of the other seven instances of the term denotes a "riddle." It occurs most frequently as a parallel for the more general term *mashal*, "proverb, saying" (Pss 49:5; 78:2; Prov 1:6; Ezek 17:2; Hab 2:6), which suggests to Yadin (414) the connotation of "a saying that requires explication or explanation." Second, Samson's saying has no formal parallels elsewhere in the Hebrew Bible (Margalith 1986a, 225–26), the closest approximation being the Philistines' "solution." Third, in fact, Samson's saying is not a "riddle" in the usual sense of the word. A "riddle" involves wordplay ("What is black and white, but re[a]d all over? A newspaper.") or misdirection ("What animal walks on four legs, then two, and finally three? A human being."). In either case, given common knowledge, a true riddle contains the information necessary for its solution. It does not assume private or undiscoverable knowledge ("What did I have for lunch yesterday?' is not a riddle; cf. Margalith 1986a, 227–28). Since Samson had not even told his parents about the lion and the honey (vv. 9, 16) and since bees simply do not build hives in carcasses, Samson's saying could not be "solved." It envisions "a topsy-turvy world where eaters are eaten" (Weitzman, 170). As Samson acknowledges (v. 18b), the answer could only be gained from Samson himself, in this case by subterfuge.

**Betrayal and Mistrust (14:15-18).** Just as the happenstance encounter with the lion set the stage for Samson's riddle, Samson's riddle sets the stage for his new wife's betrayal of his secret. Unable to crack Samson's impossible "riddle," the Philistine wedding guests approach the bride with the request that she "entice (*pth*)" her husband to disclose the answer, threatening arson against her father's household if she refuses (v. 15). The request and threat include an apparent accusation of complicity in a scheme to swindle them of the thirty linen and festal garments involved in the bet: "Have you invited us here to impoverish us?" The woman fulfills their request. She weeps and accuses Solomon of false love because he would not confide in her the secret of the riddle. No doubt, the narrator intended this stereotypical caricature of female manipulation ("if you really loved me, you would . . .") as a clue to the conflicted loyalties of both Samson and his wife. Indeed, he had not confided in her, explaining that, since he had not confided even in his parents, she could not or should not expect him to tell her. In other words, by his own confession, his new bride ranked below his parents in the hierarchy of Samson's relationships. As widely recognized, Samson's accusation that the Philistines were able to solve his riddle only because they had "plowed with [his] heifer" (v. 18) has sexual connotations (as do Samson's "riddle" and the Philistine's "solution"; see for example, Crenshaw, 115; McDaniel, 53–57; Slotkin, 158; Exum 1993, 77–78; see also Schipper's convenient and helpful discussion of scholarly interpretations of Samson's riddle and the Philistine response) and suggests that Samson has doubts about his bride's fidelity extending beyond the betrayal of his verbal confidence. Indeed, the haste with which Samson's new wife was "given" to another, namely Samson's (Philistine) "friend (*re'ah*; v. 20)" at least hints that the new husband may have been the plowman Samson suspected. Obviously, this marriage was no "union of two minds," no bond of profound intimacy. It certainly did not unite two families or provide an avenue for improving relations between two communities.

The unclear chronology of this sequence of events (vv. 14-17) may point to an intriguing aspect of this dynamic of mistrust. According to the Hebrew text, after three days of effort to solve Samson's riddle (v. 14), the Philistine young men approached Samson's wife on the seventh day (v. 15). Both versions of the Greek tradition place this conversation not on the seventh, however, but on the fourth day of the celebration, the more logical continuation of v. 14. Yet the Hebrew and the dual Greek traditions agree that Samson's wife "pressed" him for the whole seven days of the celebration (v. 17), a detail that conforms to neither chronology. The Hebrew text's seventh-day request in v. 14 is the "more difficult" reading and therefore, according to the canons of literary criticism, the more likely original. Theoretically, the Greek tradition would reflect a scribal "correction" intended to produce a more logical text. One assumes the improbability of the contrary possibility that a Hebrew scribe would alter a logical text, introducing a chronology difficulty. Neither reading of v. 14 accounts for the agreement in the textual tradition concerning the seven days of v. 17. Does v. 17 imply that Samson's wife began her efforts to learn Samson's secret even before her countrymen asked her to do so, that she mistrusted Samson's motives from the outset?

**Samson's Revenge, Samson's Character, and Foreshadowing (14:19-20).** The first act in Samson's adventures in Timnah portrays an impetuous, arrogant, egocentric, and contentious young man. He acts unwisely and rashly without carefully considering implications. Indeed, an interpretation that gives weight to the sequence of events as narrated will note that Samson decides to marry the Timnite upon merely seeing her (vv. 1-2); he "talk[s] with the woman," who "please[s him] well," only after importuning his father to arrange the marriage. With regard to this marriage, he manifests absolute disregard for his parents' wishes and for the fact that his intended belonged to those persecuting his people. One-upmanship motivates Samson's "riddle." It can only promote hostility. At least by modern standards of fair play, it is beyond the bounds. The Philistines' only hope to solve it is to resort to equally "unfair" tactics, as Samson surely knows. He is secretive, even distrustful of his parents (without reason) and his wife (apparently for good cause), although, if he suspects his wife's motives for her interest in the solution to the riddle, his acquiescence confirms a lack of wisdom and discipline. In the end, he kills thirty of Israel's Philistine enemies, not in a noble effort to deliver his people from oppression but in order to exact the cost of his defeat from his opponents, albeit indirectly.

In the broader context of the entire Samson cycle, of course, this episode prefigures the story of Samson and Delilah. As argued above (see "The Character of the Cycle and of its Central Figures" above), the similarities likely point to a complicated history of Samson traditions in which certain motifs and themes associated with the hero were realized in a variety of ways.

From the perspective of a canonical reading of the Samson cycle, however, the parallel accentuates Samson's vulnerability to "seductive" women. As the discussion below will illustrate in detail, the story of Samson and Delilah concentrates on the common motif of the Philistines' efforts to discover Samson's secret through his wife. In both cases, Samson's Philistine enemies ask his wife to "entice/seduce (*pth*)" Samson into revealing the information they seek (14:15; 16:5), and Samson ultimately complies. Judges 16 offers much greater detail concerning the interaction between Samson and his wife, however, giving the impression that the Timnite's "seduction" of Samson, which one could reasonably expect to have made Samson wary of betrayal, taught Samson nothing. Notably, the secret to Samson's strength, his Nazirite hair, plays no role in Judges 14. The elements of Samson's character and behavior common to both episodes are an arrogant sense of invulnerability and a weakness for dangerous women. The canonical arrangement of the two accounts emphasizes that, in this regard at least, Samson was a slow learner.

**Behind the Scenes 1: Reading on Two Levels.** On the level of human interactions, then, the plot of Act I of Samson's adventures in Timnah progresses through a series of events, each of which prepares for the next: Samson falls in love with a Timnite woman. On the way to visit her, he encounters and secretly kills a lion. On a return trip, he finds a colony of bees producing honey in its carcass. At the marriage celebration, he poses a challenge involving private knowledge concerning the lion and the honey. Unable to solve the "riddle," the Philistines celebrating Samson's wedding convince his wife to obtain the answer from Samson, betraying her new husband. The betrayed and enraged Samson honors the bet, in a way, but it costs thirty Philistines their lives.

On another level, however, God influences the course of events (vv. 4, 6, 19) by sending the divine Spirit upon Samson at key moments, stirring him to feats of strength. The strength Samson required to rip the lion apart barehanded resulted from the onrush of the divine Spirit (v. 6), as did the strength and anger necessary to slay thirty men in Ashkelon (v. 19). Both of these texts employ an interesting expression to describe the influence of the divine Spirit on Samson: "the Spirit of YHWH rushed upon (*tslh ʿal*) him." The phrase, which occurs in reference to Samson once more in 15:14, appears otherwise in the Hebrew Bible only in reference to Saul (1 Sam 10:6, 10; 11:6) and, in a variant with the preposition *ʾel* ("to"), once of David (1 Sam 18:10). Elsewhere, the book of Judges employs the much less forceful expression "and the Spirit of YHWH came/was upon him" (*wattehi ʿal*-X *ruah-ywhw*; 3:10—Othniel; 11:29—Jephthah), once an intriguing phrase involving the verb "to clothe" (*lbsh*, i.e., "to take possession," 6:34—Gideon), and once an equally suggestive expression with the verb "to impel, stir" (*pʿm*, 13:25—Samson again). Samson's experience of the divine Spirit stands out among these instances, regardless of the phrase describing it, in terms of the raw, violent, and immediate power the Spirit brings to Samson. The texts depict the impact of the Spirit on Othniel, Jephthah, Gideon, and David in terms of charismatic authority to lead, not of superhuman strength. The three usages of the phrase found in Judges 14 in reference to Saul portray the effect on him alternatively as prophetic ecstasy (1 Sam 10:6, 10) or as angry determination (11:6). Contrary to associations of the divine Spirit with inspiration, wisdom, guidance, prophecy, and authority, the "fruits of the Spirit" in Samson's case are sheer strength (14:6; 15:14) and "hot anger" (14:19).

Significantly, the text does not attribute to God the event that sparked the whole sequence, at least not directly. Samson's love affair with the Timnite transpires on the surface level of human motivations that dominate the account. With great subtlety, however, the editor/narrator insinuates divine purpose into the account, bringing the elements of human motivations and divine purposes into alignment in v. 4 and again, much more overtly, in v. 19. According to the editor/narrator, while it may have been true that YHWH did not direct Samson to "go down to Timnah," or exert any influence on Samson's infatuation, YHWH nonetheless recognized Samson's involvement with the Timnite as an "opportunity against the Philistines" (v. 4). The theology of God's involvement in human affairs implicit in this statement underlies several other passages in the Hebrew Bible: Joseph's recognition that, even in the absence of evidence that God had directed the course of his difficult life, events had culminated in a situation in which he would be positioned to save his whole family from starvation (Gen 45:5-8); Ruth's "happenstance" arrival in the fields of Boaz to glean (Ruth 2:3); Esther's unusual ascent to become queen of Persia at a moment when an ages-old rivalry between the Saulides and the Agagides threatened her people with extinction (Esth 4:14). Manoah and his wife did not realize it (14:4), and Samson does not seem to have understood his actions in any way as the fulfillment of his fate as the one who would "begin to deliver Israel from the hand of the Philistines" (13:5), but YHWH knows an opportunity when it presents itself. Indeed, just as, in Joseph's view, YHWH can utilize something as negative as the animosity among brothers, YHWH can also take advantage of the opportunity presented by "an obstreperous lout prepared to betray his Israelite heritage and dishonor his father and mother in order to gratify his sexual desires!" (Wharton, 58). YHWH need only nudge things along in the lion encounter and, at the end of Act I, by sending the divine Spirit "rushing" upon the angered Samson, supplying him with the raw power required to slay thirty of Israel's Philistine enemies. The number of fatalities—thirty victims of a man angry because he lost a bet—would place Samson prominently in a modern list of mass murderers; as an act of liberation, on the other hand, it hardly merits attention. As the narrators/editors portray it, however, it was at least a beginning.

**Samson in Timnah—Act II (Judg 15)**
The observations that, still angry, Samson returned to his father's household and that the Timnite's father quickly gave his daughter in marriage to one of Samson's faux Philistine friends introduce a pause in the action, as it were. When the curtain rises on Act II of Samson's Adventures in Timnah, the action resumes on the level of human motivations. Events involve a series of tit-for-tat acts of revenge that escalate from marital problems through property damage to the deaths of a thousand Philistines.

**Samson's Fiery Return to Timnah (15:1-8).** Once again, Samson's motives bear no obvious relation to his special status and calling. Time passes, his anger abates, and again (cf. 14:1) Samson's sexual appetite (the Hebrew verb "to go into" used in 15:1 commonly has sexual connotations) drives his behavior. He returns to Timnah from his father's household to find, however, that his father-in-law, who implies that Samson's angry withdrawal was tantamount to abandonment (v. 2), will not permit him "to go in" to his wife because he has given her in marriage to one of the guests at Samson's wedding celebration. Samson refuses the offer of the hand of his erstwhile bride's younger sister (cf. Laban's negotiations with Jacob, Gen 29:26-28, and Saul's with David, 1 Sam 18:17-26) and decides to take revenge for the insult. As already noted, Samson's earlier riddle challenge, which set into motion the sequence of events in Act I, seems almost to have been designed, in fact, to provoke conflict in a setting associated with the establishment and nurture of a new relationship. Samson tacitly admits that this had been his intent when he informs "them" (his father-in-law is the only figure mentioned as present) that "This time I will be blameless" when he causes Philistines harm (*ra'ah*, v. 3).

Hostilities rapidly escalate in intensity. In a manner typical of the folk hero/trickster (i.e., it is ingenious but virtually impossible), Samson knots lit torches in the tails of paired foxes and looses them in the Philistines' fields and orchards. The Philistines retaliate not by attacking Samson directly but by burning Samson's ex-wife and her father, whom they blame for inciting Samson's anger. Paradoxically, they may also have hoped to appease Samson by exacting vengeance on the individuals who had insulted him. Samson immediately "smote them hip and thigh with great slaughter" (v. 8, RSV) and withdrew, apparently intending to cease his acts of aggression (v. 7). The Philistines, however, wanted their own revenge. Repeating their mode of dealing with Samson indirectly, they threaten the inhabitants of Judah where Samson had taken up residence in a cave, coercing them to deliver Samson, bound. In turn, the Judahites approach Samson, who permits himself to be bound and delivered to the Philistines. Empowered by the onrushing divine Spirit, he breaks free and slays 1,000 Philistines with the jawbone of an ass.

Significantly, Samson's only motivation throughout this sequence of events is personal revenge, and his targets are not his former father-in-law, his ex-wife, or her new husband—the individuals who had actually insulted him—but the whole Philistine people. Samson's oath of vengeance (15:7) indicates, in fact, that the conflict with his father-in-law served for him, as for YHWH (14:4), only as an "occasion" (i.e., an "excuse") for aggression against the Philistines. In contrast, at least initially, the Philistines seem interested in limiting the scope of the conflict, placing the blame for Samson's anger where it truly belongs. The entire sequence of events amounts to an overblown illustration of the cycle of retributive violence, summarized neatly in the statements, mirror images of each other, in vv. 10 and 11. Both the Philistines and Samson explain to the Judahites that they are only doing "to him as he has done to us" and "to them as they have done to me," respectively. A contentious divorce erupts into violence that culminates in a thousand deaths.

Ironically, the Philistines bring the climactic violence on themselves. Samson's oath, which consists of three phrases exhibiting a sparse Hebrew syntax, reveals two surprising clues regarding his intentions. The first phrase, involving only one word, *kazot* ("like this"), stating the protasis of an if-then construction, offers the first surprise. Translators generally agree in extrapolating it to mean "if it is to be like this," "if this is how you are going to behave," or the like. Contrary to the Philistines' expectations that Samson would welcome their retribution against his ex-wife and father-in-law, he, in fact, views it as another provocation. The second phrase, which employs one of the standard oath formulas (*ki 'im*), presents no difficulties. According to the third, however, Samson intends only to exact vengeance for the deaths of his ex-wife and her father and has no plans to move against the Philistines in a campaign of liberation, despite the fact that, as the reader knows, he has been called to (begin to) deliver Israel, not merely to settle personal scores.

One strand of the Greek textual tradition, that represented by Codex Alexandrinus (A), offers an interesting variant on the Hebrew text of 15:7, pointing either to a conflate reading of two slightly different Hebrew originals or, more likely, to a creative attempt to rectify Samson's statement with his calling. Vaticanus (B) reads "I will exact vengeance from one and the last of you" (i.e., "each of you down to the last"). On one hand, it may have been aware of a text with "one" (*'hd*), a Hebrew variant for MT's "afterward" (*'hr*) involving confusion of the letters *resh* (r) and *daleth* (d), easily mistaken for one another in Hebrew, in which case it simply combined the readings. Alternatively, it may have taken advantage of the similarity in the letters to employ the kind of midrashic technique widely attested in literature from the period, and created the conflation. In the absence of any other manuscript evidence, the latter seems more likely. The significant aspect of the B text, then, is its attestation of an early reading of the account that grappled with the contradiction between Samson's statement that he intends to cease his aggression against the Philistines and the task of delivering Israel from Philistine oppression assigned him before his birth by the divine messenger (13:5).

**The Philistines, the Judeans, and Samson at Lehi (15:9-19).** Unable to leave well enough alone, the Philistines adopt another ironic course of action when they threaten the Judahites by raiding Lehi (v. 9). The place name, which means "jawbone" in Hebrew, foreshadows one of the two interwoven etiologies that culminate the tale of Samson's adventures in Timnah. Some form of the term *lehi* appears eight times in vv. 14-19. In fact, although the narrator employs the term anachronistically in v. 9, the account of Samson's slaughter of a thousand Philistines with a *lehi* offers an explanation of how *Ramat lehi* ("Jawbone Heights") got its name. The account abounds in such wordplay. Samson's statement celebrating his victory involves a play on words that incorporates an allusion to the place name. He boasts that "with the jawbone of an ass, heaps upon heaps, with the jawbone of an ass (*bilhi hahamor hamor hamoratayim bilhi hahamor*) I have slain a thousand men" (v. 15). The sequence of the consonants *heh, mem, resh*, and *tau* (h, m, r, and t) echoes the place name Ramat. Samson's statement itself has been the subject of scholarly debate regarding the phrase *hahamor hamor hamoratayim*. Modern translations follow the vowels supplied to the consonantal text in the Masoretic tradition and understand the second ("heap") and third ("heaps") terms as homonyms of the first ("ass"). Alternatively, the second and third words (i.e., *hamor,* and *hamor-atayim*) could be forms of the first (*hamor,* "ass"), so that the first part of Samson's statement could be translated "with the jawbone of an ass, an ass of (two she) asses" and be understood as a veiled allusion to Samson's amours. By substituting other vowels for those suggested by the Masoretes, it is also possible to translate the second and third words as "I have reddened [i.e., bloodied] (them)" (see Segert, 456–57). Such delight in the plasticity of language characterizes Hebrew literature.

A final etiology concludes the account of the incident. Apparently, the act of slaying a thousand Philistines with a bone club was strenuous work because, afterward, Samson was "very thirsty" (v. 18). In the first indication that Samson has any awareness of his role as judge ("this great deliverance"), he calls on YHWH by means of a rhetorical question to provide water. Ominously, the reference to "falling into the hands of the uncircumcised" adumbrates Samson's ultimate fate. Reminiscent of Moses' experience with murmuring Israel in the wilderness (Exod 17), Samson's request prompts God to create a spring of water to quench Samson's thirst so that he revived (lit., "and his spirit returned and he lived"). The expression *wayehi* ("he lived") precedes the last reference to Lehi (*balehi*) in the passage and serves to link the two etiologies through a rare instance in Hebrew of internal rhyme. The etiology proper consists of the explanation of the name En-hakkore, "the spring (*'en*) that [Samson] called for (*haqqore'*)" (v. 19).

Several motifs and peculiarities flavor the account of the escalation of hostilities between Samson and the Philistines. As with Gideon's marriage to a *pilegesh* from Shechem, scholars note the unusual characteristics of Samson's marriage to the Timnite (patrilocality, Samson's decision to visit his wife in her father's household, the gift/price he brings along) and speculate concerning the possibility of varieties of marriage in ancient Israel. This case invites speculation about the possibility of a kind of "visiting marriage" (see Gideon, "Conclusion," above) in particular. The "younger sister motif" is familiar from the stories of Laban deceiving Jacob into marrying Leah before Rachel (Gen 29:22-27) and of Saul's withdrawn offer of Merab, his elder daughter, to David in marriage before offering Michal (1 Sam 18:17-19). All three instances result in open hostility between son-in-law and father-in-law.

Beginning already in Act I, Samson's (*shimshon*) associations with the sun (*shemesh*) permeate the account, which depicts solar Samson as a veritable "force of nature" (Niditch 2008, 159). The Philistine wedding guests threatened the Timnite with a fiery death (14:15). In retribution, Samson set fire to the Philistine's fields using foxes and "torches" (*lapidim*; cf. Gen 15:17; Exod 20:18; and esp. Judg 7:20). Margalith (1985, 225–26), who sees in Samson's fiery foxes evidence of the Hellenistic backgrounds of the Samson material, calls attention to the colloquial Greek name for the fox, *lampouris*, "torch-tale," an obvious allusion to its bushy red tail. The Philistines, of course, retaliate with fire. At the critical moment, Samson's bonds melt away "like burning flax" (v. 14).

Samson spreads conflagration; he is a wildfire out of control, a circumstance that explains the Judeans' odd attitude toward him. Rather than welcome his actions as those of a deliverer, they cravenly collaborate with the Philistines in "capturing" Samson who has taken up residence in a rock crevice in Etam ("Eagle Eyrie," a name that seems etymologically related to a root that denotes "birds of prey," perhaps in the vicinity of Bethlehem or Zorah [so Niditch 2008, 159]; cf. 2 Chr 11:6). Apparently, the Judeans consider Samson to be "out of control." His provocation of the Philistines for what seem purely personal reasons threatens the security of the community. The picture of collaborationist Judah, unable to recognize its deliverer, is unique in the book of Judges, which is otherwise very pro-Judah (see "The Southern Campaign—Judah's Preeminence" above) and raises questions concerning the provenance of this material (does it reflect tensions between the tribes of Dan and Judah?).

Such considerations notwithstanding, the account functions in the canonical form of the Samson cycle in relation to the parallel structure of the two major sequences of events in Samson's career. Specifically, it supplies elements missing from the Timnite's betrayal to complete parallels with Delilah's betrayal. Act I featured Samson's Philistine opponents working through his wife to discover the secret of his riddle; the Samson and Delilah episode centers on the efforts of Samson's Philistine opponents to discover the secret of his strength. Both the Timnite and Delilah must importune Samson repetitively, wearying him to the point that he discloses his secret. The discovery of the secret of the riddle does not involve the binding of Samson, the wholesale slaughter of Philistines, or Samson's prayer for divine assistance. These elements that figure prominently in the Delilah episode appear only in Act II of Samson's adventures in Timnah, although Judges 16 reverses the order of the killing of large numbers of Philistines under the impulse of the divine Spirit and Samson's prayer for divine assistance, a reversal that is key to the tragic climax of the Samson cycle.

**Behind the Scenes 2: Reading on Two Levels.** As in Act I, of course, on one level, the arc of events in Judges 15 traces the contours of human emotion and motivation. Samson's riddle stokes the embers of hostilities into an open fire. Subsequently, each step that participants take fans the flames until it breaks into a raging conflagration. The Philistines "plow with [Samson's] heifer." Samson kills and steals. Samson's father-in-law further insults him. Samson destroys property. The Philistines retaliate against Samson's (former) father-in-law and wife. Samson retaliates in turn. The Philistines move en bloc against Samson, and his compatriots betray him. He kills. As in Act I, however, on a deeper level, the story of Samson's feud with the Philistines continues to manifest the theology of divine nudges to the course of human affairs. Whereas the account narrates no instance of divine direction, at two crucial moments God acts, once to fuel the flames of hostility and once to preserve Samson's life. As the editors of the Samson cycle have configured the material, God works in human affairs chiefly by accentuating certain components of the "natural" situation. Ironically, God's response to Samson's request for water to sustain his life foreshadows the only other prayer reported on Samson's lips, a prayer for the strength to commit suicide.

**Concluding Formula (15:20).** The story of Samson's adventures in Timnah ends with the typical concluding formula summarizing the activity of a judge and giving its duration. It will be duplicated at the conclusion of the Samson and Delilah narrative. From the standpoint of the history of the composition of the Samson cycle, the comment may be seen as evidence that the Timnah and Delilah stories underwent independent histories of development. In terms of a reading of the canonical text, it marks a definite caesura, a pause. As a plot device, it can theoretically signal either a turn of events (either for better or worse) or a return to original conditions for a reprise of the plot line. In fact, the brief interlude in Judges 16:1-3 narrating Samson's romantic encounter with a Philistine prostitute in Gaza and its aftermath indicates without delay that, after the pause signaled at the end of Judges 15, the story of Samson will reiterate, with variations of course, the basic plot of the account of Samson's adventures in Timnah.

## Interlude: Samson's Adventure in Gaza (16:1-3)

Once more, Samson travels to a city in Philistia, "sees" a woman there, and becomes enamoured of her. Once more, the Philistines attempt to rid themselves of the Samson menace. Once more, Samson's wit and might prevail. The essential contours of Samson's adventures in Timnah recounted in the previous section of the Samson cycle and of Samson's dealings with Delilah and the Philistines narrated in the subsequent section are obvious. Unlike either of the other two tales of Samson's complicated love affairs, however, the report of this episode lacks detail. The harlot from Gaza remains anonymous. The description of Samson's relationship with her requires only two words in Hebrew (*wayyabo' 'eleha,* "and he went in to her," v. 1). Whereas the Timnah account depends on the psychological motivation of the desire for revenge to drive events, the Gaza account omits any explicit indication of the attitudes and motivations of the central figures, Samson and the Philistines. Presumably, after the events recounted in Judges 14–15, the Philistines have become Samson's sworn enemies. Their determination to dispatch Samson requires no new impetus, only a new opportunity. Samson's sexual appetite provides it.

The similarities between the outline of this account, although truncated, and the Timnite and Delilah stories suggests that it may be regarded as a parallel tradition that may have circulated independently of the other two stories of Samson's dangerous romantic liaisons. If so, it exemplifies the germ of a tradition from which the more elaborate parallels could easily have grown, or it represents the fragmentary form of a more developed account that has been abbreviated, intentionally or accidentally, before its inclusion in the Samson cycle. Regardless of the tradition and composition history of the passage, however, it fulfills two important literary functions in the Samson cycle. First, it supplies the final element foreshadowing events to come in Samson's dealings with the Philistines as related in the Delilah episode, namely, the fact that Samson is strong enough to carry the whole assembly of the city gates of Gaza several miles to the top of a nearby city. The raw power required for such a feat far exceeds what is necessary to kill a lion barehanded or to slay a host of Philistines with a crude club. Indeed, in this instance, Samson apparently acts without the benefit of the power of the divine Spirit. The destruction of a Philistine temple should present no difficulty.

Perhaps more important from the standpoint of evaluating the Samson cycle as a whole and, in particular, of assessing Samson as an individual and a judge, this brief vignette, which brings the number of Samson's romances to three, contributes to the portrayal of Samson as a young man driven primarily by his sexual appetite unbridled by caution, morality, or ethnic and religious boundaries. Samson "sees" a woman and wants her, or takes her. He may be a Nazirite from birth, an impressive physical specimen, and even clever, but he is not pious, upstanding, wise, or admirable. In modern terms, he might be described as a playboy living a fast and dangerous life, disrespectful of his parents, willing to endanger those he claims to love, and arrogant in his strength.

## Samson's Adventures in the Valley of Sorek:
## Samson and Delilah (16:4-20)

The literary structure of the Samson cycle abounds in numerical indicators that the story constitutes its climactic episode. Samson's relationship with Delilah is his third romance. The offer of some multiple of "eleven hundred pieces of silver" (16:5) constitutes the third attempt to coerce someone close to Samson to betray him, although it is the only such effort that does not involve a threat (the Timnite 14:15; the Judeans, 15:9-10). After the Timnite and the Judeans, Delilah will be the third actually to betray him. The triplet pattern also appears within the Samson and Delilah account itself. Three times the text refers to the Philistines "lying in wait ('*rb*, 16:2, 9, 12). Three times Delilah asks Samson to tell her "how you might be bound (*bammeh te'aser*)" (vv. 6, 10, 13).

Subtly, another numerical pattern involving four elements calls attention to the decisive fourth element, which differs significantly in every case from its predecessors. Samson's four explanations of how he might be subdued involve the shared apodosis "then I shall become weak and be like any other man" (vv. 7, 11, 13, and 17). In three of these four explanations, Samson responds deceptively to Delilah's questions concerning the source of his strength. The fourth, honest response brings disaster. Four times she acts on the information. Four times the Philistines emerge from concealment to seize Samson as Delilah exclaims to him, "the Philistines are on you!" (vv. 9, 12, 14, and 20). Samson's three easy escapes from his bonds occasion Delilah to accuse him three times of mocking (*hetalta*, vv. 10, 13, 15) her and twice of telling her lies (*kezabim*, vv. 10, 13). In this story, for Delilah, the fourth time is the charm. Samson even participates in the numerical game with his references to "seven" wet bowstrings, presumably freshly harvested animal tendons favored as bowstrings because of their strength and elasticity, and the "seven" locks of his hair.

If, as the saying goes, the third time is the charm, the question raised involves who will benefit from the repetition. Will Samson finally recognize the pattern of betrayal, or will Delilah finally succeed in "enticing" (16:5; cf. 14:15) her husband to reveal the truth about his strength? To refine the question given the outcome, does Samson's acquiescence to Delilah's persistence, which parallels his behavior in relation to his Timnite bride, reveal naiveté (since he did not learn the lesson of the Timnite), disregard for the holiness of his vow (since he revealed his secret), or overconfidence (cf. 16:20)?

## Samson Marries Delilah from Sorek (16:4)

In contrast to the account of Samson's marriage to the Timnite, the narrative of Samson's affair with Delilah moves apace to the tale of deception. The text devotes only one verse to the description of the context for what follows: "Samson fell in love with a woman from the Valley of Sorek named Delilah" (16:4). Probably to be identified with the modern Wadi es-Surar about thirteen miles southwest of Jerusalem (Boling, 248), the Valley of Sorek would have been situated at the boundary between the Philistines and Samson's tribe of Dan. Timnah (modern Tibneh), Zorah, and Eshtaol were all nearby. Segert (458) sees in the name (*srq*, "red grapes"), which probably refers to the chief agriculture product of the region at the time, a double allusion to the Nazirite prohibition against alcohol consumption and, since the term can also mean "to comb," to the hair about to be cut. Perhaps significantly, Delilah is the only one of Samson's paramours named in the text. Her name may also be allusive, although scholars have difficulty narrowing the etymological possibilities. Hebrew *dll* means either "loose, long hair" or "small," while in Arabic the root means "flirtatious" (see Segert, 460). The possibility of a play on words with *laylah*, the Hebrew word for "night," may lend the Samson (*shmsh*, "sun," see "The Character of the Cycle and of Its Central Figures" and "The Philistines, the Judeans, and Samson at Lehi" above) and Delilah story the character of an allegory for the battle between night and day. Plausible etymologically, all these options also suit the themes and motifs of the story. Conceivably, the tradition, the author, or the editor responsible for both the names Sorek and Delilah may have chosen them precisely for this wealth of associations.

Not only does Delilah's name represent a puzzle but her identity and behavior are also highly ambiguous (cf. C. Smith). First, the text does not make clear whether she was Samson's wife (as was the Timnite) or his paramour, perhaps a harlot (as was the Gazite). Second, the text does not specify her ethnicity. Although she collaborates with the Philistines, her name is apparently Hebrew. In the parallel sequence of events centered in Timnah, both his Philistine wife and his Judean countrymen have already betrayed Samson, establishing a precedent for either interpretation of Delilah's ethnicity. Since the Valley of Sorek demarcated the apparently porous boundary between Israelite and Philistine territories (see Weitzman, 160–62), Delilah's residence there manifests the ambiguity.

The question of Delilah's identity bears directly on how one assesses both her behavior and Samson's. Several scholars, who argue for the more traditional understanding that Delilah was Philistine (whether wife or harlot), have recently called attention to the implications of the reader's perspective for an evaluation of Delilah's actions (Klein 1993; Smith; Ackerman). For a Philistine reader, Delilah would be the heroine of the story, a Philistine Jael (or Judith, so Ackerman, Exum 1993, 88). Like Jael, she vanquished the enemy when the male leadership could not; like Sisera, Samson was unable to withstand her. Klein (1993, 66) concludes that, from a Philistine point of view, Delilah may be seen as "a resourceful woman, possibly a heroine to her own people, who perpetrates an age-old and repugnant ruse: using a man's love to bring him down." One nation's liberator is another's rebel. To the Philistines, Samson, Israel's judge, was a terrorist.

The text presents a significant obstacle to this understanding of Delilah as a Philistine Jael, however. Notably, whereas the canonical text assumes the Philistines' motives, it suggests greed as Delilah's motivation, not solidarity with the Philistine people, leaving open the possibility that she was an Israelite (Exum 1993, 69), even Samson's Israelite wife. Arguably, however, the greed motive supports the notion that the text envisions her as Samson's paramour.

If one views Delilah as a harlot, whether Philistine or Israelite, one can consider her behavior solely as a quite profitable (v. 5—1,100 pieces of silver from each of the Philistine lords!) business transaction. Her objective was not Samson's capture but a sizeable fortune. In any case, the final form of the Samson cycle opens the possibility that readers are to assume that Delilah knows of Samson's past exploits. If so, she may well anticipate that, once again, the Philistines will ultimately fail to subdue Samson, but not before she collects her fee. On the assumption that Delilah is a harlot out for profit, Samson's behavior, on the other hand, exemplifies folly. He can have no reasonable expectation of Delilah's loyalty. If his Timnite wife would betray him under threat, a harlot from Sorek will certainly do so for money.

If one views Delilah as Samson's Israelite wife, one can classify her behavior as a parallel to that of the Judeans who handed Samson over to the Philistines at Lehi. The possibility that Delilah was Israelite underscores, then, the impression that Samson's own people viewed him as an unpredictable, volatile, and erratic loner—beyond the influence of parents, living in caves, at the fringes of civil society—whose amorous excesses and outbursts of retaliatory violence endangered the welfare of the community. The assumption that the account depicts Delilah as Samson's Israelite wife results in many of the same dynamics as the harlot interpretation. She took advantage of the opportunity to acquire such wealth while ridding her people of a reckless troublemaker, knowing that, in fact, the whole enterprise had the potential to backfire on the Philistines. In any reading, it seems, Samson cannot expect fidelity or solidarity. If his Judean countrymen would betray him under threat, an opportunistic wife will certainly do so for money.

### Seduction and Complicity (16:5-20)

In any case, after the succinct indication of the place and the persons, the account progresses to the contrasting detailed game of seduction and deceit that results in Samson's capture. In its current context, the Philistines' motive for seeking to "bind and subdue" Samson, a motive that the text fails to specify, must be the history of conflict recounted in Judges 14:1–16:3. Now, however, the Philistines do not seek to retaliate for some distinct mischief. Instead, they think much more strategically. They have learned the lessons of the Judeans' ropes (15:12-13) and the Gazites' gate (16:3). They can only hope to rid themselves of the Samson menace by neutralizing the source of his incredible strength, which they must first discover. Unfortunately for them, their strategy of neutralization (they say nothing of killing Samson and, when they succeed in capturing him, choose to humiliate rather than execute him) proves insufficiently radical.

So much for the secondary characters in the intrigue. The motivations and behaviors of the key figure, Samson, are obviously central to an interpretation of the passage. Since this account is typical of Hebrew narrative, which rarely reports information about the subjective state of characters, one must deduce Samson's state of mind from his actions and the literary structure of the story. In this regard, it is significant that the structure of vv. 4-21 noted above may be repetitive, but it is not static. Instead, it serves as the vehicle for a subtle but definitive progression driven, significantly, by Samson's actions. Any reader, ancient or modern, will react with a degree of incredulity to the fact that Samson continues his relationship with Delilah after her first act of betrayal, not to mention after the second and third. She makes no effort to conceal her intentions; she does not resort to trickery or deceit (cf. Exum 1993, 83). Given the improbability that the story intends to portray Samson as downright stupid, one can only conclude that Samson knowingly chooses to play Delilah's game. Furthermore, his responses to her questions about the source of his strength move ever closer to the ultimate revelation of the truth: seven (bow) strings, seven ropes, seven braided locks of his hair, the seven locks shorn. Samson seems to toy with Delilah. She repeats her questions, accusations, and exclamations almost without variation; he controls the progression of events toward the climactic moment. He can halt it at will.

Why did he persist, then? The text offers a partial, unsatisfying answer with a parallel in the story of the Timnite: Samson gave in to Delilah's charges that his unwillingness to reveal the secret of his strength demonstrated that he did not truly love her (16:16), just as he gave in to the Timnite (14:16). He could not withstand either woman's unrelenting pressure (*hetsiqathu*, 14:17; *hetsiqah lo*, 16:16). In fact, Delilah's persistence was withering. Hyperbolically, the text reports that she "vexed" (*qtsr*, lit., "shortening") Samson "to death" (v. 16). Certainly, yielding to such persistent pressure is understandable on one level, but Samson's secret in this case will cost much more than thirty suits of fine clothing (14:12). More to the point, in contrast to the Timnite's one-time betrayal, Delilah has already demonstrated her intention. Of course, the text also abounds in language that suggests that Samson has fallen prey to Delilah's charms. Repeatedly, mighty Samson permits Delilah to bind him while he sleeps. Furthermore, the text reports that, after Samson revealed the secret of his strength, Delilah "made him sleep upon her knees" (v. 19). Does the text portray Samson, if not as mentally deficient, as emotionally weak? Does it attribute Samson's downfall to his inability to withstand the wiles of a desirable but manipulative woman? Is mighty Samson "henpecked"?

While the overall tone and dynamics of the account raise these questions, Samson's final statement before the Philistines seize and blind him coupled with the narrator's comment on Samson's state of awareness point in another direction, but under careful scrutiny provide only enough information to raise other questions about Samson's thinking. By this juncture in the Samson cycle, of course, the hero has many times escaped bonds, eluded ambushes, and survived betrayals, sometimes acting under the direct influence of the divine Spirit, sometimes in his apparently native strength. His expectation that he will "go out as at other times and shake [himself] free" (v. 20) seems, therefore, at first glance, very reasonable, since he has not yet realized what the narrator and readers already know. The haircut has ended his Nazirite status; both his strength (v. 19) and YHWH (v. 20) have left (*sur*, cf. 1 Sam 16:14) him. So much is clear. It is unclear, however, whether Samson's expectation was sensible in this particular circumstance. Judging from Delilah's behavior in the first three betrayals, Samson surely would have assumed that she would act on the information he had given her. Nonetheless, he fell asleep with his head in her lap. She summoned the barber, had him cut Samson's hair, and presumably bound Samson—all while he slept. Samson stated his confidence that he would escape yet again when startled awake by her fourth announcement that the Philistines were about to pounce. The narrator informs readers that Samson did not know that YHWH had departed but says nothing about whether Samson realized that his hair had been cut.

There are two possibilities. First, Samson may have spoken before he had time to realize that he had been shaved. He did not know about the haircut administered in his sleep, therefore he did not know that both YHWH and his strength had left him. His mistaken statement of confidence reflected his ignorance of the data. Second, if, as seems most likely, he would have expected Delilah to act on the information he had given her, and would have immediately become aware of the haircut upon awaking, his ignorance of the fact that YHWH had left him would reveal something about his attitude toward his strength and his vow. This moment is the crux of the Samson story. Although in his disclosure to Delilah, he correctly attributes his strength to his unshorn Nazirite hair, the fact that he willingly risks his status and continues to trust his strength even after the haircut suggests that his many escapes from close calls have instilled in him an arrogance, an over-reliance on his own strength, a recklessness born of outrageous success, a sense of invincibility. His confession to Delilah may be orthodox, but his behavior is presumptuous, selfish, even self-centered.

The common interpretation of the function of Samson's Nazirite vow in the Samson cycle understands this moment in Samson's life as his violation of the vow. In some versions of this interpretation, in fact, this violation is only the culmination of a series of violations of Samson's Nazirite vow (see "Samson's Birth Narrative" and "The Focal Issue, Then: Samson, the Nazirite" above). In light of the observations offered above, however, and noting especially that Samson does not administer the haircut, the common interpretation must be modified. Samson does not violate his Nazirite vow; rather, he disdainfully puts it at risk, perhaps because he has come to think of his strength as inherently his own. Samson dares Delilah, as he did the Timnites and the Judeans, and like them she takes the dare. This time, however, unlike his secretive treatment of the lion and the honey, Samson has *willingly* given away the key to his might. In the end, Samson is neither stupid nor a violator of his vow, but lustful and arrogant. "He is susceptible to women's attractions and to the delusion that his great power is self-generated" (Niditch 2008, 168).

### Samson in Gaza (16:21-31)
The scene that plays out in vv. 21-31 will have been familiar in ancient Mediterranean and Near Eastern cultures in which it was not sufficient to defeat an enemy. He must also be humiliated. The Philistines humiliated powerful Samson first by blinding him, a practice frequently mentioned in reports of the treatment of vanquished enemies of Assyrian and Babylonian kings. Shalmaneser I of Assyria boasted, for example, of blinding 14,400

soldiers in the defeated army of Shattuara, king of Hanigalbat (Ashur-Nasir-Apli I and II made similar claims; see Grayson, 82, 126, 145). The Bible records that Nebuchadnezzar blinded the rebellious Judean king Zedekiah after first making him witness the execution of his sons (2 Kgs 25:7; Jer 52:10-11). Another common form of humiliation involved the feminization of captives that extended to homosexual abuse. The Judges account implies that Samson suffered such mistreatment in its references to the Philistines forcing Samson to "grind (*thn*)" at the mill, a term that can be a euphemism for sexual activity (Job 31:10; cf. esp. Isa 47:2, where it refers to the mistreatment of military captives) and to "make sport (*tshq/shq*)," another term with sexual connotations (see Gen 26:8; 39:14, 17; and 2 Sam 6:21 [=1 Chr 15:29], cf. Niditch 1990, 617). Duped by a woman, shorn, blinded, and bound by his Philistine enemies, held captive in one of their leading cities, Gaza, and led about by the hand like a child or an old man (v. 26), Samson must now "make sport" in a public spectacle (vv. 25-27). How the mighty has fallen!

**Behind the Scenes 3: Reading on Two Levels**
A number of details strengthen the irony inherent in the stark contrast between Samson before his haircut and after. Immediately following the summary report of Samson's blinding, capture, and imprisonment in Gaza, for example, the narrator offers the portentous aside concerning the regrowth of Samson's hair. Although the comment does not state whether Samson's strength will return with his hair, the possibility hangs over the continuation of the story. Consequently, although the Philistines seem to have good cause for their celebration, they unwittingly create the situation that Samson will exploit for revenge. From the reader's perspective, the Philistines' repeated statement of faith, "Our god has given our enemy into our hand," made first by the Philistine leadership (v. 23) and then by the people (v. 24), compounds the irony. Formally, it is indistinguishable from similar statements made about Israelite successes on other occasions recorded in the book of Judges (1:4; 3:10, 28; 4:7, etc.), a circumstance that subtly raises a theological claim concerning the identity of the deity managing events in the Philistine-Israelite conflict. As subsequent events will demonstrate, in fact, the capture of Samson, like the capture of the ark of the covenant recorded in 1 Samuel 4–6, does not demonstrate the superiority of the Philistine deity. Rather, it introduces into the very sanctuary of Philistine religion the means of its destruction in a demonstration of the might of Israel's God.

Along another ironic axis, Samson's blindness and his request that YHWH renew his strength so that he "may be avenged . . . for one of [his] two eyes" manifest the substance of irony itself, namely the question of whether one is able to discern the truth in complicated, multi-layered reality. Can one see clearly what is really happening? Like the Johannine story of the man blind from birth who could see Jesus more clearly than even the religious authorities (John 9), the account of blinded Samson who recognizes the opportunity presented him while the Philistines see an opportunity to celebrate the end to the Samson threat represents the contrast between those who can and those who cannot truly perceive.

The ironic perspective that runs, in fact, throughout the Samson cycle culminates in the narrator's concluding comments in vv. 30 and 31. Beginning no later than the messenger's statement to Samson's mother that her son would "begin to deliver" Israel from its enemies, Samson's role and behaviors have exhibited a complex interrelationship, especially with regard to the presence and purposes of YHWH. As demonstrated above in the analysis of events that transpired in Timnah and later in the Valley of Sorek, Samson manifests virtually no concern for fulfilling a calling at YHWH's direction and very little, if any, awareness that his behavior advances YHWH's purposes. Samson satisfies his appetites for women and revenge, incidentally vexing the Philistine enemies of Israel and of YHWH. His behavior is erratic and reckless. From the perspective of the Judeans at Lehi, and perhaps of Delilah if she is to be understood as an Israelite, Samson is far from a deliverer. His provocations only incite the Philistines to move against Israel. In the end, his game of brinkmanship leads to his debilitation and capture. The narrator's conclusion reminds readers that, Samson's lack of discipline notwithstanding, on another level, YHWH was still able to utilize Samson's selfish behaviors to "begin" delivering Israel from the Philistines (for a similar reading of the Samson cycle, see Exum 1983). Indeed, Samson's suicide attack proved to be the climactic act of deliverance: "So the dead he killed in his death were more than those he killed while alive" (v. 30). The remarks reporting Samson's burial in his father's tomb located somewhere "between Zorah and Eshtaol" (v. 31) recall the earlier comment concerning the onset of Samson's ecstatic experience (cf. 13:25) and reprise the summary report of the duration of his judgeship (cf. 14:20), bringing the Samson cycle to an anti-climactic conclusion.

# The "Appendices"—
# Disarray and Disorder

Judges 17–21

In a book characterized by the peculiar, the block of material in Judges 17–21 stands out because of the overtly negative pictures it paints for readers. Whereas often in the earlier sections of the book it is difficult to determine whether the depiction of a figure or an event intends to leave a generally positive or negative impression (Gideon, Jephthah, and Samson, for example), the portrayals of persons and actions in the concluding block of material unmistakably describe moral, religious, and social disarray, even decadence. The foreign oppressors who represent the threat in the earlier chapters of the book yield the stage to internal forces of social disorder. In fact, the intertribal tensions evident as early as the Song of Deborah escalate in the final section of the book into fullscale civil war. This civil war results in the near-total collapse of the standards of decency necessary for civil society. Jephthah's crass disregard for the life of his daughter pales in comparison to the deteriorated level of the treatment of women (abandonment, rape, mutilation, kidnapping) reported in the unit that concludes the book. The section begins with the first overt treatment of Israelite religious practice since Gideon's inconsistent destruction of the Baalist cultic site in his hometown only to later set up a heterodox ephod there. Anti-Bethel polemic, which first appeared in subtle form in the opening chapters of the book, reemerges in this account of the founding of cultic sites with much greater force and blatancy.

Perhaps the most striking oddity of the concluding section involves the nature of the protagonists. No judge figure appears in the concluding section of the book of Judges, a circumstance that has contributed to the tendency, described above ("Preface/Appendicies Outer Envelope"), to view the unit as a collection of "appendices." The problem here, however, may involve the reader's expectation based more on the traditional title of the book, which derives from the LXX tradition, than on the book itself. The book begins not with an account of a judge's career or a programmatic statement concerning judgeship (such references begin to appear only as late as 2:18) but with a summary of the relative successes and failures of the conquest. As discussed above ("Theological Assessment(s) of Israel's History"), even the so-called "Deuteronomistic Paradigm" devotes greater attention to a variety of theological explanations for Israel's failure to take total possession of the land than to the nature of judgeship. From the perspective of the editors responsible for the final form of the book, it depends for its coherence not on the judge figures but on the fact that, during the period in question, judges were necessary because Israel had failed to attain control over the territory and, more important, to maintain its religious (and ethical) identity. In other words, in a real sense, the final block of materials in the book returns to an advanced state in the development of conditions set at the outset.

In this regard, the refrain that appears throughout Judges 17–21, "in those days there was no king in Israel" (17:6; 18:1; 19:1; 21:25), which appears parenthetically in its first and last instances in a form amplified by the explicatory phrase "every man did what was right in his own eyes" (17:6; 21:25), "holds [the] stories together as evident illustrations of the religious and social anarchy to which Israel was subject without the centralizing control of the monarchic institution" (Mayes 1983, 242). The careers of the judges themselves played out in the vacuum of royal leadership and represented evidence of the chaotic state of Israelite social and political organization in the period. In the history of modern scholarship, of course, the question of the book's stance on Israel's monarchy has been a focal point of discussion (see "Abimelech" above) and will be considered in the course of the interpretation of the material below. At this point, however, it is worthwhile to note that the absence of judges from the last five chapters of the book now called "Judges" represents not an anomaly but a continuation of the conditions that made the judges necessary in the first place.

## Bi-Partite Structure of the Block

Judges 17–21 divides neatly into two narrative units (chs. 17–18 and 19–21) with similarly shaped plots, although they differ significantly in the details. Both begin with the questionable actions of an individual Israelite (Micah and the anonymous Judean Levite, respectively), actions that soon prove to have much broader, in the second case even pan-Israelite, ramifications (cf. Satterthwaite 1993, 77). In both cases, the ironic elaboration of the consequences of the individuals' deeds reveals the inconsistencies inherent in their actions. In his mistaken efforts to secure God's blessing, Micah succeeds only in attracting the attention of the opportunistic Danites. The equally opportunistic Levite-for-hire demonstrates his devotion to financial prosperity, not his piety or his loyalty to Micah. The Danites, by contrast, attain their objectives through thievery, chicanery, and violence, potentially ruinous foundations for a city or a society.

Similarly, the Judean Levite, like his immediate predecessor, demonstrates unreliability and disloyalty to his concubine/wife. The motivations of the Levite's father-in-law are opaque, but the Ephraimite who offered the Levite and his concubine/wife protection from the worthless inhabitants of Gibeah proves to be perfectly willing to expose even his own daughter to abuse. After nearly eradicating the tribe of Benjamin and vowing not to intermarry with the Benjamites, Israel reconsiders the implications of the disappearance of a whole tribe and resorts to subterfuge in order technically to keep its vow while actually contravening its intention (see Amit 1999, 7). Along the way, through allusions of varying degrees of transparency, the block undermines the legitimacy of the northern sanctuaries of Bethel and Dan and casts aspersions on the Benjamite tribe (and, perhaps not coincidentally, the Gibean home of Saul), while affirming, by divine oracle no less, the supremacy and priority of the tribe of Judah (cf. Mayes 1983, 245). Editorial comments, which are slightly more frequent and more transparent than elsewhere in Judges, reinforce the ironic character of the actions and behaviors of the participants in the events narrated. In outline form, the structure of the "appendices" illustrating the prominence of these editorial comments is as follows:

Micah, the Levite, the Danites, and the Sanctuaries in Bethel and Dan, chs. 17–18
    Micah, the Levite, and the Sanctuary in Bethel, 17:1-13
        Micah Founds a Sanctuary and Installs a Cultic Object, 17:1-5
        *Editorial Comment, 17:6*
        Micah Installs a Priest-for-hire, 17:7-13
    The Danites and their Sanctuary, 18:1-31
        *Editorial Comment—Reprise, 18:1a*
        The Danite Espionage Mission, 18:1b-10
        The Danite Raids on Micah and Laish, 18:11-26, 27-31
The Rape and Murder of the Levite's Concubine and Its Aftermath, Judg 19–21
    The Levite's Concubine, Judg 19
        *Editorial Comment as a Temporal Clause, 19:1a*
        A Troubled and Troubling Marriage, 19:1-11
        Hospitality and the Criminally Inhospitable, 19:12-21

"Worthless Fellows," Abomination, and Ambiguity, 19:22-30
Consequences: Civil War, Judg 20
    Gathering at Mizpah, 20:1-10
    Benjamin Refuses Terms, 20:11-13
    Three Days of Battle, 20:14-48
        The First Two Days of Battle: Benjamin Routs the Israelite Army, 20:20-25
        The Third Day of Battle: Ambush, 20:26-48
Seven Wrongs Do Not Make a Right, 21:1-25
    Once More at Bethel, 21:1-14
    More Wives for Benjamin, 21:15-25
    Collective Punishment Gone Wild
    *Concluding Editorial Comment, 21:25*

## Micah, the Levite, the Danites, and the Sanctuaries in Bethel and Dan (Judg 17–18)

Irony pervades the account of the establishment of the two shrines associated with the anonymous young Levite first employed by Micah at his private chapel. Events unfold in three acts. In the first (17:1-13), Micah uses tainted money consecrated for the purpose by his mother to finance the manufacture of an idol to serve as the cultic object for his personal sanctuary, and he employs a wandering Levite as his personal priest. The first act concludes with Micah's statement of satisfaction that he has undertaken the steps necessary to procure God's favor. The ironic contrast between the source of the funds and the heterodox nature of the sanctuary established, on the one hand, and Micah's confidence that he has won God's favor, on the other, sets the stage for the second act (18:1-10). The topic shifts to the tribe of Dan and the dilemma of its lack of territory. An espionage mission to Laish in the far north becomes the occasion for the Danite spies to encounter Micah, his sanctuary, his cultic object, and his priest on their way northward. In Laish, they find not only a desirable locale but also a population unprepared to defend itself. The spies recommend a campaign against Laish, their kinsfolk endorse their recommendation, and, in the third and final act of the drama (18:11-31), a force of 600 retraces the route taken by the espionage party. Not only do they go on successfully to capture Laish but also, remembering what they have seen at Micah's home, they stop by there on the way to their victorious campaign to appropriate Micah's ready-made sanctuary, complete with clerical staff and cultic symbol, to be transplanted to their new home in Laish/Dan.

### Micah, the Levite, and the Sanctuary in Bethel (17:1-13)

The story of the founding of Micah's sanctuary, which sets the conditions for the Danites' theft, divides neatly into two subsections (vv. 1-5, 7-13) marked by parallel introductions ("Now there was a [young] man from . . .") and separated by the editorial comment concerning the absent monarchy (v. 6) thematic of the conclusion to the book of Judges. The first subsection narrates how Micah came to establish his shrine and the process he followed. The second recounts how Micah seized an opportunity to upgrade his sanctuary by staffing it with a genuine Levite. Every step along the way involves morally and religiously questionable behavior. In particular, theft and a curse taint the financing of the shrine; its central feature implicates Micah and his mother in blatant idolatry; and its priesthood, entirely illegitimate from the outset, rests on the mercenary opportunism of a migrant Levite apparently seeking his fortune. Allusions to the heterodox sanctuary in Bethel underlie the entire account, suggesting that, in the context in which it was composed and included in the book of Judges, polemic against the religious policies of Jeroboam I of Israel and his successors would have resonated with a readership.

**Micah Founds a Sanctuary and Installs a Cultic Object (17:1-5).** The story wastes no time. Immediately after introducing Micah, it begins *in media res* with his admission to his mother that he had stolen 1,100 silver coins (intriguingly, the amount the Philistine lords offered Delilah for betraying Samson) from her (v. 2). His admission presupposes the theft and his mother's public pronouncement of a curse on the thief, neither of which need be recounted now. In response to his admission, his mother blesses him and returns to him a portion of the money, which she has consecrated for the purpose, to be used for the production of cultic objects. There is some question as to whether the text refers to one ("an idol image, that is to say a cast figure," so Boling 1975, 256, and others) or two ("a carved image and also a cast figure"), although the reference in v. 6 to an ephod *and* teraphim suggests the latter. In any case, the text raises two other questions that prove more fruitful for understanding the dynamics at work between Micah and his mother. It is unclear, first, when she consecrated the money and, second, whether she consecrated the entire amount (v. 3) then, in fact, to devote only 200 silver coins to the project (v. 4). A long tradition of interpretation seizes on the apparent discrepancy between the statements in vv. 3 and 4 to suggest that not only was Micah a thief but his mother was also greedy (see Moore, 376, in disagreement; Burney, 420; and recently Yee, 158).

In a recent study of evidence for similar curses in other eastern Mediterranean cultures (Canaanite, Greek, and Latin), Faraone, Garnand, and López-Ruiz (165) have argued, rather, that the intensifying grammatical construction of the mother's statement in v. 3, a so-called *figura etymologica*, underscores the certainty of the consecration ("I have *indeed* consecrated it") not the amount ("I have consecrated it all"). Further, based on parallels especially in Greek and Latin curses, they contend that she likely consecrated the specific amount as an element of the curse she had pronounced on the unknown thief. Such dedications of some portion of the missing property to a deity were made "at the very beginning as a precondition for getting the deity to punish the malefactor." Finally, the purpose of publishing the curse ("you uttered a curse, and even spoke it in my ears," v. 2) was to "[frighten] the thieves and thereby [force] them to confess or return the stolen property or both" (Faraone, Garnand, and López-Ruiz, 176; see also Fox).

Thus, with stolen money, consecrated under curse, Micah and his mother commission the production of an idol image or idol images. As McCann (120) pointedly observes, "Micah and his mother [break] at least half of the Ten Commandments in only five verses." In the view of the prophetic and deuteronomistic theologies that predominate in the Hebrew Bible, however, this violation of Israel's covenant with its God typifies Israel's paramount failure. Rather than recognize the error, however, Micah only compounds it. First, in direct contradiction to the biblical requirement that priests be Levites, he installs one of his sons as the priest in his private sanctuary (v. 5), and then he hires a young Judean Levite who was apparently wandering the region in search of a sinecure (vv. 8-11).

**Micah Installs a Priest-for-hire (17:7-13).** Certain details related in vv. 7-13 may reveal information concerning a period in ancient Israel before the Torah's regulations governing cultic practices had been standardized. The identification of the young Levite as a member of "the family of Judah" contradicts the normal biblical position that the term "Levite" denotes a member of the tribe of Levi. The Levite's search for a sinecure suggests the existence of multiple sanctuaries throughout Israel, despite the Deuteronomic Code's insistence that there could be only one legitimate, central sanctuary (Deut 12:5-14, 17-18). No other text in Scripture suggests that Levites received what would essentially be tantamount to a salary. Instead, Levites were entitled to a proportion of the tithes and offerings presented in the sanctuary. Their livelihoods were linked to Israel's faithfulness to YHWH, not to the wishes of an employer. The possible wordplay in v. 7 (*ger sham*, "sojourn there") on Gershom, the name of Moses' son, who is also mentioned in 18:30 in connection with the sanctuary in Dan (cf. 20:26-28, which links Phinehas, Aaron's grandson, with the sanctuary in Bethel; cf. further Josh 21:27-33; 1 Kgs 2:27; 11:29-39; 12:28-29; 1 Chr 6:71-76; 2 Chr 11:13-15; 13:8-11), leads Halpern (1976, 37) to conclude that the Micah story points to political rivalries among Israel's priests, specifically between those tracing their lineage back to Moses and others to Aaron. In his view, Judges 17 is an "Ephraimite White Paper" claiming "antiquity and nobility for the cult at Bethel."

Even acknowledging the intriguing evidence for such political rivalries between sanctuaries and local priesthoods, Micah's theft hardly lends the account the air of nobility. Even if the current form of the text conceals an earlier pro-Bethel tradition, later editors and redactors have co-opted it for an antithetical purpose, namely to argue that the aberrant sanctuary at Bethel was founded from the outset on robbery, cursedness, and opportunism. Indeed, given all these flaws associated with Micah's sanctuary and its cultic practices, his statement of confidence, "Now I know that YHWH will cause me to prosper" (v. 13), effuses irony. The irony of Micah's statement only culminates an extensive array of links between his shrine and the infamous sanctuaries established by Jeroboam I in Bethel and Dan (1 Kgs 12:26-33; see Boling, 258–59 and Amit 1999, 14). The most obvious such linkage surfaces in the next chapter when the Danites transport Micah's shrine to their new home in the far north. Allusions to Bethel already begin, however, in 17:1 where the expression "mountain/hill of Ephraim" conceals a reference to Bethel (cf. Judg 1:22-26; Jer 4:15; 2 Kgs 5:22; Halpern 1976, 36; Amit 199, 12–13, and see Amit's discussion of v. 5, which links "Dan[ites] and Bethel" by association [1999, 14]). Furthermore, the depiction of Micah's shrine as a "house of God (*bet 'elohim*)" in v. 5 echoes the name Bethel (*bet-'el*, "house of God"). Finally, Micah's "molten" image ties the episode both to Aaron and the golden calf (Exod 32:4, 8; 34:17; Lev 19:4; Deut 9:12, 16; 27:15; see Butler, 379) and to Jeroboam's golden bull figurines at Bethel and Dan (1 Kgs 14:9; 2 Kgs 17:16; Hos 13:2). Founded with stolen money, centered on an idol, in competition with the "house of God at Shiloh" (18:31), and administered by a mercenary Levite, Micah's shrine could well be expected to bring catastrophe rather than the prosperity of which he is so confident.

### The Danites and their Sanctuary (Judg 18:1-31)
The account of the "Migration of Dan" recorded in Judges 18 constitutes the only extended narrative dealing with the Danites recorded in Scripture. By virtue of this uniqueness and because of the unusual nature of the events

recorded here, it represents a puzzle for historians interested in conditions pertaining to the tribal and territorial structure of pre-monarchial Israel. Spina conveniently summarizes the difficulties raised by the biblical text for a reconstruction of the history of the tribe of Dan: (1) Some texts say that Dan held no territory (Josh 19:47; Judg 18:10-3), others that its territory was extensive (Josh 19:40-46; 21:23-24). (2) One tradition associates it with seafaring (Judg 5:17), an unlikely way of life for a people situated in the region between "Zorah and Esthaol," well inland from the Philistine seacoast. (3) Judges 17–18, the major narrative of Dan's history, is tendentious; it devotes greater attention to discrediting the sanctuary in Dan than to the actual conquest of Laish, the translocation of the people of Dan, and the construction of the new city of Dan. (4) The situation is further complicated by the intriguing similarity of the name of a Greek tribe with ties to Egypt, the *Dny(n)*, to the name of biblical *Dn/Dny*, which calls attention to "the connection of the Danite Samson with Philistines, and the similarity of certain episodes in the Samson saga to Sea Peoples legends" (Spina, 62). Additionally, archaeological evidence from the site of ancient Dan also raises questions as to the Israelite character of its population during the early biblical period. In particular, some scholars have interpreted the Tel Dan inscription as an indication that the patron deity of the ancient city was the Canaanite god Hadad (see Noll).

Scholars have proposed a number of theories to explain this scant but intriguing evidence. A harmonization of statements concerning Dan in biblical sources results in a picture of Dan as a small or weak group who, unable to withstand pressure exerted by the Philistines to the west and the Ammonites to the east, in fact migrated northward. Another hypothesis, which focuses on the biblical reference to Dan's seafaring lifestyle and on the similarities between biblical Dan and the Greek *Dny(n)*, posits the identity of biblical Dan and this originally non-Israelite group (see Y. Yadin). In this reading, the account in Judges 18 (cf. Gen 49:17; 1 Kgs 12; Amos 8:14, etc.) reflects Israelite suspicions of the (foreign) cult in Dan (see Arbeitman).

Based on archaeological evidence and texts such as 1 Chronicles 2:50-54, 4:2, and Nehemiah 11:29, yet a third theory conjectures that traditions such as Judges 17–18, which speak of Dan's migration north, were composed in a late period when, in fact, Danites had migrated south from their original northern home. According to this view, the author or authors of the Judges account projected contemporary tensions back into Israel's earliest period, a well-known but in this case unverifiable phenomenon in the ancient literature (see Niemann; on the complicated situation involving Joshua's list of

Danite cities [21:23], which seem to reflect Solomonic administrative districts, see Kallai-Kleinmann).

Since resemblances between names can easily be coincidental, the biblical evidence is sparse, and the archaeological evidence is open to interpretation, any reconstruction of the history of the Danites must remain speculative for now. The interpretation of Judges 18 itself benefits from an element shared by all the theories concerning Dan's history, namely, Dan's reputation as an eccentric, strange, even dangerous group within Israel, with heterodox propensities. From the perspective of the Judahite groups responsible for the Deuteronomistic History, including the editors of Joshua (22:10-34; see Biddle 1998, 194–95, 199, 200) and Judges, tribes distant from the central sanctuary in Jerusalem were susceptible to idolatry and apostasy. Judges 18 purports that these tendencies took root in Dan from the earliest days in the land.

**The Danite Espionage Mission (Judg 18:1b-10).** On one level, the story of the Danites' espionage mission and subsequent conquest of Laish/Dan serves to further link Dan and Bethel, the two heterodox cultic sites. Just as the tribe of Joseph reconnoitered Luz, took it, and established Bethel as their own (Judg 1:22-26), the tribe of Dan will now send spies to Laish, capture it, and rebuild it as Dan. Bethel and Dan share similar backgrounds and a common illegitimate cult. The depiction of Dan's dangerous eccentricity depends heavily on the ironic configuration of this standard genre, the spy story, found also in the conquest narratives of the books of Numbers and Joshua (Böhler, 21–23; Spina, 65). Although the basic outline of the account of Dan's migration follows the standard pattern, certain components do not conform to genre expectations, and the overall outcome of the episode portrays "unscrupulous plunderers, [whose] cult is corrupt, and [who] destroy an innocent city" (Satterthwaite 1993, 84). Wagner (261–62) has identified six typical elements of spy stories in the Hebrew Bible: (1) the commissioning of spies (18:2a ); (2) the sending of spies with a specified mission (18:2aβ-5); (3) the report of the spies' execution of their mission (18:2b-7), often with elaborate operational details (missing in Judg 18), with reference to some confirmation of the expectation of success in accomplishing the ultimate objective such as an oracle (18:5-6), or with an appeal to some previous situation in which YHWH gave Israel success; (4) the announcement of the spies' return of and their report (18:8-10*); (5) the spies' declaration that YHWH has given the reconnoitered territory to Israel or some group of Israelites (18:10*); and (6) the conquest mission itself (18:11-31).

Whereas the account of the espionage mission launched from Kadesh-barnea (Num 13) departs from the standard genre with regard to the sixth element (the people hesitate to embark on the conquest mission), the account of the Danites' espionage mission diverges obviously at two points. First, its elaboration of the third element lingers over the encounter between the five Danite spies and Micah's Levite. Second and similarly, even though the text ostensibly deals with the conquest of Laish and its reestablishment as the city of Dan, the sixth element of the genre, which deals with the conquest mission proper, involves only vv. 27-29. Just as the spies had stopped by Micah on their way northward, the Danite expeditionary force of 600 men make a point of revisiting Micah on their way to battle. In fact, situated at the center of the account, the report of that visit requires fifteen verses, almost half of the overall.

Other distinctives of Judges 18 in comparison to the generic standard are more subtle but no less significant. When the spies came to Micah's house in the hills of Ephraim, they "turned aside" because they "recognized the voice of the young Levite." Since the account gives no indication that the Levite and the Danites had ever been acquainted, the statement must refer to a quality of the Levite's voice, probably his accent. Significant dialectic variations between North and South have already played an important role in the book of Judges (12:6) in the context of inter-tribal rivalry, even outright conflict. The Danites' "recognition" of the Levite's accent, which motivated them to "turn aside" and interrogate the Levite regarding his reasons for living in Ephraim, hints that their deeper motivations may have been fueled by inter-tribal tensions and serves to warn that they may be contemplating mischief.

Equally suggestive, the diction of the Levite's oracle, which the Danites find encouraging, hints at a more ominous reality. The RSV renders the oracle, "Go in peace. The journey on which you go is under the eye of the LORD" (v. 6). The Hebrew reads, "your journey . . . is before YHWH (*nokah YHWH*)," a unique phrase in the Hebrew Bible. Similar phrases (i.e., "before the eyes of/the face of *someone*") do not connote affirmation, as the Danites seem to assume, but awareness or wary observation (see Prov 5:21; Jer 17:16; Lam 2:19; Ezek 14:3, 4, 7). Thus, the Levite's oracle might better be translated idiomatically, "YHWH has his eye on you."

Finally, contrary to the normal pattern of espionage and conquest stories in the Bible, a pattern that involves the complementary emphases on the weakness of the Israelites relative to their opponents and on Israel's reliance on YHWH for victory (cf. Num 13:32-33; 14:8-9), the Danite spies recommend Laish as a target for conquest largely because the Laishites seem poorly prepared to defend themselves. They do not represent a challenge to be overcome with God's help, but an easy target well within the capabilities of an army of 600. In fact, the text repeats characterizations of the Laishites as "trusting (*bth*)" (vv. 7, 10, 27, the RSV translates variously "in security" and "unsuspecting" in an effort to capture the connotation of naiveté). Their confidence in their safety was not well founded. Although the text suggests that the population was somehow related to the Sidonians (whether ethnically, politically, or commercially, although the latter may be the most obvious interpretation of the statement that they lived "in the Sidonian manner"), they apparently did not maintain strong ties to their Sidonian kinsfolk, allies, or trading partners, as the case may be, due to distance (v. 28). In short, despite the spies' formulaic reference to God in v. 10, the account of their victory over Laish fails to mention divine intervention or assistance and leaves the impression that, in the Danites' understanding, the victory was Dan's, not God's.

**The Danite Raids on Micah and Laish (18:11-26, 27-31).** In addition to the nuance provided by the generic characteristics of the account, its characterization of major figures emphasizes their negative aspects (Amit 1999, 7–8; cf. Davis, 158). Beginning with the observation that the Danites had not yet found "an inheritance among the tribes of Israel," the portrayal of the Danites underscores their desperate opportunism. It echoes the comment in Judges 1:34, contextualizes Dan's failures in relation to the generalized failure of tribes other than Judah (Judg 1:27-36), and recalls the rebuke delivered by the angelic messenger at Bochim (2:1-5; see "Growing Internal Disharmony" and "Weeping at Bochim" above). The pregnant question posed by the five original spies to their comrades-in-arms when they reach Micah's home vibrates with premeditation and calculation. "Do you know that in these houses there are . . . ? Decide what you will do" (v. 14). What options do they imply? Significantly, when they then "turn aside," the five spies go to the house of the Levite, apparently a separate structure in Micah's compound ("in these houses [plural]"), ominously leaving their 600 comrades "armed with weapons of war" standing at the gate with the Levite. He is effectively in custody. Apparently, the decision has been made. The Danites, on their way to steal a city, have decided to steal a sanctuary and its priest, too. The ironies multiply. The sanctuary in Dan depends for its existence on a double theft; with origins in Micah's theft, theft brought it to Dan. Furthermore, the account leaves no room for any interpretation other than that the Danites act with full awareness that they have stolen. As they leave Micah's compound, they place their families and goods at the front of the column

(v. 21), presumably to distance them from the approach of any counter-attacking force Micah may muster when he discovers the theft. When, just as they have anticipated, Micah and a posse of his neighbors overtake them, they compound their crime with threats of murder. Describing themselves as "desperate men (*'anashim marey nefesh*—"men bitter in spirit," v. 25)," they admit what the narrator implies and the careful reader will have already concluded.

The Levite fares no better. His interactions with Micah have already raised suspicions as to the ignobility of his motives. A young man searching for his fortune, he had no qualms about assuming the priesthood of a private sanctuary centered on idolatrous cultic objects produced with funds a son had once stolen from his mother! At first, he objects to the Danites' theft of Micah's cultic emblems, but when the Danites offer him a new sinecure with a much larger parish (and the implicit promise of greatly increased income), "his heart was glad." The narrator confirms the reader's suspicions that the Levite is as interested in his own fortunes as he is in fulfilling his priestly role. The surprise in store for readers regarding the fortune-seeking Levite awaits the end of the account, which, for the first time, mentions him by name (Jonathan) and lineage (the son of Gershom and grandson of Moses). This opportunist priest of a heterodox sanctuary was Moses' grandson! The ancient scribes found this information so shocking that, in an attempt to shield Moses' reputation, they inserted a so-called "suspended *nun*" (*nun* is the Hebrew letter "n") into Moses' name (Hebrew *mshh*), thereby converting it into the name of the heretical king, Manasseh (Hebrew *mnshh*). The original text, however, testifies to the willingness of the authors of Hebrew Scripture to report unpleasant truths about even Israel's heroes.

In a perverse dynamic of justice, the third figure in the story, Micah, becomes the victim of his own misguided aspirations. The opening scene of the account concludes with the statement of Micah's confidence that the fact that he has created a sanctuary and acquired a priest will ensure his standing before God (17:13). In his final appearance in the episode, however, Micah recognizes the overwhelming strength of the Danites and returns home without his prized cultic emblems or his priest (18:26). They have by no means secured him God's favor. In fact, both Micah (v. 24) and the narrator (vv. 27, 31) suggest an explanation for God's failure to intervene on Micah's behalf. The cultic objects are "[Micah's] gods which [he] made." By implication, of course, the Danites' shrine, stolen from Micah, made by Micah, and financed with tainted wealth, can hardly be expected to benefit them any more than it had benefitted Micah. Ominously, in fact, the narrator's description of the Danite sanctuary refers to the ultimate fate of the northern kingdom ("the captivity of the land")," a fate the Deuteronomistic History attributes in great part to the apostasy represented by the sanctuaries in Dan and Bethel.

## The Rape and Murder of the Levite's Concubine and Its Aftermath (Judg 19–21)

The book of Judges concludes with a lengthy account of a series of astonishing and disturbing events sparked by an episode involving yet another itinerant Levite, associated, like Micah's priest, with Bethlehem of Judah (cf. 17:7 and 19:1). In response to the outrageous rape and murder of this Levite's anonymous concubine, the united tribes of Israel take punitive action against the inhabitants of Gibeah, where the crime occurred, and, because it refused to identify and surrender the actual perpetrators, against the whole tribe of Benjamin. Furthermore, in their outrage, the eleven tribes swear not to intermarry with Benjamin. When military reprisals succeed in virtually annihilating the Benjamite population, their fellow Israelites recognize the danger that a whole tribe could be lost, a danger compounded by their rash oath against intermarriage. They devise a means to secure wives for the Benjamites without technically violating their oath while simultaneously punishing Jabesh-Gilead for its failure to participate in the action against Benjamin. Finding that "four hundred young virgins" of Jabesh-Gilead (21:11), the only inhabitants of the city spared, were not enough to supply the surviving Benjamites with wives, they devise yet another technique that will enable them to acquire wives for Benjamin without technically violating their oath. They instruct the Benjamites to kidnap young women from Shiloh during a festival and persuade the fathers of the young women not to resist the scheme, but to accept the *fait accompli*. Episodes in this comedy of horrors unfold in a grotesque downward arc that begins with marital strife and ends with captive brides, including along the way betrayal, rape, murder, and the near-eradication of an Israelite tribe. Event follows event as though no force could impede the momentum of violence and atrocity. The editorial refrain surrounding the section ("in those days there was no king in Israel," 19:1; 21:25) and the Israelites' comment concerning the unprecedented nature of the crime committed in Gibeah (19:30) aptly set the tone.

### The Levite's Concubine (Judg 19)

Perhaps the most obvious feature of the opening account in this unfolding sequence of mayhem involves its unmistakable similarity to the account of

Sodom and Gomorrah (Gen 19). Both stories involve travelers arriving in the evening with the intention of spending the night outdoors; an alien resident in the city who insists on extending hospitality to the visitors; the performance of the hallmarks of hospitality (footwashing and a shared meal); a gang of ruffians who surround the host's home, demanding that the host surrender his guests whom they intend to rape; and the host's objection and ultimate willingness to surrender a female in his household as a substitute. Similarities extend to a number of verbal parallels (*lyn*, "to lodge," Gen 19:2 || Judg 19:4, 6, 7, 9 twice, 10, 11, 13, 15 twice, 20; *swr*, "to turn aside," 19:2 || 19:11, 12, 15; "rising early and going one's way" 19:2 || 19:9; *htmhmh*, "to linger, tarry," 19:16 || 19:8; "wash feet," 19:2 || 19:20; "eat," 19:3 || 19:21; *b'rb*, "in the evening," 19:1 || 19:16; "house," 19:2, 3, 4, 11 || 19:18, 21-23; for a detailed analysis of the parallels, see Block, 326–27).

The self-evident similarities between the two accounts raise a number of questions. Scholars debate the nature of the genetic relationship between the two texts, arguing for the literary dependence of one account on the other. Some (for example, Block, 336) conclude that the intention of the Judges passage is to liken Gibeah (copy) to Sodom (model). Israel has descended to the level of Sodom and Gomorrah. Others (for example, Niditch 1982, 375–78, although she later [2008, 192] argues for the possibility that both accounts represent independent realizations of a "type scene" or stock plot), argue that the Genesis text depends on Judges.

Regardless of whether one text served as the model for the other, the high degree of similarity between them invites comparative interpretation and, especially in the context of the contemporary public debate concerning homosexuality, promises at first glance to yield insights into the Bible's potential to inform a responsible Christian sexual ethic. Specifically, Genesis 19 is often read as primarily a condemnation of homosexuality. Compared to Judges 19, however, Genesis 19 appears instead as a tale of disregard for standards of hospitality and of brutal violence, not as a blanket condemnation of homosexuality. In both texts, the gangs of ruffians who accost the visitors to their city seem motivated not by sexual desires but by suspicion of and animosity toward outsiders (cf. Gen 19:9). In the Judges text, the Levites' host acknowledges their intention to humiliate the outsider when he offers his daughter and the concubine to be "humbled" (*'nh*, v. 24; cf. 20:5). In the context of ancient Israel's shame and honor culture, the term he uses occurs elsewhere in relation to sexual conduct to denote not the act of rape but the condition of shame brought upon the victim as the consequence of her change in social status (cf. esp. Gen 34:2; Deut 21:14; 22:24, 29; Ezek 22:10, 11; Lam 5:11). From a sociological perspective, such acts of calculated debasement continue to be evidenced in the behaviors of Latin American death squads, in the prison rape phenomenon, and even in the shameful actions of members of the United States military at the Abu Ghraib facility in Iraq. The perpetrators' objectives in such cases do not involve (homo-) sexual gratification, but the assertion of dominance over their debased victims. Significantly, the "base fellows" in Judges 19 were evidently determined to abuse someone; in the end, they proved indifferent regarding the gender of the victim.

This reading of Genesis 19 and Judges 19 as tales of sexual violence, not as condemnations of homosexuality *per se*, finds support in the reactions of the hosts in both stories and in references to the Sodom and Gomorrah incident elsewhere in the Bible. Most often, biblical authors cite the fates of these two cities as an example of destruction (Isa 1:9; 13:19; Jer 49:18; 50:40; Lam 4:6; Amos 4:11; Zeph 2:9; Matt 10:15; 11:24; etc.). Biblical authors describe the sin committed in Sodom and Gomorrah in terms of arrogance (Isa 3:9), specifically arrogant mistreatment of the needy (Ezek 16:49), or in comparison to the behavior of the angelic "sons of God" who, as reported in Genesis 6:1-4, crossed the boundary between human and divine in their pursuit of the "daughters of men" (see 2 Pet 2:4, 6; Jude 6-7). Apparently, in the widely attested view of biblical authors, the crimes committed in Sodom and Gomorrah and in Gibeah consisted in acts of violence and violations of the standards of hospitality, not in the sexual orientation of the perpetrators. The central concern for Lot ("only do nothing to these men, since they have come under the shelter of my roof," Gen 19:8) and the Levite's anonymous host ("no, my brothers, please do not commit this wrong, since this man has come into my house," Judg 19:23) was the expectation that a host extend protection to his guests.

As a prelude to a more detailed examination of the account in Judges 19, then, it is important to set aside any expectation that this text will contribute to an understanding of the biblical stance on sexual orientation. Instead, as Stone (1995b, 89) observes, this story deals with a nexus of "gender, power, homosexuality and hospitality" that must be analyzed as a whole. Surprisingly, such an examination reveals an account rich in subtlety and suggestion, an account that resists a simplistic moral assessment. The account of the abhorrent rape and murder of the anonymous concubine hints throughout that the reader should also look beyond the obvious crime and the obvious criminals to an even more profound and pervasive indecency.

**A Troubled and Troubling Marriage (19:1-11).** The horrific events narrated in Judges 19 hinge on the troubled and troubling dynamics of the relationship between the Levite and his *pilegesh*. As in the earlier instances of *pilegesh* marriages (Gideon's wife and Abimelech's mother and at least one of Samson's relationships), features of the Levite's marriage hint that the term *pilegesh* may describe a unique institution, "patrilocal" or "visiting" marriage in which the wife continues to reside in her father's household (see Gideon, "Conclusion" above). The woman's return to her father's household, for example, would be consistent with such an institution. Of course, as indicated above, a precise description of *pilegesh* marriage suffers from a lack of data.

In fact, the textual tradition of v. 2, which evidences confusion concerning the woman's return to her father, suggests that the institution had been largely forgotten as early as the period of the translation of the LXX. The Hebrew MT reads *wattizneh 'alayw pilegsho*, "and his concubine played the harlot against him." The Greek versions offer two variants: LXX A reads "and his concubine became angry with him," while LXX B reads simply "and she departed from him," possibly representing a confusion of *poreuo*, "to go," for *porneuo*, "to commit sexual immorality." Although the Hebrew reading is more likely the original, it presents a number of difficulties on its own. Grammatically, the expression involves a preposition, translated "against" above, that occurs in conjunction with the verb only here and in Ezekiel 16:15 and 16, where, however, it has the meanings "because of" (16:15) and "on" (16:16). More significantly, the structure of Judges 19:2 parallels the phrase with the statement concerning the woman's return to her father so that the whole clause could be translated "and his concubine played the harlot against him, that is, she went from him to her father's household." Thus, the term *znh*, "to play the harlot," may function hyperbolically, as it were, characterizing the woman's departure itself as a kind of infidelity. Zakovitch (39; cf. Exum 1993, 178) speculates that, in some cases, women who have chosen to leave their husbands' homes, and who would therefore be without resources, may have found it necessary to resort to prostitution. This understanding comports well with the woman's behavior, her father's willingness to receive her (i.e., so that destitution did not push her into prostitution), and the Levite's decision to pursue her, "to speak to her heart and bring her back" (v. 3). Indeed, Bohmbach (90) points out that an adulterous woman would not likely have returned to her father's household, bringing shame on him and risking the penalty for adultery, and an ancient Near Eastern father would certainly not have welcomed her home. In addition to Bohmbach's observations, the interpretation of the woman's behavior not as sexual immorality but as "infidelity" to her husband's household finds support in the unexpected comment in the Hebrew text of v. 3 that the *pilegesh* brought the Levite "into her father's house" (LXX has "when *he* reached her father's house"), in the father's joyful reception of the Levite (v. 3), in his keen interest in delaying the Levite's departure (vv. 4-9), and in the text's silence regarding the woman during the Levite's five-day stay with his father-in-law. The centrality of the woman's father and his household is unmistakable:

> . . . after four months the Levite travelled to his father-in-law to "speak to his wife's heart" and to bring her back. But when he arrived at her father's house he did not speak to his wife at all. The conversations were between the Levite and his father-in-law, as was also the eating and drinking together that went on for four full days. The concubine was excluded from all this. (Eynikel, 105; cf. Bohmbach, 93–94)

Bal (1999, 327) pursues a similar line of reasoning even further, theorizing that the term *pilegesh* denotes a woman originally from a patrilocal culture who marries into a virilocal culture, that is, one in which a woman lives in her husband's household. Bal (332) interprets material in Judges concerning marriage customs as evidence of a transition in forms of patriarchy during Israel's early history. In this reading, the woman's "unfaithfulness" would consist of her vacillation between the two systems, her fluid loyalty to her husband versus to her father. Given the theoretical nature of Bal's reconstruction and the unfortunate dearth of documentary evidence, her reading, while attractive, remains only plausible (see further, Ng, 205).

Nonetheless, an interesting pattern in the distribution of relationship terms strengthens the impression that the character of the Levite's marriage was linked somehow to location. The text concentrates references to the woman as the Levite's *pilegesh* at the beginning of the story, where it relates her departure from the Levite's household (vv. 1, 2); at the end of the section that describes the Levite's stay in Bethlehem of Judah, where it reports that the Levite took his *pilegesh* and departed (vv. 9, 10); and in the account of their experiences in Gibeah (vv. 24, 25, 27, 29). Notably, the account of events in Bethlehem of Judah refers to the woman only indirectly through her father, who is consistently identified as the Levite's "father-in-law, the girl's father" (*hotno 'abiy hannarah*, vv. 4, 5, 9; "father-in-law" alone in v. 7; "the girl's father" alone in v. 8). In other words, in Ephraim the woman was the Levite's *pilegesh* and he was her husband, but in Bethlehem of Judah she was her father's daughter and the Levite was his son-in-law. In his household, her father occupied the central and dominant position in the nexus of relationships, a circumstance that may explain his joyful reaction when his daughter "brought [her husband] into her father's household." The Levite's entry into his father-in-law's household implies incorporation into its power structure in secondary status. Remarkably, the text refers to the Levite as the woman's husband only just before he enters her father's household (v. 3). After her ordeal in Gibeah, it identifies him as the woman's "master/lord" (*'adoneyha*, vv. 26, 27), hinting at another transformation in their relationship not occasioned by a change of location, but manifesting the Levite's willingness to treat his wife as property.

**Hospitality and the Criminally Inhospitable (19:12-21).** The text takes pains to specify the location of events and the tribal affiliations of the participants. The Levite made his home in the hills of *Ephraim* (vv. 1, 18). Similarly, his anonymous host, an alien resident in Gibeah, was also originally from the Ephraimite hills (v. 16). The Levite's concubine was from *Bethlehem* in *Judah* (vv. 1, 2, 18). Their journey back to Ephraim took them by the city of the *Jebusites*, which, as the text reminds its readers, will one day be David's capital city, *Jerusalem* (v. 11). The horrific rape and murder of the Levite's concubine takes place in Gibeah in *Benjamin* (vv. 12, 13, 14, 15, 16) and its perpetrators are *Benjamites* (v. 16). The constellation of place and group names—Bethlehem, the ancestral city of David; Gibeah in Benjamin (distinct from cities by the same name located in Judah [Josh 15:57] and Ephraim [Josh 24:33]), the ancestral city of Saul, which was sometimes even called "the Gibeah of Saul" (1 Sam 11:4; 15:34, Isa 10:29); Jerusalem, David's capital—suggests to many commentators that, just as the story of the founding of the sanctuary in Dan functions as polemic against Jeroboam's royal sanctuaries in Dan and Bethel, this account of the atrocity committed by the Benjamites of Gibeah alludes to relations between Saul and David, depicting Saul's ancestors as rapists and murderers (see Moore, 407).

Although it is plausible, perhaps even likely, that the editors of the book of Judges meant to draw such a comparison, the text cannot be reduced to this polemical function since its many details cannot be mapped seamlessly onto the dynamics of the Saul-David relationship. Most prominently, the central section of Judges 19, which contains the significant parallels to Genesis 19 discussed above, explicitly introduces the theme of hospitality that will become central as the story progresses. Because his father-in-law successfully delayed his departure until late into the fifth day of his stay in Bethlehem of Judah, the Levite was able to travel only as far as Jebusite

Jerusalem as evening approached. In response to his servant's suggestion that they spend the night in Jebus/Jerusalem, the servant's sole act in the story, the Levite expresses his unwillingness to gamble on the reception they might receive from these "foreigners, not of the sons of Israel" (v. 12). The harsh reception he fears contrasts with the insistent, even manipulative, hospitality his father-in-law has already shown him. Like many other biblical characters who fear mistreatment at the hands of non-Israelite hosts, often without reason (cf. Abraham's sojourns in Egypt and Gerar; Gen 12:10-20 and 20:1-18, respectively), the Levite's apprehensions, which imply the reliability of Israelite hospitality, ultimately prove unfounded.

In fact, pressing on to Gibeah, approximately eighteen miles from Bethlehem, the Levite found the inhabitants singularly inhospitable (v. 15). The anonymous old man confirms and amplifies the impressions that arise from the fact that initially no one in Gibeah offered lodging to the travelers. The Levite, who apparently interprets the situation solely in terms of hospitality customs and the disgrace associated with shirking the responsibility, seems to think that the locals see hosting him as a potential inconvenience. He quickly asserts to the old man that, although hosting his company of concubine, servant, and pack animals could prove a substantial responsibility, he has brought along provision enough not to constitute an imposition (v. 19). Since the old man does not specify grounds, his insistence that the Levite abandon plans to overnight in the city square can be taken on first reading as confirmation of his embarrassment or shame that the locals have so neglected the commonly accepted standards of hospitality. He can and will gladly meet all their needs, he assures the Levite, but the Levite and his companions must not overnight in the square. In fact, as v. 21 reports succinctly, the old man models the behavior of the ideal host, not only providing lodging but also tending to the livestock, allowing his guests to bathe their feet, and offering food and drink. Indeed, their dinner and drink was apparently of such quality and quantity that the text can describe the meal as an occasion of merrymaking (v. 22).

**"Worthless Fellows," Abomination, and Ambiguity (19:22-30).** The events reported in 19:22-30 cast a new light on the anonymous host's insistence that the Levite and his company accept his hospitality. As an alien resident in Gibeah, he would have been familiar with the character of the native population. Apparently, he recognized their failure to extend hospitality not as an affront to the requirements of civility but as a symptom of a much more threatening criminality. It would have been far more than a disgrace for the Levite to camp overnight in the city square; it would have been dangerous. In the middle of dinner, a group of locals, whom the narrator identifies from the outset as criminals ("base fellows," *'anshey beney-beliya'al*, lit., "men who were sons of worthlessness," v. 22) burst onto the scene. As events unfold, the narrator's harsh characterization of these Gibeans proves almost understated. With no apparent provocation, they demand custody of the visitor, boldly stating how they intend to treat him. The absence of any explicit information concerning the motives of this crowd of ruffians invites attention to subtleties. These clues suggest that their sole motivation was a determination to humiliate an outsider, or perhaps to humiliate both the Levite and his host (see Eynikel, 109). The anonymous host objects strenuously that such an act would be a gross breech of hospitality. Should he deliver his guest to them, he would be equally guilty of the crime. "But the men would not listen to him" (v. 25); instead, they savagely raped the Levite's concubine—who was shoved out the door to them as a substitute for the Levite—until dawn.

Clearly, the narrator's initial characterization of the Gibeans was accurate. If, however, these "worthless" men are the villains in the story, who is the hero? At the critical moment, in an effort to spare the Levite, the anonymous host, who seemed a likely candidate for the hero role earlier in the story, offers a bargain that modern readers will find cowardly and downright repugnant. Why would the host prefer to surrender his own daughter and presume to offer his guest's concubine to avoid surrendering the Levite? Common interpretations of his motivation suggest, alternatively, in essence, that the host acted in accordance with a presumed Israelite cultural morality that viewed heterosexual rape as a lesser evil than homosexual rape or that his willingness to sacrifice women in his household testifies to the distorted values of Israelite patriarchy. Neither interpretation salvages the host's honor. The notion that, in his view, he had at least prevented the ruffians from committing homosexual rape paints him as a cynic. In the alternative, it is equally difficult to imagine that the Israelite patriarchy in any form would condone, let alone promote, such attitudes toward one's own daughter. Rather than explain the host's behavior as a choice between the lesser of two evils or blame it on a warped values system, a third alternative posits that the narrator/editor of this account and its ancient readers may well have reacted to the host's behavior much as moderns do. His actions do not reveal a moral flaw in Israelite patriarchy—it is susceptible to ample criticism on other grounds—so much as they manifest his personal callousness and cowardice.

Significantly, the account of the incident the Levite later gives to the assembled tribes of Israel (20:4-7) omits references both to the danger of homosexual rape that he faced and to the fact that his host offered the women as substitutes. Instead, he reports only, "*me*, they intended to kill and *my concubine*, they raped; she is dead" (20:5; the translation reflects the unusual emphatic word order of the Hebrew). His omissions confirm the hypothesis that he understood the threat primarily in terms of violence, not sexuality, and forestall any question concerning his or his host's complicity in the death of his concubine. In fact, although the host offered the "worthless men" of Gibeah both his own virgin daughter and the Levite's concubine, the text specifies that, when the mob refused to be dissuaded from their intentions, the Levite himself "grabbed (*wayihazeq*) his concubine and shoved her out to them" (v. 25).

The narrator continues with a skillful depiction of the Levite's repulsive behaviors, subtly alluding to the characterization of the troubled state of the relationship that opens the story. The account does not dwell on the events of the night (v. 25) but slows the pace of its report of the following morning to observe disturbing details. When the gang has finished with her, the woman makes her way to the door of the house where her "master" had spent the night indoors, safe and apparently untroubled (v. 26). In stark disharmony with the circumstances, he rises matter-of-factly that morning and sets out to continue his journey—not to search for her or to seek justice from city elders but simply to escape and go about his business in safety. When he opens the door, he finds his *pilegesh* "fallen (*nofelet*) in the doorway of the house, with her hand on the threshold" as though she were reaching for the door or had been knocking on it (v. 27). She spends her strength at the threshold of safety. Crassly, rather than rushing to comfort her, to tend to her injuries, or even to inquire about her welfare, he issues a succinct command: "Get up! Let's go!" (v. 28).

She does not respond. Oddly, the text does not state whether she was already dead or merely unconscious, leaving the reader to speculate. The text does not report that the Levite made any effort whatsoever to determine her condition. In any case, the Levite's subsequent actions are inconsistent with those of a loving husband. He loads his unresponsive concubine on one of the asses as though she were cargo and sets out for home. If she were still alive, the journey would have surely contributed to her death, deepening the Levite's complicity in her murder. Even on the assumption that she was already dead, the Levite's behavior is offensive. As the text reports the incident, he remains emotionless. Indeed, when he returns home, he "grabs (*wayahazeq*)" her again (v. 29), now not to shove her out the door (v. 25) but to butcher her body.

The victim of this crime is obvious. The identity of the guilty parties, of the "worthless fellows," on the other hand, is open to discussion. As the tale transitions into the account of the corporate revenge taken by the united tribes of Israel against Benjamin, it reports the ironic response of all who received one of the twelve pieces of the concubine's body. "Nothing like this" had ever happened in Israel since its departure from Egypt (v. 30). At this point, before the Levite explains events to the assembly, the comment can only refer to the dismembered body itself (see Keefe, 82–83). The Israelite assembly cannot know what the reader knows, namely, that the woman whose body has been butchered by her husband had already been the object of a power struggle between him and her father, that her husband had "grabbed" her like chattel and, in cowardly and craven indifference to her welfare, delivered her into the hands of murderers, that "this" dismemberment was but the final injury of many done to this anonymous woman from Bethlehem in Judah. No wonder the Levite omits certain details from his report to the assembly. It comes as no surprise that the Levite's duplicity leads Lasine (48) to call him "an irresponsible liar."

## Consequences: Civil War (20:1-48)

No doubt as the Levite had intended, the dispersal of his dismembered concubine's corpse throughout the tribes of Israel prompted a chain of reactions that progresses grimly and grotesquely toward ironic outcomes. An entire Israelite tribe faces near extinction, and overblown retribution for the rape and murder of the concubine culminates in the perverse kidnapping of hundreds of young women from Jabesh-Gilead and Shiloh. Grotesquely, this version of retributive justice reproduces the crime it seeks to punish. The lengthy and somewhat complicated account of the virtual civil war between Benjamin and the other tribes of Israel, the events that connect the crime and its incongruous by-product, details without comment the duplicitous (the Levite), inexplicable (Benjamin), and precipitous (Israel) actions of the participants. The warfare itself takes place over the course of three days of battle in which, paradoxically, Benjamin first prevails over the assembled forces of Israel. In each case, the text reports that the forces of Israel muster, seek divine guidance, take up position for battle, and attack. The account of each day's battle concludes with an assessment of the outcome. Some scholars have suggested, not implausibly, that the convoluted account results from the compilation of variant source materials (cf. Moore, 407–408, 421–22; Burney, 447; Soggin, 293–94; Hentschel, 36–38; contra Revell; Satterthwaite 1992). As it stands in the final form of the text, however, the repetition serves to delay Benjamin's ultimate defeat and ominously introduces a mood of uncertainty in Israel (cf. Niditch 2008, 204): Benjamin's repeated successes raise doubts in Israel concerning the course of action undertaken. The Israelites would have no doubt expected, if their cause were just, to prevail over Benjamin easily and quickly. Although the narrator remains silent on the issue, readers know, of course, that, in fact, the Levite's complicity in the death of his concubine taints Israel's cause. Israel is now also complicit. In the end, the contagion of violence spreads throughout Israel, implicating virtually the whole nation as "worthless fellows."

**Gathering at Mizpah (20:1-10).** To their credit, the Israelites, shocked to receive such missives, quickly assembled at Mizpah to inquire as to the meaning of this outrage. Presumably, the Levite will have engaged messengers to transport his concubine's corpse to the various tribes of Israel. The text does not indicate that he instructed them to convey a verbal message to accompany the physical evidence of the crime, calling, perhaps, for a convocation at Mizpah. In fact, contrary to the impression that may arise from English translations, the admonition that opens the convocation ("Tell how this evil has happened!" v. 3), which employs a plural verb (*dabberu*), does not address the Levite. It has the force of an impersonal usage ("*someone* speak up"). Apparently, then, the Levite had not sent a verbal communication along with the dissected corpse—at least not one that identified the sender or included any explanation of the meaning of its grotesque physical message, and probably not even one convening an assembly in Mizpah. Evidently, he had counted on the shocking nature of his communication to excite outrage and ensure Israel's response. Further, Mizpah may have been simply assumed as the logical location for such a gathering. It often served as the location for similar convocations of Israel (Judg 10:17; 11:11; 1 Sam 10:17); there, Jacob and Laban made their parting covenant (Gen 31:49); it was associated with Samuel and his judgeship (1 Sam 7); later it functioned as the seat of Gedaliah's temporary governorship (2 Kgs 25:23; Jer 43–41); and it was remembered even later as having once been a cultic site (1 Macc 3:46). Niditch (2008, 202) calls attention to the fact that the people initially act in accordance with the prescription found in Deuteronomy 13:12-18 concerning how to deal with the crimes of "worthless fellows" (*'anshey beney-beliya'al*, Deut 13:14; Judg 19:22; 20:13). Deuteronomy calls, first, for a diligent and thorough investigation.

Indications that, before the Levite offers his statement at Mizpah, the gathered Israelites have no detailed information concerning the significance of the grotesque communication they have received add weight to the suggestion offered above that, in actuality, the Levite was complicit in the death of his concubine. Ironically, given the state of their knowledge at the time, the Israelites' statement concerning "this evil" can only refer to the dismembered body, itself an abomination. In response to their call for someone to explain, the Levite steps forward to offer an account that conveniently omits details concerning his own actions. Instead, he justifies the desecration of his concubine's body with the poignant clause "for they have committed immorality (*zimmah*) and wantonness (*nebalah*)." The Levite employs first a term that can refer to immoral behavior generally (e.g., Ps 26:10; Prov 10:23; Isa 32:7), but most often has sexual connotations (Lev 18:17; 19:29; 20:14; Job 31:11; Jer 13:27; Ezek 16:27, 43, 58; 22:9, 11; 23:21, 27, 29; etc.; Hos 6:9); appropriately, the Levite's vocabulary includes a term favored in priestly strands of material in the Hebrew Bible. The second of the paired terms, *nebalah*, is a near homonym to *nebelah*, a common word for "corpse" in contexts dealing with ritual purity (cf. Lev 5:2; 7:24; 11:8, etc; Deut 21:23), another paradoxical hint that the immediate abomination was the desecration of the woman's corpse.

The Levite's rhetoric not only subtly diverts attention away from his complicity in the death of his concubine but also pointedly shifts responsibility for avenging her death and punishing the criminals onto the people. The conclusion to his speech involves a prepositional phrase that is difficult to translate. Literally, the Hebrew of v. 7 reads, "Now, all of you sons of Israel, give yourselves (*lakem*) a word (*dabar*) and counsel here." Many English translations render the prepositional phrase as a possessive (e.g., "give your advice and counsel here," RSV), although Hebrew has a ready mechanism for denoting such possessive relations. The prepositional phrase seems, rather, to function more like the redundant indirect object in familiar, especially southern American, English ("I am going to get myself a dog"). Indeed, both of the major Greek manuscript traditions translate the phrase with a reflexive pronoun (*heautois*). In other words, contrary to the impression left by translations such as RSV, the Levite does not ask the assembly to give its advice (presumably to him), but to take counsel among themselves, to decide on a course of action. Furthermore, the last word he speaks (*halom*, "here") implies a demand for urgent action (i.e., "here and *now!*").

The Israelite assembly accepts the challenge. "[Arising] as one man" (cf. v. 1), they vow not to return to their homes until they make Gibeah pay for the crime committed there. This emphasis on Israelite unity continues an overarching theme announced earlier in the account, beginning with the observation that "all of Israel . . . from Dan to Beersheba" responded to the Levite's grotesque summons. The narrator specifies that even the Gileadites, inhabitants of the region east of the Jordan who, because of their remote location, often constituted a threat to Israelite unity (see "Conflict with Ephraim" above), came to Mizpah. This observation incidentally foreshadows the marked absence of representatives from Jabesh in Gilead. Similarly, the narrator explicitly notes that the entire tribe of Benjamin was aware of the assembly but sent no representatives, an indication that Benjamin has already adopted an uncooperative stance toward the proceedings, foreshadowing their later unwillingness to agree to the terms offered by the unified tribes.

Even the Israelites' methodical planning for conflict with the inhabitants of Gibeah, planning that assumes Gibeah's resistance, includes a component designed to protect Israelite unity and perhaps also to involve the deity in their endeavor. By means of a lottery, seen in ancient Israel not as a matter of chance but of divine direction, ten percent of the men from each of the assembled tribes (4,000) will be chosen for special duty. They are "to get provisions for the people," that is, to serve as the quartermaster corps handling the logistics for provisioning the larger militia (400,000; v. 2). The phrasing of the continuation of v. 10 involves an awkward string of infinitives that almost defies translation (lit., "to do, to come them, to Gibeah according to all the wantonness that it did in Israel"). The second of these infinitive phrases (*lebo'am*) presents the greatest difficulty. Without it, the clause can be translated "to get provisions for the people, in order to do Gibeah according . . . ." The problem phrase consists of a prefixed prepositional particle (*le-*, usually "to" or "for"), the infinitive proper (*bo'*, "to come" or "to go"), and a third person pronominal suffix (*-am*, "them"). Since the pronominal suffix is masculine plural and cannot refer to "provisions," which is a feminine singular noun in Hebrew, it must refer to the collective masculine noun "people." The fact that, in the qal (or simple) tense, *bo'* denotes "to come" or "to go" and not "to bring" further supports this understanding. Thus, the phrase can be understood as an example of the infinitive with an object functioning as the logical (but not grammatical) subject of the infinitive, a common phenomenon in Hebrew, and rendered "their coming" or better simply "they come." The chief difficulty lies with the Hebrew preposition, which most commonly expresses direction or purpose, meanings that do not suit the context. Although Hebrew usually employs one of two other prepositions (*beth* and *kaph*) to express time in such phrases, most translations render the preposition in this case as a temporal, "when they come," a solution almost dictated by the elimination of viable options.

This comment concerning a detail of the Israelites' preparations for confronting Gibeah stands out in the Hebrew Bible as the only such record of an Israelite concern for the logistical aspect of a military campaign (cf., however, the commentary on 7:8 regarding the rare term "provisions"). Taken together, the apparent triviality of this logistical concern in relation to the weighty matter at hand and the tendency of Hebrew narrative to avoid providing any but the most essential information suggest that the comment conveys more information than might be obvious at first glance. Evidently, the people had not come to the assembly fully prepared to engage in a military action, a circumstance that gives additional support to the notion that the Levite's outrageous communiqué had consisted only of the physical evidence of a crime. The assembly learned the details only from the Levite's report at Mizpah. Furthermore, the concern for provisioning the fighting force now that the assembly has learned what has transpired and has decided to punish the wrongdoers suggests that they anticipate a major conflict. That is, they already anticipate that Benjamin, who had sent no representatives to the assembly, will refuse to hand over the perpetrators of the atrocity. Seen from these perspectives, the apparently offhand observation concerning logistical preparations strengthens the force of several undercurrents running throughout the overall narrative: the lottery emphasizes their concern for unity and their interest in the divine imprimatur; their lack of preparation confirms that initially their sole source of information was the dismembered corpse; and their decision to dedicate ten percent (40,000) of those assembled to provisioning the full fighting force of 360,000 men sounds a note of foreboding. They expect Benjamite resistance and are willing to see the conflict escalate into full-fledged warfare.

**Benjamin Refuses Terms (20:11-13).** Quite logically, the united Israelite forces first offer Benjamin the opportunity to surrender the guilty parties (the *beney beliyya'al* from Gibeah) to face justice (v. 13a). Quite illogically, Benjamin refuses (v. 13b), setting the stage for all-out conflict. The narrator does not indicate the reasoning or motivation of the Benjamites, and any hypothesis would be mere speculation. The narrator's interests lie rather in continuing the theme of unity that figured so prominently in vv. 1-12. "All the men of Israel" gather to confront Gibeah, "a company acting as one man" (v. 11). The eleven tribes were resolute in their determination to eradicate evil from their midst. Mirroring this unity, they send messengers throughout Benjamin with their offer of a solution to the situation. In response, Benjamin demonstrates a perverse unity of its own. The narrator's comment summarizes the tension between Benjamite unity (with Gibeah) and Benjamin's place in a united Israel: "the Benjamites would not heed the voice of their brothers, the people of Israel." Although the narrator gives no clue as to Benjamin's motives, guilt spreads as each successive party implicates itself in the crime of the ruffians from Gibeah. Just as the anonymous host and the Levite were complicit in the concubine's death before the fact, the Benjamites become accomplices after the fact, harboring murderers in their midst. Guilt spreads like a contagion.

**Three Days of Battle (20:14-48).** The lengthiest section of the tale of the punishment of Benjamin for the crimes of Gibeah reports the conduct and outcomes of the armed conflict between the united forces of Israel against one of its smallest, most vulnerable tribes. According to the canonical form of the text, the campaign consisted of three distinct battles fought on successive days. Although the accounts of these three battles vary with regard to the level of detail reported, with the account of the third and decisive battle understandably receiving the greatest attention, the sequence of events in all three cases follows a common pattern (see Niditch 2008, 203). The opposing forces gather (vv. 14-17, 22, 26), and Israel makes inquiry to God concerning some aspect of the conduct of its impending attack on Benjamin (vv. 18, 23, 26-28). Receiving affirmative responses from the deity (vv. 18, 23, 28), the Israelite forces make final preparations for battle (vv. 19-20, 24, 29-30) and then engage the Benjamites (vv. 21, 25, 31-45). The account of each day's fighting concludes with a report of the outcome, including fatality statistics (vv. 21, 25, 46-47). As already noted (see "Consequences: Civil War" above), the repetitive structure of the extended account raises the issue of whether the final form of the text represents a composite of several originally independent traditions. An investigation of this possibility lies outside the scope of this commentary (see Satterthwaite 1993, 80–81), although it may be significant that the accounts of the first two days of battle devote much greater attention to the inquiries put to God and to fatality statistics than to the details of the battle itself.

Besides the question of the possibility of multiple sources underlying the current text, the effect of the intricate and repetitive character of 20:14-48 is to raise a number of theological and ethical questions. According to the final form of the text, Israel achieves its objective only after days of costly warfare. If Israel's cause were just and since its forces vastly outnumbered the Benjamites, what accounts for its initial lack of success and for the great cost in human lives paid for Israel's ultimate victory? Certainly, the Israelites seem to have been puzzled, as evidenced by their multiple, and apparently successful, attempts to obtain the divine imprimatur (cf. Niditch 2008, 204). Given Israel's theology of warfare, they certainly had reason to doubt that God supported their endeavor. In contrast, modern readers may rightly doubt the morality of the form of justice Israel practiced in this case. The narrator's only interpretive comments, however, remain the framing refrain concerning the absence of a king and the virtual anarchy that resulted "in those days" (19:1; 21:25).

*The First Two Days of Battle: Benjamin Routs the Israelite Army (20:14-25).*
The accounts of the first two days of battle merely state the fact that a battle occurred, placing much greater emphasis on the numbers of combatants and fatalities and on the divine oracles received in each case. According to v. 2, a total of 400,000 armed men from throughout Israel assembled at Mizpah, ten percent of whom were assigned responsibility for logistics, leaving 360,000 to array against Benjamin's force of 26,700, including 700 "left-handed" "sons of the right hand" (on the implicit pun, see the commentary on Judg 3:15 in "Ehud" above) from Gibeah who were particularly skilled with the slingshot. By the end of the first day of battle, Benjamin's army had slain 22,000 of the Israelites (v. 21), and by the second, 18,000 (v. 25), for a total of 40,000 or ten percent of the overall force. By omitting any reference to Benjamite casualties, the text gives the impression that Benjamin's forces did not sustain significant losses. After two days of battle, Israel's effort to avenge the horrendous murder of one Judean woman has resulted not in victory over Benjamin but in the deaths of 40,000 of their own militia.

This apparent defeat obviously contrasts, even conflicts, with the assumption that YHWH supports the Israelites' effort to obtain justice for the anonymous murder victim. After all, they had gathered in Mizpah, a sometime holy site associated with justice, and had vowed to punish the wrongdoers. Benjamin had refused their reasonable offer to resolve the situation, thereby becoming accomplices to the crime. Now, the Israelites have even sought YHWH's council and affirmation. The form of their inquiries (vv. 18 and 23) suggests that they employed the common technique of seeking to discern the divine will through lots, perhaps the *urim* and *thummim* (cf. Exod 28:30; Lev 8:8; Num 27:21; Deut 33:8; etc.). In such cases, the inquirer phrased a question designed to elicit a yes-no response or to arrive at an answer by the process of binary elimination (cf. Josh 7; 1 Sam 14:41). They have already determined to do so without consulting YHWH and thus seem to have assumed YHWH's approval of their decision, so the Israelite's first inquiry focuses not on whether to move against Benjamin but on which tribe should lead the attack. Both the inquiry and God's response echo the opening of the book of Judges (1:1), recalling the heightened status of the tribe of Judah in the initial portions of the book. Perhaps significantly, God's response does not include an assurance of success. Similarly, the second question Israel puts to God, which asks the more important question as to whether they should, in fact, engage Benjamin in a second day of battle, does not ask whether their campaign against Benjamin aligns with God's will. Again, God's response, which can be read either as an expression of assent ("Go ahead, if you insist") or of approval, does not offer an assurance of success. As Eversmann (29) has noted, "God's extended period of obscure behavior before God ultimately becomes involved in the situation irritates readers and raises the question as to whether Israel's actions were truly proper" (trans. mine).

Joshua 7 records another instance in which Israel assumed YHWH's support for a military campaign only to suffer initial defeat. On that occasion, Joshua complained to YHWH only to learn that Israel had sinned with regard to objects under the ban of holy war. Until Joshua identified and punished the guilty party, YHWH would refuse to fight on Israel's side (Josh 7:7-13). Apparently, the Israelites assembled to fight against Benjamin suspected that their two days of losses indicated that they faced a similar situation. At Bethel, the sanctuary that housed the ark of the covenant at the time (v. 27), they "wept, sat before YHWH until evening, and offered burnt and peace offerings before YHWH" (v. 26) before making their third inquiry. Their behaviors, consistent with mourning, penitence, and sacrifice for sin, represent an effort to appease the deity for some potential unknown offense.

The content of this third, much more specific inquiry also suggests that they may have reconsidered their assumption of divine support for their cause and may have even developed a hypothesis concerning the reason for YHWH's apparent displeasure. It acknowledges that the enemy consists of "our brothers" and states the option of ending the conflict. Do they suspect that YHWH disapproves of intra-Israelite warfare? YHWH's response ignores the implication concerning the internecine character of Israel's campaign and finally supplements the permission to conduct another attack on Benjamin with the assurance of success ("for tomorrow I will give him [i.e., Benjamin] into your hand," v. 28). Although neither YHWH nor the narrator/editor addresses the problem of a house divided, the issue once raised, even if subtly, moves to the center of attention as the story unfolds. An attentive reader may wonder whether the account means to suggest that YHWH lent only qualified support to the Israelite campaign against Benjamin. By the end of the account, the Israelites themselves regret their zeal.

*The Third Day of Battle: Ambush (20:26-48).* Events on the third and decisive day of battle receive the greatest attention. Assured of success in their third inquiry of YHWH, the Israelites engage Benjaminite forces yet a third time, employing the same tactics as on the two previous days of battle (*kepa'am bepa'am*, "as at other times," 20:30 RSV) and, at first, obtaining similar negative results (*kepa'am bepa'am*, "as at other times," 20:31 RSV). On this third day of battle, however, the Israelite force quickly adapts its strategy, luring the Benjaminites away from Gibeah in pursuit of a portion of the Israelite army in feigned retreat. Simultaneously, two other segments of the Isrealite force array themselves in ambush along the retreat route at Baaltamar, one somewhere west of Gibeah (apart from Geba and Gibeah, none of the place names in this section of the account have been identified with any degree of certainty), and the other around Gibeah, the Israelite objective. Ultimately, the pursuing Benjaminite forces fall into the trap and are decimated, but initially the first ambush unit continues to "give Benjamin space" (*wayyitnu 'ish-yisra'el maqom lebinyamin*, v. 36), luring them even further away from Gibeah so that the second ambush could be sprung on Gibeah itself. A column of smoke arising from Gibeah signals the retreating Israelites to turn against the pursuing Benjaminites, who, recognizing their situation, flee the battlefield toward Nohan east of Gibeah, toward the rock of Rimmon, and to Gidom. The Israelites show no mercy, pursuing and slaughtering the Benjaminites.

In fact, as a tally of casualty figures given in the account indicates, this civil war cost both sides dearly. According to vv. 21, 25 and 31, Israelite losses exceeded 40,000. According to v. 35, Benjamin lost 25,000 men in the first ambush and, according to v. 45, an additional 5,000 in the Israelite "mop-up" operations. The account does not report the numbers of casualties inflicted when, not satisfied with merely defeating the Benjaminite army, the Israelites rampaged throughout Benjaminite territory, slaughtering "men and animals, and everything they found" (v. 48). Because of the attention given to casualty figures, the account leaves the impression that the 600 Benjaminite men who took refuge for four months in the wilderness area of Rimmon (v. 47) constituted the sole survivors of the tribe, all adult males.

In retaliation, then, for the outrage in Gibeah, the assembled forces of the eleven tribes, acting in unison for the first time recorded in the book of Judges, nearly exterminate the male population of Benjamin. Along the way, it seems, the original victim had been forgotten. Even the Levite disappears from the story. Was this justice? The near silence of God in the account coupled with the reticence of the narrator to characterize events sharpens the impression that united Israel has exceeded its mandate, as it were. Notably, Israel's ultimate victory was achieved neither because of their application of overwhelming force nor by God's intervention on the field of battle (cf. Judg 5:4-5; 7:22; 11:32), but by means of ingenious battlefield strategy. Indeed, the Israelites' repeated appeals to God to approve their course of action and, especially, their acts of penitence at Bethel before the third day of battle suggest that they feared that their lack of success resulted from some fault.

**Seven Wrongs Do Not Make a Right (21:1-25)**
As has already been observed at several points above, the narrator of the story of the gruesome fate of the anonymous woman and its aftermath exercises remarkable restraint with regard to voicing any explicit moral judgment. This silence invites commentators and readers to wonder not only about the moral stance of the narrator but also about the ethical values held by the society that produced and originally read this account. Did the surrender of the woman to the brigands in Gibeah imply that the relatively greater value placed on the lives of men in comparison to women was an accepted cultural norm in ancient Israel? Why were the Israelites so quick to resort to genocide and abduction as solutions to the "Benjaminite problem"? Fokkelman (40–41) points out the central significance of the storyteller's sole explicit indication of his (or her) moral assessment of the criminals in Gibeah when they first appear in the story (19:22). Further, she calls attention to the fact that "the quasi-objective narration and the precise description of horrors is a much more effective critique of violence than snorting out moral indignation . . . ."

The presence of Phinehas, the grandson of Moses (20:28), and the narrator's description of the young women abducted from Jabesh-Gilead may provide additional clues as to the narrator's disapproval of the events he recounts (see Organ). Phinehas figures prominently in only three other contexts: the accounts of the apostasy at Peor (Num 25), of the war with Midian (Num 31), and of the controversy concerning the heterodox cultic site in the Transjordan (Josh 22). The expression in Judges 21:12, "who have not known a man by lying with a male (*lo yade'a 'ish lemishkab zakar*)," that describes the young women from Jabesh-Gilead taken captive as brides for Benjamin constitutes a suggestive intertextual nexus. Its only other occurrences in the Hebrew Bible refer to Lot's daughters (Gen 19:8), to the Midianite young women whom the Israelites spared and took as captive brides, equated in the context in Numbers with the dangerous women of Baal-peor (Num 31:17-18), and to Jephthah's daughter (Judg 11:30). Together, Phinehas's presence and the rare phraseology describing the young women captives allude to Israelite apostasy and suggest a comparison between the offer of Lot's daughters to the men of Sodom and Gomorrah, the unnecessary sacrifice of Jephthah's daughter, and the abduction of the young women of Jabesh-Gilead—all of whom were (at least potentially) victims of unwise, if not cowardly, male conduct. The Levite's *pilegesh* is the implied link in this nexus of relationships. Although not a young woman who had "not known a man by lying with a male," she was, nonetheless, offered to appease a violent mob (Lot's daughters), sacrificed unnecessarily (Jephthah's daughter), and forcibly taken (the daughters of Jabesh-Gilead). Her fate colors the account of the capture of wives for Benjamin. Ultimately, Israel's unrestrained revenge on Benjamin led them to replicate 600 counts of the original crime.

In addition to key verbal clues, the bizarre conclusion to this grotesque series of events confirms the assumption that the narrator condemns the actions of the major participants, albeit indirectly. In the narrator's view, there are no "good guys" here; nothing laudable transpires in this sequence of occurrences. The circumstances of the initial rape and murder highlight the Levite's complicity and duplicity, which, in turn, generate the deaths of 40,000 Israelites, the near eradication of the tribe of Benjamin, an unwise vow, the annihilation of Jabesh-Gilead, the capture of the young Jabeshite women intentionally spared for that purpose, and the abduction of hundreds of young women from Shiloh. Seven wrongs do not make a right.

**Once More at Bethel (21:1-14).** The narrator's flashbacks in vv. 1 and 5 that report decisions made in the assembly at Mizpah set the conditions for the next act in the unfolding series of outrages. First, even before conducting the campaign against Benjamin in such a way that the tribe was reduced to only 600 warriors, much like Jephthah, they had made a vow that, while seeming noble on its face, entailed an undesirable contingency, an unintended consequence. Only after making this rash vow and nearly exterminating the tribe of Benjamin, both actions that Israel undertook of its own volition apparently without divine prompting, the "men of Israel" suddenly recognized the situation they had created. Since they had vented their anger against even the women and children in Benjamin and had sworn, furthermore, not to allow intermarriage with Benjamin, this small tribe now faced extinction. In light of the fact that Israel's voluntary actions produced this crisis, their plaintiff question recorded in v. 3 confirms the impression that their decisions at Mizpah manifested moral confusion and that their subsequent actions were unconsidered expressions of a bloodthirsty and blind desire for vengeance. "Why, O YHWH, God of Israel, has this happened in Israel, that one tribe would be missing from Israel today?" They did not need to address this question to YHWH. The answer lay not in the realm of divine mystery but in the sphere of their own choices and behaviors. Benjamin faced extinction because they had knowingly nearly eradicated its population and had made a vow that virtually guaranteed its demise. Nothing in the text attributes either the vow or the extreme measures taken in battle to YHWH's will or instruction. Israel did this of its own volition.

Second, also at Mizpah, the assembled Israelite forces had entered into a previously unreported "great oath," swearing to punish with death any tribal group that did not participate in the campaign against Benjamin. Now this oath afforded them the opportunity to execute a clever gambit that would allow them to provide wives for the 600 surviving Benjaminites while simultaneously both keeping their vow against intermarriage with Benjamin and exacting the penalty called for by their oath. Determining that, in fact, Jabesh-Gilead had not responded to the muster at Mizpah, the "congregation (*'edah*)" sent a force of 12,000 to Jabesh-Gilead with specific instructions to slaughter the entire population, even "the women and children," except for the virgin young women (vv. 10-11). The language invokes the ban (*hrm*, v. 11). The congregation evidences no awareness of the perversity of their actions. A campaign launched in pursuit of justice for the rape and murder of one Bethlehemite woman results in the mass murder of innocent women and children, setting aside the question of whether the people of Jabesh-Gilead had made a conscious decision to abstain from the punitive campaign. Notably, the narrator includes no account of the attack as though he or she considered such an account superfluous or even distasteful. Instead, the narrative hastens to report the outcomes of the action against Jabesh-Gilead. Israelite forces captured 400 young women and brought them to Shiloh, whereupon, ironically, the congregation made "peace" overtures to the 600 surviving Benjaminite warriors in their refuge at Rimmon. Unceremoniously, the Benjaminites "returned," presumably to Shiloh, and the congregation of Israel awarded them their captive brides, only then to realize that there remained a shortage of 200!

**More Wives for Benjamin (21:15-25).** The final unit in the book of Judges and in the horrific saga engendered by the fate of the Levite's anonymous *pilegesh* appears to be a doublet or parallel of the tale of the capture of the young women from Jabesh-Gilead (see Gnuse, 232). The statement of the Israelites' concern for the survival of the tribe of Benjamin in v. 15 replicates the basic sentiment already expressed in v. 3, although it adds the novel attribution of the conflict between Benjamin and the other tribes to YHWH. The question concerning the appropriate remedy for the situation recorded in v. 16 corresponds almost verbatim to the question posed first in v. 7. For the second time, the account reports the vow, now described more as a self-imprecatory oath, that no one in the other tribes would allow their daughters to marry a Benjaminite (cf. vv. 7, 18). As in the previous case of the abduction of the young women from Jabesh-Gilead to be wives for the Benjaminite survivors (vv. 10-12), the proposed solution involved a clever stratagem that permitted the Israelites technically to honor their vow/oath while meeting the need for Israelite women as brides for Benjamin (vv. 19-22).

While one could speculate as to whether the two episodes represent independent traditions or variants of a single tradition, the coupling of the two accounts in their current context serves to compound the terrible irony inherent in Israel's decisions and actions in response to an unnecessary crisis of their own making. Just as they first seek to remedy the problem created by their near annihilation of Benjamin by nearly eradicating the population of Jabesh-Gilead, they now seek, for the second time, to remedy the problem that originated in the rape (and murder) of a single woman by sanctioning the forcible abduction and marriage of hundreds of young women, in essence by sanctioning hundreds of rapes. Indeed, the language describing the measures that the Israelites endorse and execute highlights their violent and hostile nature (cf. Bach, 10–16). The plan called for the Benjaminites to conceal themselves in the vineyards surrounding Shiloh during the annual festival there. When the young women of Shiloh appear at the dances associated with the festival, the Benjaminites are to spring their ambush (*'rb*, "to lie in wait, ambush," v. 20), and each Benjaminite is to "seize" (*htf*, v. 21) a young woman to be his wife. Occurrences of the verb "to ambush" earlier in Judges suggest the hostile, violent, and even treacherous connotations of the term. It describes the actions of the bandits from Shechem (9:25) against whom Abimelech retaliated mercilessly (9:32, 34, 43), the tactics employed by the Gazites (16:2) and later by Delilah's co-conspirators (16:9, 12) against Samson, and, in the immediate context of the passage under consideration, the strategy Israel finally employed against the Benjaminites of Gibeah on the third and final day of battle (20:29, 33, 36, 37, 38). The verb "to seize" found here occurs only twice elsewhere in the Hebrew Bible, both in Psalm 10:9, significantly, perhaps, together with the verb "to ambush" (also twice) in a lengthy meditation on the crimes of the wicked individual who is compared to a lion "lying in wait" for the opportunity to "seize" the poor.

Only the perversity of the Israelite's plan for the mass abduction at Shiloh surpasses its violence. Anticipating that the male relatives of the abductees from Shiloh will object to this mistreatment of their daughters and sisters, the Israelite leadership prepares a two-pronged argument designed to coerce the men of Shiloh to acquiesce to the forcible seizure of their young women. When the fathers and brothers of the kidnapped women raise their wholly justifiable objections, the Israelite leadership will ask the plaintiffs to accept the state of affairs, first because the Israelites "did not take them . . . in battle," an implicit threat: "Yes, your daughters and sisters have been abducted, but we did not kill any of you (as we did at Jabesh-Gilead) in the process. Be grateful and be quiet." The second argument the Israelite leadership has ready relates to the vow that all Israel, including presumably the inhabitants of Shiloh, had taken regarding intermarriage with Benjamin. "By stealing your young women," the Israelite leadership will argue, "we *spared* you from violating the vow and incurring guilt. In effect, we have done you two favors. No need to thank us."

The Shiloh episode, the tale of the rape and murder of the Levite's *pilegesh* and its aftermath, and, indeed, the book of Judges end abruptly and jarringly. In a terse, straightforward, and matter-of-fact fashion, the narrator/editor reports first that the Benjaminites executed the plan devised by Israel's leadership ("the Benjaminites did so," v. 23). Apparently, the attendance at the Shiloh dances afforded a surfeit of young women since the Benjaminites were able to "take wives according to their number." Quietly, taking their captive wives with them, the Benjaminites then returned home, rebuilt the cities and villages destroyed in the civil conflict, and "lived in them." The understated implication that circumstances have reattained equilibrium clashes with the unbounded violence and the abuses that led to this resolution.

Similarly, the penultimate verse in the book of Judges, the conclusion to the series of events unleashed at Gibeah (v. 24), contributes to the strident irony. With the Benjaminites penalized for the crime at Gibeah by near extinction and the incongruous success of measures undertaken to assure the continuation of the tribe of Benjamin, the assembled Israelite forces simply and quietly return to their homes, "every man to his tribe and family . . . every man to his inheritance." They do not mark the profound horror of the actions they have taken or enabled with ceremony or memorial. They do not pray, make confession, or seek blessing. They just go home. The final verse in the book of Judges, the fourth statement of the refrain that frames chapters 17–21, explicates the events involving Micah's anonymous Levite and the anonymous Levite's anonymous *pilegesh* as examples of the anarchy that prevailed in Israel before the establishment of the monarchy.

Looking back over the entire chain of occurrences that began when the Levite's *pilegesh* left her husband to return to her father's household, the eerie symmetry evident in the account highlights the perversity of the whole affair. The *pilegesh* spends four months with her father before the Levite comes to seek reconciliation, just as the surviving Benjaminites reside four months in their refuge at the Rock of Rimmon before the Israelite assembly extends peace to them. Both the Levite and his Ephraimite host in Gibeah are sojourners. The sexual violence perpetrated on Jabesh-Gilead and Shiloh by those who had set out to avenge the rape and murder of the *pilegesh* not only mirrors the original crime but also exceeds it by a multiple of 600. The Israelites coerce the fathers of the young women captured in the dances at Shiloh into a complicity in the abduction of their daughters that recalls the willingness of the Levite and his host in the face of danger to deliver one's wife and the other's daughter into the hands of rapists and murderers. Unbridled liberty easily degenerates into libertine anarchy.

**Collective Punishment Gone Wild.** Like perhaps no other section in the book of Judges, the stories of Micah and the Danites' sanctuary and of the rape and murder of the Levite's concubine with its aftermath pose the problem of what message the editors intended to convey regarding the character of Israel's leadership during the period of the judges, especially as it contrasted with that of the monarchial period. Typically, commentators properly focus attention on the editorial comment concerning the libertine behaviors of Israelites in the days when "there was no king in Israel," a comment that functions as a refrain in this section of the book. Clearly, Israel's behaviors, especially as described in Judges 18–21, fell short of the standards of religious fidelity (Judg 17–18) and social solidarity (Judg 19–21) to be expected of God's covenant people. The issue, stated bluntly, concerns whether the editors meant to attribute Israel's misbehaviors to the lack of steady leadership represented by the monarchy, a common interpretation of the refrain. As Satterthwaite (1993) has recently observed, however, according to the continuation of the Deuteronomistic History in the books of Samuel and Kings, the monarchy did not succeed in eradicating the religious and ethical "deviancy" reported in Judges 17–18 (and 19–21) either. Instead, in a standard reading of the account of the establishment of the Danite shrine, events during the period of the Judges merely foreshadowed the establishment of the royal sanctuaries in Dan and Bethel under Jeroboam I (1 Kgs 12:26-33). Inter-tribal tensions manifest in the book of Judges ripen into the schism between Israel and Judah that was marked by periods of border conflict (1 Kgs 15:6–16:22). The horrific rape of the Levite's concubine finds a parallel in Amnon's rape of his half-sister, Tamar. The complicity of both the Levite and his host hardly seems more repugnant than David's inability or unwillingness even to reprimand his son (2 Sam 13). Already a problem in the period of the Judges, the tribe of Benjamin would later give rise to Israel's first, equally problematic king. Satterthwaite (1993, 88) concludes, "Judges 17–21 contains, so to speak, the protases of a number of narrative analogies whose apodoses occur only in Samuel and Kings. In other words, Judges 17–21, so far from being unqualifiedly pro-monarchic, is intended to lead one towards a highly critical evaluation of much of what the kings described in Samuel and Kings actually do."

The counterbalance, in a sense, to the editorial refrain concerning Israel's anarchic behavior prior to the institution of a monarchy occurs in Samuel's statement of displeasure when Israel asked him to anoint a king, a statement echoed in YHWH's response (1 Sam 8:7-9). Both the prophet and his God viewed the request for a king as at least a partial rejection of YHWH's direct rule over his people. An obvious reading of this reaction would see it as a statement of preference for the charismatic style of leadership characteristic of the judges—deliverers like Moses who arose under the direct inspiration and empowerment of YHWH to save their people from oppression. Nonetheless, the editorial comment about the lack of a king, positioned in a section of the book of Judges remarkable for its lack of a deliverer figure, provokes an assessment not only of the monarchy to come but also of the judges that have preceded the events of Judges 17–21. While they succeeded in varying degrees in temporarily liberating their people from oppressors, or, as in Samson's case, in "beginning" (Judg 13:5; see "The Focal Issue, Then: Samson, the Nazirite" above) to do so, a significant point of the book arguably highlights the failures of the judges to deal with Israel's tendencies toward apostasy, civil contention, and immorality, especially with regard to the treatment of women.

In the end, given the editorial techniques employed in the book of Judges, techniques that rely on suggestion rather than declaration, the question of how the final form of the history of Israel that begins in Joshua and ends in 2 Kings views the monarchy defies a simple answer. As an institution, the monarchy manifested the same shortcomings already evident in the judgeship. Both the institutional office of king and the charismatic function of judge failed to address Israel's tendencies toward apostasy, incivility, and immorality. The words of the prophets Jeremiah (4:4; 9:26; 17:1; 24:7; 31:31-34) and Ezekiel (11:19; 36:36), echoing those of Moses in Deuteronomy (30:6), come to mind. Israel's shortcomings did not result from its form of leadership but from the constitution of the human heart. While modern political institutions differ significantly from ancient Israel's judgeship and monarchy, the human heart has not changed in the intervening years.

# Works Cited

Ackerman, Susan. 2000. "What if Judges Had Been Written by a Philistine?" *BibInt* 8:33–41.

Albertz, Rainer. 1994. *A History of Israelite Religion in the Old Testament Period.* Volume 1: *From the Beginnings to the End of the Monarchy.* Translated by John Bowden. OTL. Louisville: Westminster John Knox.

Albright, William F. 1950–1951. "A Catalogue of Early Hebrew Lyric Verse (Psalm LXVIII)." *HUCA* 23:1–39.

———. 1968. *Yahweh and the Gods of Canaan: A Historical Analysis of Two Contrasting Faiths.* London: Athlone.

Alt, Albrecht. 1925. *Die Landnahme der Israeliten in Palästina: Territorialgeschichtliche Studien.* Leipzig: Werkgemeinschaft Leipzig.

Alter, Robert. 1981. *The Art of Biblical Narrative.* New York: Basic.

———. 1985. *The Art of Biblical Poetry.* New York: Basic.

Amit, Yairah. 1999. *The Book of Judges: The Art of Editing.* Translated by Jonathan Chipman. Biblical Interpretation Series 38. Leiden: Brill.

———. 2000. "Bochim, Bethel and the Hidden Polemic (Judg 2:1-5)." In *Studies in Historical Geography and Biblical Historiography: Presented to Zecharia Kallai,* ed. G. Galil and M. Weinfeld, 121–31. VTSup 81. Leiden: Brill, 2000.

Arbeitman, Yoël. 1994. "Detecting the God Who Remained in Dan." *Hen* 16:9–14.

Assis, Elie. 2004. "The Choice to Serve God and Assist His People: Rahab and Yael." *Bib* 85:82–90.

Auld, Graeme. 1975. "Judges I and History: A Reconsideration." *VT* 25:261–85.

Bach, Alice. 1998. "Rereading the Body Politic: Women and Violence in Judges 21." *BibInt* 6:1–19.

Bal, Mieke. 1988. *Death and Dissymmetry: The Politics of Coherence in the Book of Judges*. CSJH. Chicago: University of Chicago.

Barré, Michael. 1991. "The Meaning of PRŠDN in Judges III:22." *VT* 41:1–11.

Beck, John. 2008. "Gideon, Dew and the Narrative-Geographical Shaping of Judges 6:33-40." *BibSac* 165:28–38.

Becker, Uwe. 1990. *Richterzeit und Königtum: Redaktionsgeschichtliche Studien zum Richterbuch*. BZAW 192. Berlin: de Gruyter.

Becker-Spörl, S. 1996. "Krieg, Gewalt und die Rede von Gott im Deboralied (Ri 5)." *BK* 51:101–106.

Biddle, Mark E. 1998. "Literary Structures in the Book of Joshua." *RevEx* 95:189–202.

———. 2003. *Deuteronomy*. Smyth & Helwys Bible Commentary 4. Macon: Smyth & Helwys.

———. 2004. "Contingency, God, and the Babylonians: Jeremiah on the Complexity of Repentance." *RevExp* 101:247–65.

———. 2007. "Obadiah-Jonah-Micah in Canonical Context: The Nature of Prophetic Literature and Hermeneutics." *Int* 61:154–66.

Blenkinsopp, Joseph. 1963. "Structure and Style in Judges 13–16." *JBL* 82:56–76.

Block, Daniel. 1990. "Echo Narrative Technique in Hebrew Literature: A Study in Judges 19." *WTJ* 52:325–41.

Böhler, Dieter. 2008. *Jiftach und die Tora: Eine Intertextuelle Auslegung von Ri 10,6-12,7*. OBS 34. Frankfurt am Main: Peter Lang.

Bohmbach, Karla. 1999. "Conventions/Contraventions: The Meanings of Public and Private for the Judges 19 Concubine." *JSOT* 83:83–98.

Böhme, W. 1885. "Die älteste Darstellung in Richt. 6, 11-24 und 13, 2-24 und ihre Verwandtschaft mit der Jahveurkunde des Pentateuch." *ZAW* 5:251–74.

Boling, Robert. 1963. "'And Who is Š-K-M?' (Judges IX 28)." *VT* 13:479–82.

———. 1975. *Judges: Introduction, Translation, and Commentary*. AB 6A. Garden City: Doubleday.

Boogaart, Thomas. 1985. "Stone for Stone: Retribution in the Story of Abimelech and Shechem." *JSOT* 32:45–56.

Bowman, Richard. 1995. "Narrative Criticism of Judges: Human Purpose in Conflict with Divine Presence." In *Judges and Method: New Approaches in Biblical Studies*, ed. Gale A. Yee, 17–44. Minneapolis: Fortress.

Brensinger, Terry. 1999. *Judges*. Believers Church Bible Commentary. Scottsdale PA: Herald.

Brettler, Marc. 1989. "Jud 1,1-2,10: From Appendix to Prologue." *ZAW* 101:433–35.

———. 1991. "Never the Twain Shall Meet? The Ehud Story as History and Literature." *HUCA* 62:285–304.

———. 1995. "The Ehud Story as Satire." In *The Creation of History in Ancient Israel*, 79–90. New York: Routledge.

———. 2002. *The Book of Judges*. Old Testament Readings. New York: Routledge.

Brooks, Simcha. 1996. "Saul and the Samson Narrative." *JSOT* 71:19–25.

Brown, Cheryl. 2000. "Judges." In *Joshua, Judges, Ruth*, ed. J. Gordon Harris, Cheryl Brown, and Michael S. Moore, 121–289. NIBCOT 5. Peabody MA: Hendrickson.

Budde, Karl. 1897. *Das Buch der Richter Erklärt*. KHAT 7. Freiburg: Mohr.

Burney, Charles. 1970. *The Book of Judges with Introduction and Notes and Notes on the Hebrew Text of the Book of Kings With an Introduction and Appendix*. Library of Biblical Studies. New York: Ktav.

Bustenay, Oded. 1986. "The Table of Nations (Genesis 10): A Sociocultural Approach." *ZAW* 98:14–31.

Butler, Trent. 2009. *Judges*. WBC 8. Nashville: Thomas Nelson.

Camp, Claudia, and Carole Fontaine. 1990. "The Words of the Wise and Their Riddles." In *Text and Tradition: The Hebrew Bible and Folklore*, ed. Susan Niditch, 127–51. SemeiaSt 20. Atlanta: Scholars Press.

Chisholm, Robert, Jr. 2009. "Identity Crisis: Assessing Samson's Birth and Career." *BSac* 166:147–62.

Christiansen, Eric. 2003. "A Fistful of Shekels: Scrutinizing Ehud's Entertaining Violence (Judges 3:12-30)." *BibInt* 11:53–78.

Cook, Stanley. 1927. "The Theophanies of Gideon and Manoah." *JTS* 28:368–83.

Crenshaw, James. 1978. *Samson: A Secret Betrayed, A Vow Ignored*. Atlanta: John Knox.

Craig, Kenneth M., Jr. 2003. "Judges in Recent Research." *Currents in Biblical Research* 1:159–85.

Craigie, Peter. 1972. "A Reconsideration of Shamgar ben Anath (Judg 3:31 and 5:6)." *JBL* 91:239–40.

Cross, Frank M. 1973. *Canaanite Myth and Hebrew Epic*. Cambridge MA: Harvard University Press.

Crown, Alan. 1967. "Judges V 15b-16." *VT* 17:240–42.

Danelius, Eva. 1963. "Shamgar ben 'Anath," *JNES* 22:191–93.

Davis, Dale. 1984. "Comic Literature—Tragic Theology: A Study of Judges 17–18." *WTJ* 46:156–63.

Day, Peggy L. 1989. "From the Child Is Born the Woman: The Story of Jephthah's Daughter." In *Gender and Difference in Ancient Israel*, ed. P. L. Day, 58–74. Minneapolis: Fortress.

Diebner, Bernd. 1995. "Wann Sang Debra ihr Lied? Überlegungen zu zwei der ältesten Texte des TNK (Ri 4 und 5)." *ACEBT* 14:106–30.

Drews, R. 1989. "The 'Chariots of Iron' of Joshua and Judges." *JSOT* 45:15–23.

Echols, Charles. 2005. "The Eclipse of God in the Song of Deborah (Judges 5): The Role of Yhwh in the Light of Heroic Poetry." *TynBul* 56:149–52.

Emmrich, Martin. 2001. "The Symbolism of the Lion and the Bees: Another Ironic Twist in the Samson Cycle." *JETS* 44:67–74.

Eversmann, Anke. 2008. "Gottesbefragung und Bruderkrieg in Ri 20." *BibNot* 136:17–30.

Exum, J. Cheryl. 1980. "Promise and Fulfillment: Narrative Art in Judges 13." *JBL* 99:43–59.

———. 1981. "Aspects of Symmetry and Balance in the Samson Saga." *JSOT* 19:3–29.

———. 1983. "The Theological Dimension of the Samson Saga." *VT* 33:30–45.

———. 1993. *Fragmented Women: Feminist (Sub)versions of Biblical Narratives*. JSOTSup 163. Sheffield: Sheffield Academic.

Eynikel, Erik. 2005. "Judges 19–21, an 'Appendix:' Rape, Murder, War and Abduction." *CV* 47:101–15.

Fager, Jeffrey. 1993. "Chaos and the Deborah Tradition." *QR* 13:17–30.

Faraone, Christopher, Brien Garnand, and Carolina López-Ruiz. 2005. "Micah's Mother (Judg. 17:1-4) and a Curse from Carthage (*KAI* 89): Canaanite Precedents for Greek and Latin Curses against Thieves?" *JNES* 64:161–86.

Fewell, Dana, and David Gunn. 1990. "Controlling Perspectives: Women, Men, and the Authority of Violence in Judges 4 and 5." *JAAR* 58:389–411.

Fleishman, Joseph. 2006. "A Daughter's Demand and a Father's Compliance: The Legal Background to Achsah's Claim and Caleb's Agreement." *ZAW* 118:354–73.

Fokkelman, Jan. 1992. "Structural Remarks on Judges 9 and 19." In *Sha 'arei Talmon: Studies in the Bible, Qumran and the Ancient Near East Presented to Shemaryahu Talmon,* ed. Michael Fishbane and Emanuel Tov, 33–46. Winona Lake: Eerdmans.

Fox, W. Sherwood. 1913–1914. "Old Testament Parallels to *Tabellae Defixionum*." *AJSL* 30:111–24.

Fretheim, Terence. 2005. *God and World in the Old Testament: A Relational Theology of Creation*. Nashville: Abindon.

Friedman, R. E. 1981. *The Exile and Biblical Narrative: The Formation of the Deuteronomistic and Priestly Works*. HSM 22. Chico CA: Scholars.

Fritz, Volkmar. 1982. "Abimelech und Sichem in Jdc. IX." *VT* 32:129–44.

Fuchs, Esther. 1989. "Marginalization, Ambiguity, Silencing: The Story of Jephthah's Daugher." *JFSR* 5:35–45.

Gerbrandt, Gerald. 1986. *Kingship according to the Deuteronomistic History*. SBLDS 87. Atlanta: Scholars.

Giles, Terry, and Wiliam J. Doan. 2009. *Twice Used Songs: Performance Criticism of the Songs of Ancient Israel*. Peabody MA: Hendrickson.

Gnuse, Robert. 2007. "Abducted Wives: A Hellenistic Narrative in Judges 21?" *SJOT* 22:228–40.

Gottwald, Norman. 1979. *The Tribes of Israel: A Sociology of the Religion of Liberated Israel, 1250–1050 B.C.E.* Maryknoll: Orbis.

Gray, John. 1964. *I and II Kings*. OTL. London: SCM.

Grayson, Albert. *Assyrian Royal Inscription, Volume 1: From the Beginning to Ashur-resha-ishi I*. Records of the Ancient Near East. Wiesbaden: Otto Harrassowitz.

Gressmann, Hugo. 1914. *Die Anfänge Israels: Von 2. Mosis bis Richter und Ruth*. Göttingen: Vandenhoeck und Ruprecht.

Guest, Deryn. *When Deborah Met Jael: Lesbian Biblical Hermeneutics*. London: SCM.

Guillaume, Philippe. 2004. *Waiting for Josiah: The Judges*. JSOTSup 385. New York: T & T Clark.

Gunn, David M. 2005. *Judges*. Blackwell Bible Commentaries. Oxford: Blackwell.

Habel, Norman. 1965. "Form and Significance of the Call Narratives." *ZAW* 77:297–323.

Halpern, Baruch. 1976. "Levitic Participation in the Reform Cult of Jeroboam I." *JBL* 95:31–42.

———. 1988. "The Assassination of Eglon: The First Locked-Room Murder Mystery." *BR* 6:32–41.

Hamlin, E. John. 1990. *At Risk in the Promised Land: A Commentary on the Book of Judges*. ITC. Grand Rapids: Eerdmans.

Handy, Lowell. 1992. "Uneasy Laughter: Ehud and Eglon as Ethnic Humor." *SJOT* 6:233–46.

Hauser, Alan. 1975. "The 'Minor Judges'—A Re-evaluation." *JBL* 94:194–96.

———. 1979. "Unity and Diversity in Early Israel Before Samuel." *JETS* 22:289–303.

———. 1992. "Judges 5: Parataxis in Hebrew Poetry." *JBL* 99:23–41.

Hentschel, Georg. 2008. "Der Bruderkrieg zwischen Israel und Benjamin (Ri 20)." *Bib* 89:17–38.

Hess, Richard. 1997. "The Dead Sea Scrolls and Higher Criticism of the Hebrew Bible: The Case of 4QJudg$^a$." In *The Scrolls and the Scriptures: Qumran Fifty Years After*, ed. Stanley Porter and Craig Evans, 122–28. Roehampton Institute London Papers. Sheffield: Sheffield Academic Press.

Hillers, Delbert. 1965. "Miscellanea Biblical: A Note on Judges 5, 8a." *CBQ* 27:124–26.

Hobsbawm, Eric. 1969 (rev. 2001). *Bandits*. London: Weidenfeld & Nicolson.

Hübner, Ulrich. 1987. "Mord auf dem Abort? Überlegung zu Humor, Gewaltdarstellung und Realienkunde im Ri 3, 12-30." *BN* 40:130–40.

Janzen, J. Gerald. 1987. "A Certain Woman in the Rhetoric of Judges 9." *JSOT* 38:33–37.

———. 1989. "The Root *pr'* in Judges V 2 and Deuteronomy XXXII 42." *VT* 39:393–406.

Jobling, David. 1995. "Structuralist Criticism: The Text's World of Meaning." In *Judges and Method: New Approaches in Biblical Studies*, ed. Gale A. Yee, 91–118. Minneapolis: Fortress.

Jost, Renate. 2006. *Gender, Sexualität, und Macht in der Anthropologie des Richterbuches*. BWANT 164. Stuttgart: Kohlhammer.

Jull, Tom. 1998. "מקרה in Judges 3: A Scatological Reading." *JSOT* 81:63–75.

Kallai-Kleinmann, Zekharyah. 1958. "The Town Lists of Judah, Simeon, Benjamin and Dan." *VT* 8:134–60.

Keefe, Alice. 1993. "Rapes of Women/Wars of Men." *Semeia* 61:79–97.

Kegler, Jürgen. 1985. "Simsson—Widerstandskämpfer und Volksheld." *CV* 18:97–117.

Kisch, Guido, editor. 1949. *Pseudo-Philo's Liber Antiquitaum Biblicarum*. PMS X. Notre Dame: Notre Dame.

Kingsbury, Edwin. 1967. "He Set Ephraim before Manasseh." *HUCA* 38:129–36.

Klein, Lillian. 1988. *The Triumph of Irony in the Book of Judges*. JSOTSup 68. Sheffield: Almond.

———. 1993. "The Book of Judges: Paradigm and Deviation in Images of Women." In *A Feminist Companion to Judges*, ed. Athaliah Brenner, 55–71. The Feminist Companion to the Bible 4. Sheffield: Sheffield Academic.

Knauf, Ernst. 1991. "Eglon and Ophrah: Two Toponymic Notes on the Book of Judges." *JSOT* 51:25–44.

———. 2000. "Does 'Deuteronomistic Historiography' Exist?" In *Israel Constructs Its History*, ed. A. de Pury and T. Römer, 388–98. Sheffield: Sheffield Academic.

Köhler, Ludwig. 1956. *Hebrew Man*. Translated by Peter R. Ackroyd. Nashville: Abdingdon.

Kratz, Reinhard. 2000. *Die Komposition der erzählender Bücher des Alten Testaments: Grundwissen der Bibelkritik*. Uni-Taschenbücher 2157. Göttingen: Vandenhoeck & Ruprecht.

Kübel, Paul. 1971. "Epiphanie und Altarbau." *ZAW* 83:225–31.

Lasine, Stuart. 1984. "Guest and Host in Judges 19: Lot's Hospitality in an Inverted World." *JSOT* 29:37–59.

Lemche, Niels Pieter. 1984. "'Israel in the Period of the Judges': The Tribal League in Recent Research." *ST* 38:1–28.

Levenson, Jon. 1984. "The Last Four Verses in Kings." *JBL* 103:353–61.

Levin, Yigal. 2003. "Who was the Chronicler's Audience? A Hint from his Genealogies." *JBL* 122:229–45.

Lewis, Theodore. 1996. "The Identity and Function of El/Baal Berith." *JBL* 115:401–23.

Lilley, J. P. U. 1967. "A Literary Appreciation of the Book of Judges." *TynBul* 18:94–102.

Lindars, Barnabas. 1995. *Judges 1–5: A New Translation and Commentary*. Edinburgh: T & T Clark.

Liptzin, Sol. 1992. "Jephthah and his Daughter," in *A Dictionary of Biblical Tradition in English Literature*, ed. D. J. Lyle, 392–94. Winona Lake: Eerdmans.

Lowery, Kirk. 1992. "Jael." In *ABD* 3, 610–11. New York: Doubleday.

Maisler, Benjamin. 1929. "Die Landschaft Bašan im 2. Vorchristlichen Jahrtausend." *JPOS* 9:80–87.

Marais, Jacobus. 1998. *Representation in Old Testament Narrative Texts*. Biblical Interpretation Series 36. Leiden: Brill.

Marcos, Natalio. 2003. "The Hebrew and Greek Texts of Judges." In *The Earliest Text of the Hebrew Bible: The Relationship between the Masoretic Text and the Hebrew Base of the Septuagint Reconsidered*, ed. Adrian Schenker, 1–16. SBLSCS 52. Atlanta: Society of Biblical Literature.

Margalith, Othniel. 1985. "Samson's Foxes." *VT* 35:224–29.

———. 1986a. "Samson's Riddle and Samson's Magic Locks." *VT* 36:225–34.

———. 1986b. "More Samson Legends." *VT* 36:397–405.

———. 1987. "The Legends of Samson/Heracles." *VT* 37:63–70.

Margulis, Baruch. 1965. "An Exegesis of Judges V 8a." *VT* 15:66–72.

Matthews, Victor. 1989. "Freedom and Entrapment in the Samson Narrative: A Literary Analysis." *PRSt* 16:245–57.

———. 1991. "Hospitality and Hostility in Judges 4." *BTB* 21:13–21.

———, and Don Benjamin. 1992. "Jael: Host or Judge?" *TBT* 30:291–96.

Mayes, A. D. H. 1969. "The Historical Context of the Battle against Sisera." *VT* 19:353–60.

———. 1983. *The Story of Israel between Settlement and Exile: A Redactional Study of the Deuteronomistic History*. London: SCM.

Mayfield, Tyler. 2009. "The Accounts of Deborah (Judges 4–5) in Recent Research." *Currents in Biblical Research* 7:306–35.

McCann, J. Clinton. 2002. *Judges*. Interpretation. Louisville: Knox.

McDaniel, Karl. 2001. "Samson's Riddle." *Did* 2:47–47.

McKenzie, Steven. 1991. *The Trouble with Kings: The Composition of the Book of Kings in the Deuteronomistic History*. VTSup 42. New York: Brill.

Milton, John. 1649. *The Tenures of Kings and Magistrates: That it is Lawful, and hath been so through all the Ages, for any, who have the Power, to Call to Account a Tyrant, or Wicked King, and After Due Conviction, to Depose, and Put him to Death, if the Ordinary Magistrate have Neglected, or Deny'd to doe it*. London: Matthew Simmons.

Mobley, Gregory. 1997. "The Wild Man in the Bible and the Ancient Near East." *JBL* 116:217–33.

Mosca, Paul. 1984. "Who Seduced Whom? A Note on Joshua 15:18 || Judges 1:14." *CBQ* 46:18–22.

Moore, George. 1949. *A Critical and Exegetical Commentary on Judges*. ICC. Edinburgh: T. & T. Clark.

Mullen, E. Theodore, Jr. 1982. "The 'Minor Judges': Some Literary and Historical Considerations." *CBQ* 44:185–201.

Muller, Hans-Peter. 1966. "Das Aufbau des Deboraliedes." *VT* 16:446–59.

Neef, Heinz-Dieter. 1999. "Jephta und Seine Tochter (JDC. XI 29-40)." *VT* 49:206–17.

Nelson, Richard D. 1981. *The Double Redaction of the Deuteronomistic History*. JSOTSup 18. Sheffield: JSOT Press.

———. 2005. "The Double Redaction of the Deuteronomistic History: The Case Is Still Compelling." *JSOT* 29:319–37.

Ng, Andrew Hock-Soon. 2007. "Revisiting Judges 19: A Gothic Perspective." *JSOT* 32:199–215.

Niditch, Susan. 1982. "The 'Sodomite' Theme in Judges 19-20: Family, Community, and Social Disintegration." *CBQ* 44:365–78.

———. 1990. "Samson as Culture Hero, Trickster, and Bandit: The Empowerment of the Weak." *CBQ* 52:608–24.

———. 2008. *Judges: A Commentary*. OTL. Louisville: Westminster John Knox.

Niemann, Hermann. 1999. "Zorah, Eshtaol, Beth-Shemesh and Dan's Migration to the South: A Region and Its Traditions in the Late Bronze and Iron Ages." *JSOT* 86:25–48.

Noll, Kurt. 1998. "The God Who Is Among the Danites." *JSOT* 80:3–23.

Noth, Martin. 1966 [= 1930]. *Das System der zwölf Stämme Israels*. BWANT 4/1. Darmstadt: Wissenschaftliche Buchgesellschaft.

———. 1981. *The Deuteronomistic History*. JSOTSup 15. Sheffield: University of Sheffield.

O'Doherty, Eamonn. 1956. "The Literary Problem of Judges 1,1-3,6." *CBQ* 18:1–7.

Organ, Barbara. 2001. "Pursuing Phinehas: A Synchronic Reading." *CBQ* 63:203–18.

Peckham, Brian. 1985. *The Composition of the Deuteronomistic History*. HSM 35. Atlanta: Scholars Press.

Rake, Mareike. 2006. *"Juda wird aufsteigen!" Untersuchungen zum ersten Kapitel des Richterbuches*. BZAW 367. Berlin/New York: de Gruyter.

Reinhartz, Adele. 1992. "Samson's Mother: An Unnamed Protagonist." *JSOT* 55:25–37.

Revell, E. J. 1985. "The Battle with Benjamin (Judges XX 29-48) and Hebrew Narrative Techniques." *VT* 35:417–37.

Richter, Wolfgang. 1963. *Traditionsgeschichtliche Untersuchungen zum Richterbuch*. BBB 18. Bonn: Peter Hanstein.

Rüdiger, Bartelmus. 1991. "Forschung am Richterbuch seit Martin Noth." *TRu* 56:221–59.

Rofé, Alexander. 2005. "The Biblical Text in Light of Historico-Literary Criticism: The Reproach of the Prophet-Man in Judg 6:7-10 and 4QJudg." In *On the Border Line: Textual Meets Literary Criticism. Proceedings of a Conference in Honor of Alsander Rofé on the Occasion of his Seventieth Birthday*. Beer-Sheva 18. Beer-Sheva: University of the Negev Press.

Römer, Thomas. 1998. "Why Would the Deuteronomists Tell about the Sacrifice of Jephthah's Daughter." *JSOT* 77:28–37.

———. 2005. *The So-Called Deuteronomistic History: A Sociological, Historical and Literary Introduction*. London: T. & T. Clark.

———, and Albert de Pury. 2000. "Deuteronomistic Historiography (DH): History of Research and Debated Issues." In *Israel Constructs its History*, ed. A. de Pury and T. Römer, 24–141. Sheffield: Sheffield Academic.

Rüdiger, Bartelmus. 1991. "Forschung am Richterbuch seit Martin Noth." *TRu* 56:221–59.

Saarisalo, Aapeli. 1927. *The Boundary between Issachar and Naphtali: An Archaeological and Literary Study of Israel's Settlement in Canaan.* Suomalaisen Tiedeakatemian Toimituksia B/21/3. Helsinki : Suomalaisen Tiedeakatemian Toimituksia.

Sarna, Nahum. 1972. "Gideon." *EncJud* 7:557–60.

Satterthwaite, Philip. 1992. "Narrative Artistry in the Compilation of Judges XX 29ff." *VT* 42:80–89.

———. 1993. "'No King in Israel': Narrative Criticism and Judges 17–21." *TynBul* 44:75–88.

Schmid, Konrad. 1999. *Erzväter und Exodus: Untersuchungen zur doppelten Begründung der Ursprünge Israels innerhalb der Geschichtsbücher des Alten Testaments.* WMANT 81. Neukirchen-Vluyn: Neukirchener.

Schipper, Jeremy. 2003. "Narrative Obscurity of Samson's חידה in Judges 14.14 and 18." *JSOT* 27:339–53.

Segert, Stanislav. 1984. "Paronomasia in the Samson Narrative in Judges XIII-XVI." *VT* 34:454–61.

Slotkin, Edgar. 1990. "Response to Professors Fontaine and Camp." In *Test and Tradition: The Hebrew Bible and Folklore*, ed. Susan Niditch, 153–59. Semeia Studies. Atlanta: Scholars.

Smend, Rudolf. 1971. "Das Gesetz und die Völker: Ein Beitrag zur deuteronomistischen Redaktionsgeschichte." In *Problemer biblischer Theologie: Gerhard von Rad zum 70. Geburtstag*, ed. H. W. Wolff, 494–509. Munich: Chr. Kaiser.

Smith, Carol. 1997. "Samson and Delilah: A Parable of Power?" *JSOT* 16:45–57.

Smith, Michael J. 2005. "The Failure of the Family in Judges, Part 1: Jephthah." *BibSac* 162:279–98.

Snyman, S. D. 2005. "Shamgar ben Anath: A Farming Warrior or a Farmer at War?" *VT* 55:125–29.

Soggin, J. Alberto. 1981. *Judges: A Commentary*, trans. John Bowden. OTL. Philadelphia: Westminster.

———. 1989. "'Ehud und 'Eglon: Bemerkungen zu Richter III 11b-31." *VT* 29:95–100.

Soisalon-Soininen, Ilmari. 1951. *Die Textformen der Septuaginta-Übersetzung des Richterbuches*. AASF B 72/1. Helsinke: Suomalainen Tiedeakatemia.

Speiser, Ephraim. 1964. *Genesis: Introduction, Translation, and Notes*. AB 1. Garden City NY: Doubleday.

Spina, Frank. 1977. "The Dan Story Historically Reconsidered." *JSOT* 4:60–71.

Stager, Lawrence. 2003. "The Shechem Temple: Where Abimelech Massacred a Thousand." *BAR* 29/4:26–35, 66–69.

Steinberg, Naomi. 1995. "Social Scientific Criticism: Judges 9 and Issues of Kinship." In *Judges and Method: New Approaches in Biblical Studies*, ed. Gale A. Yee, 45–64. Minneapolis: Fortress.

Stevenson, Jeffery. 2002. "Judah's Successes and Failures in Holy War: An Exegesis of Judges 1:1-20." *ResQ* 44:43–54.

Stipp, Hermann-Josef. 1995. "Simson, Der Nasiräer." *VT* 45:337–69.

Stone, Ken. 1995a. "Gender Criticism: The Un-manning of Abimelech." In *Judges and Method: New Approaches in Biblical Studies*, ed. Gale A. Yee, 183–201. Minneapolis: Fortress.

———. 1995b. "Gender and Homosexuality in Judges 19: Subject-Honor, Object-Shame?" *JSOT* 61:87–107.

Sweeney, Marvin. 1997. "Davidic Polemics in the Book of Judges." *VT* 47:517–29.

Täubler, Eugen. 1947. "Cushan-Rishathaim." *HUCA* 20:137–42.

———. 1958. *Biblische Studien: Die Epoche der Richter*, ed. Hans-Jürgen Zöbel. Tübingen: Mohr (Siebeck).

Thompson, Stith. 1979. *Motif-index of Folk-literature: A Classification of Narrative Elements in Folktales, Ballads, Myths, Fables, Mediaeval*

*Romances, Exempla, Fabliaux, Jest-books, and Local Legends.* Bloomington: Indiana University, 1955–1958. Repr., Bloomington: Indiana University.

Trebolle Barrera, Julio. 1991. "Edition préliminaire de 4QJuges$^b$: Contribution des manuscripts qumrâniques des Juges à l'étude textuelle et littéraire du livre." *RevQ* 15:79–100.

Trible, Phyllis. 1981. "A Meditation in Mourning: The Sacrifice of the Daughter of Jephthah." *USQRSup* 36: 59–73.

Tsevat, Matitiahu. 1952–1953. "Some Biblical Notes." *HUCA* 24:107–14.

Van Selms, Adrianus. 1964. "Judge Shamgar." *VT* 14:294–309.

Von Rad, Gerhard. 1947. *Deuteronomium Studien.* Göttingen: Vandenhoeck & Ruprecht.

———. 1962. *Old Testament Theology.* Volume 1. Translated by D.G.M. Stalker. New York: Harper & Row.

Wagner, Siegfried. 1964. "Die Kundschaftergeschichten im Alten Testament." *ZAW* 76:255–69.

Webb, Barry. 1987. *The Book of the Judges: An Integrated Reading.* JSOTSup 46. Sheffield: Sheffield.

Weinfeld, Moshe. 1972. *Deuteronomy and the Deuteronomic School.* Oxford: Clarendon.

———. 1993. "Judges 1:1–2:5: The Conquest under the Leadership of the House of Judah." In *Understanding Poets and Prophets: Essays in Honour of George Wishart Anderson,* ed. A. G. Auld, 388–400. JSOTSup 152. Sheffield: Sheffield.

Weitzman, Steve. 2002. "The Samson Story as Border Fiction." *BibInt* 10:160–73.

Wharton, James. 1973. "The Secret of Yahweh: Story and Affirmation in Judges 13–16." *Int* 27:48–66.

Willis, Timothy. 1997. "The Nature of Jephthah's Authority." *CBQ* 59:33–44.

Wilson, Robert. 1975. "Old Testament Genealogies in Recent Research." *JBL* 94:169–89.

Wong, Gregory. 2006. *The Compositional Strategy of the Book of Judges: An Inductive, Rhetorical Study*. VTSup 111. Leiden: Brill.

Yadin, Azzan. 2002. "Samson's *îdâ*." *VT* 52:407–26.

Yadin, Yigael. 1968. "And Dan, Why Did He Remain in Ships?" *AJBA* 1:9–23.

Yee, Gale. 1995. "Ideological Criticism: Judges 17–21 and the Dismembered Body." In *Judges and Method: New Approaches to Biblical Studies*, ed. Gale Yee, 146–70. Minneapolis: Fortress.

Younger, K. Lawson, Jr. 1991. "Heads! Tails! Or the Whole Coin?! Contextual Method and Intertextual Analysis: Judges 4 and 5." In *The Biblical Canon in Comparative Perspective: Scripture in Context IV*, ed. K. Lawson Younger, Jr., William Hallo, and Bernard Batto, 109–46. Ancient Near Eastern Texts and Studies 11. Lewiston: Edwin Mellen.

———. 1995. "The Configuration of Judicial Preliminaires: Judges 1.1–2.5 and Its Dependence on the Book of Joshua." *JSOT* 68:75–92.

Zakovitch, Yair. 1981. "The Woman's Rights in the Biblical Law of Divorce." *The Jewish Law Annual* 4:28–46.

Zertal, Adam. 1992. "Bezek." In *ABD* 1, 717–18. New York: Doubleday.

www.ingramcontent.com/pod-product-compliance
Lightning Source LLC
Chambersburg PA
CBHW051540230426
43669CB00015B/2670